W9-ASW-203

GOOD SCRIPTS, BAD SCRIPTS

Good Scripts, Bad Scripts

Learning the Craft of Screenwriting
Through 25 of the Best and Worst Films in History

THOMAS POPE

THREE RIVERS PRESS
NEW YORK

Published by Three Rivers Press, New York, New York.

Random House, Inc. New York, Toronto, London, Sydney, Auckland
www.randomhouse.com

THREE RIVERS PRESS is a registered trademark and the
Three Rivers Press colophon is a trademark of Random House, Inc.

Printed in the United States of America

Library of Congress Cataloging in Publication Data
Pope, Thomas,
    Good scripts, bad scripts : learning the craft of screenwriting
through 25 of the best and worst films in history / by Thomas
Pope.—1st ed.
    1. Motion picture authorship. I. Title.
PN1996.P66 1998
808.2'3—dc21   97–45528

ISBN 0-609-80119-8

10   9   8

Contents

Acknowledgments   ix
Preface   xi

Introduction: The Theory   xv

PART ONE: STRUCTURE

1. **The Abyss**
   The Narrative Spine Needs a Chiropractor   3
2. **Cutthroat Island**
   Shiver Me Structure!   8
3. **Inherit the Wind**
   The Play's the First Thing, the Screenplay's
   the Second   14
4. **Singin' in the Rain**
   The Perfect Film That Shouldn't Work   27
5. **Pulp Fiction**
   Reinventing Structure   40
6. **The Usual Suspects**
   The Great Script That Could Have Been Greater   52

7. High Noon
   Aristotle Goes Out West   60
8. Citizen Kane
   Flashback As Narrative   70
9. The Bonfire of the Vanities
   Third Act Suicide   80
10. Last Action Hero
    Deconstruction Self-Destructs   92
11. Fargo
    Satire Isn't Always What Closes on Saturday Night   102
12. The Jewel of the Nile
    Your Subtext Is Showing: The Problem of the False
    Second Act   108
13. Groundhog Day
    The Unexpected, Expected Structure   119
14. The Searchers
    The Third Act Hiccup   125
15. The Verdict
    Dialogue As Litany   133
16. Tender Mercies
    Less Is More, Lots More   140
17. Some Like It Hot
    Fewer Scenes, Bigger Laughs   147

PART TWO: CHARACTER

18. Prizzi's Honor
    The Passive Second Act Protagonist   157
19. The Day of the Jackal
    The Antagonist As Protagonist   166
20. Network
    The Catalytic Monster   175
21. Chinatown
    The Elusive Antagonist   183
22. Casablanca
    The Antihero As Protagonist   193

23. Havana
    Casablanca Lite   204
24. The Treasure of the Sierra Madre
    The Greatest Adventure   210
25. Falling in Love
    The Good Guys Ought to Be the Bad Guys   223

    Resources   231

Acknowledgments

No book is written truly alone. My thanks begin with Professor Irwin Blacker of the University of Southern California, who first introduced me to the mysteries and wonders of screenwriting. Walker Pearce, director of Film in the Cities in Minneapolis, allowed me to invent a new course called Good Scripts, Bad Scripts. Walker was always supportive in a thousand small and big ways. Dr. Jeff Hansen of the Blake School of Minneapolis encouraged me to explore *Inherit the Wind*. Michael Dennis Browne and Claire Walter-Marchetti, both of the University of Minnesota, also sponsored later classes of Good Scripts, Bad Scripts and acted above and beyond the call of duty. I want to thank all of the students who took my classes and offered numerous opinions and ideas, but I must especially thank Paul Wardell, Susan Lenfestey, Lindsey Nelson, Lynn Lukkas, Elaine Duffy, and Marisha Chamberlain for their many observations and insights.

I also want to thank my agent, Jonathon Lazear, who was always energetic and passionate. Andrew Stuart was a meticulous, insightful, and conscientious editor, exacting in his advice and generous with his time.

And I thank my father, Henry Pope, for his support and love, and my sister, Beth Eden, for her steady interest. My two sons,

ACKNOWLEDGMENTS

Ethan Rowan and Nicholas Bly, were unstinting in their opinions and advice. Thanks, guys.

But above all, I want to thank Freya Manfred: my wife, editor, counselor, agent, and most loving friend, who spent countless hours giving invaluable advice and assistance. Without her, this book truly could not exist.

Preface

▬ ▬ ▬ ▬

It all began at Harvard. Things weren't going well at the business school. Graduates armed with the latest theories of efficient management were sailing out into the marketplace and making post-graduate fools of themselves. All that they'd learned from their very expensive education turned out to be too theoretical, too pie-in-the-sky, too, well . . . Harvard. The best and the brightest turned out to be the lame and the halt. And from this debacle sprang the Harvard Case Study Method. Classes in theory were eliminated and replaced by those studying actual problems of management and production. Specific examples of both successful and troubled companies were cited and examined in depth. Not only that, but students were asked the most important question a teacher can ask of any student: "What would you do?" They asked that question because they'd learned that theory isn't enough.

I'll say that again: Theory isn't enough. Not in war, not in peace, not in the Harvard Business School, and certainly not in screenwriting. Unfortunately, virtually all the screenwriting books available are theoretical. And while some of these are splendid works and should be read by all aspiring screenwriters, or by anyone interested in the ghost in the machine of moviemaking, they are ultimately examples of principle without application, ideas without facts, words without deeds. I remember as a young screenwriting student wondering what exactly to do with advice such as "Keep your dialogue brief," "Express character through action," "Structure is everything," and so on. There were a million bits of wisdom like that, but I'd find myself thinking, How brief is brief? Must I always reveal character through action? And just what exactly does structure mean? I wanted examples to back up all those fine-sounding theories, but whenever examples were given, they were often of classic films I held in so much awe that I hesitated to apply what they had to teach. It was as if the Ten Commandments had been rolled out to demonstrate why I shouldn't rob from a five-and-dime.

I also found I was learning as much from the mistakes of bad films as from the triumphs of great ones. But when I asked why *The Jewel of the Nile* didn't work as well as the original, why *Falling in Love* fell on its face, why *Havana* was revolting, or why so many films simply didn't work, all I got was a shrug and a smile. The idea that as much could be learned from failure as from success, or that bad films should be studied in juxtaposition with good ones, was anathema to traditional teaching. Better to genuflect in the direction of *High Noon* than to roll up our sleeves over the miscalculations of, say, *The Bonfire of the Vanities*. This reverence for the canon of film classics just led to more theory; what I wanted were examples.

This book attempts to give such examples. It was born from a series of lectures I conducted through the Minneapolis-based Film in the Cities and through the University of Minnesota. It is the Harvard Business School gone Hollywood. Each film is chosen to illustrate a different problem of screenwriting. In general I won't include what would normally constitute a complete film analysis or review; any discussion of acting, directing, photography, editing, theme, or aesthetics will be in the context of screenwriting and how it helped or hurt the films in question. I've selected the successful films because an examination of what problems they overcame can be applied to other screenplays. The failed films I've selected give insights on how better to approach these same problems. They are also chosen because whatever flaws or virtues they possess are ones that the filmmakers could have reasonably known about and been responsible for before the cameras rolled. The films are roughly mixed in genre and period and include a grab bag of westerns and comedies, dramas and satires, taken from the golden age of movies up to the present day. I've also chosen them because their videotapes are available from most rental stores; I suggest you first see the film and then read the chapter discussing it. Similarly, the screenplays of the films discussed are available from bookstores or from several screenplay dealerships in the Los Angeles area, listed in the back of this book; if possible, the script should be read in juxtaposition with each chapter discussion. Most chapters contain a brief history of the film, and all contain a plot summary and an examination of its structure. "Good" scripts (I use that word advisedly, because the judgment is my own) and "bad" scripts (I use that judgment with even more trepidation) are about equally represented, and I mix things up. Too many bad scripts in a row could drive us all to artistic impotence, and too many good scripts could drive us, frustrated, to suicide. Nor is there a strict division between "good" and "bad": *The Searchers,* surely one of the great scripts, has a nearly fatal flaw, and *The Usual Suspects,* a wonderful script, is filled with problems; similarly, *The Bonfire of the Vanities,* which is a greatly miscalculated script, nevertheless contains some very fine writing. As for the table of contents, while I've placed the scripts in the two areas "Structure" and "Character," in fact there is tremendous overlap within each chapter, and this organization is a guide of the loosest and roughest nature.

A quick warning: Filmmaking is a mysterious process and one finally hidden, even for the filmmakers themselves. Ask a great filmmaker how some wonderful film moment came about, and often as not the answer will be (especially if it's an honest answer), "Damned if I know; we just sort of got together and thought it up; I don't remember who first came up with it." Also, memory is elusive at best and usually self-serving. I'll mention anecdotes that, while as accurate as film histories can make them, should be taken with a Buick-size grain of salt. Maybe it happened that way, maybe it didn't.

The same goes for credits. They'll state that someone directed a film, but the real creative force may have been the cinematographer, the editor, or (heaven forbid) the screenwriter. Screenwriting credits themselves are derived from a process called arbitration, wherein the scripts of all the (often numerous) screenwriters involved on a film are submitted to a panel of professional screen-writers, who wade through the material and try to come up with whoever is largely responsible. A calculus of credit has been invented, a rough guideline by which the panel can ascribe credit. But in the process, important contributions often go uncredited. And equally important ideas, conceived on the production floor, are given to a screenwriter who had nothing to do with them. So when I mention So-and-so as having written a wonderful or terrible script, So-and-so may in fact have had nothing to do with it. I have to use a name, so I use the name on the credits, but that person may be completely innocent of the deed.

However, before I can begin the main body of this book, I find I'm forced to discuss exactly what I wrote this book to avoid: I have to talk about theory. I have to define the rules, terms, and ideas that I'll use to examine our films. But first a warning: There are no rules. In fact, that may be the single most important idea to come from this entire book. There are guidelines, there are accepted means of approach, there are theoretical constructs, all of which may help in understanding the amazingly difficult and glorious craft of screenwriting; but the only rule is that the script must work, and if it works by breaking all the accepted rules, then more power to it. As an example, take a look at *Singin' in the Rain*. Better yet, take many looks.

But first, on to the theory.

Introduction

The Theory

Many books are devoted to the fundamentals of screenwriting. The works of Irwin Blacker, William Froug, and many others hold valuable insights. This book is intended to complement rather than compete with them. Nevertheless, just to make sure we're starting on the same page, here's a brief outline of the ground rules under which we'll be working.

If case analysis begins at Harvard, then dramatic theory begins with Aristotle. His *Poetics* was the first attempt to make sense of why one play succeeds while another fails. And while some of his thinking on aesthetics is outdated—his belief in the unity of time and space, for example, or his placing of major action offstage—a great deal remains that is of value. In particular, there's much to be gained from his belief that a drama begins when a problem begins and ends when the problem is resolved. Stated this way, his belief may sound simple, or even simpleminded, yet it's the basis of all drama.

Here's a graph that illustrates Aristotle's idea: the bottom line represents time and the vertical line a rising force of tension, whether physical or psychological or both. Since a problem by its very nature contains some level of tension, a drama can't begin at the exact bottom left, as that's a point of no tension. But neither should we start at the top of the tension line, because that would mean we'd have nowhere to go for the rest of the story except straight ahead or down, either of which is guaranteed to alienate the audience. So we begin just a few points above the bottom. Ideally each succeeding scene should increase in tension, building gradually until it reaches its point of highest tension at the climax. From there, with our problem resolved, we get out of the story as fast as possible, in the denouement:

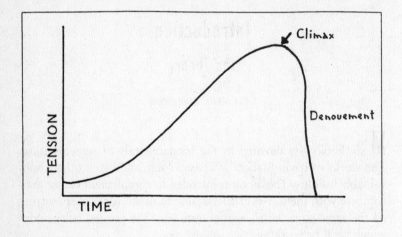

Theory Chart #1

This elegant curve is the basis of all drama. However, it's complicated by the fact that all dramas contain both external and internal problems. That is, when bad guys ride into town gunning for the sheriff, as they do in the classic western *High Noon,* they are a purely external problem since they represent a purely physical threat. A psychological or internal problem is introduced when the sheriff admits his fear that his fighting will cost him the love of his wife. Ideally these internal and external problems will resolve themselves at the same point of highest tension. To resolve them at separate times would mean we'd have two climaxes: one for the external and another for the internal. Two climaxes mean two resolutions, which means a story that can't make up its mind when to end, and that means an angry audience. These internal and external problems thread through the main tension line of a story, in a hemstitch fashion, thus:

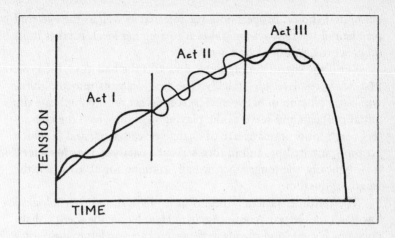

Theory Chart #2

Notice that this curve also breaks down into three segments, called acts. Over time, this three-act structure has become the mortar and brick of drama. The old saying goes that in the first act you get your hero up a tree (that is, you create an initial problem), in the second act you throw things at him (you complicate the initial problem), and in the third act you get him out of the tree (you resolve the initial problem).

Location of act breaks is tricky. Typically the first act is the shortest, beginning with the introduction of the initial problem and major characters and ending with the protagonist's decision to grapple with the initial problem. In a way, the first act tells the audience, "Here's what the movie's about, and here's whom we'll be dealing with." The first act is the "play fair" act, which lays out the ground rules of style, the internal and external problems, and the nature of the characters. It often ends at a point of moral conflict for the protagonist, or hero. In *High Noon* it ends when the sheriff decides to return to town to fight the bad guys. If he had decided to run—that is, if he'd decided to morally abdicate the challenge placed before him—there'd be no further story. The bad guys would have had no good guy to fight, and the hero would have ethically damned himself. End of first act and end of story. The decision to fight, whether as a physical action or as an existential choice, propels both the internal as well as the external problem of the first act and takes it to a higher level. It takes it, in other words, to the second act.

But if the sheriff simply fights and kills the bad guys, then our first act is resolved too quickly. The first act runs into the third, without a pit stop in between. The second act must complicate the initial problem and serve as the playing field on which the characters reach for a dramatic arc of change or catharsis, and in which action is initiated by, and in turn serves to catalyze, the characters. It is, typically, the longest act, usually running for at least half the length of the film.

The third act generally begins at a physical and psychological low point for the protagonist. Again in *High Noon,* the sheriff, abandoned by his wife and friends in the second act and left to die, writes his last will and testament. It's then, in his darkest moment, that the train whistle blows, announcing the arrival of the noon train carrying the final antagonist. At the point when all seems lost, the hero walks out of his office and into the third act, where he will resolve the external and internal crises generated in the first act.

Now a brief word about reality: This elegant form, so perfect a vehicle for relating dramatic collisions and revealing the deepest parts of the human soul, has little to do with real life. Let's chart a typical real life:

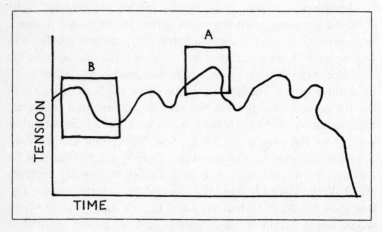

Theory Chart #3

As you can see, life is one damned thing after another, without apparent structure or meaning. F. Scott Fitzgerald said Americans have no second act, but he was only partially right. No one has a second act, or a first, or a third; life doesn't have acts because life has no structure; life just is. There are times (A) when some small section of our lives reflects the artificial shape of a dramatic curve. But just as often, real life is a graph of irrational, or even tragic, lines (B). Art doesn't try to imitate life, but rather distills its essence to find and reveal the truth beneath the lies, the meaning behind the meaninglessness, the structure within the randomness. Even when it doesn't show those deeper truths, it can at least let people see, for a few, popcorn-drenched moments, a better world, where heroes triumph and life has structure and meaning.

The building block of the classic dramatic curve is the scene. In the thirties and forties, a typical scene ran five pages, and a movie, with its 120 pages (assuming roughly a page a minute), usually contained about twenty or twenty-five scenes. Each scene was viewed as a minimovie, containing a beginning, middle, and end. A typical scene might introduce a problem (such as the bad guys are coming into town), complicate that problem (there are four bad guys, they are ruthless, they're after the sheriff), and then resolve the problem (the sheriff decides to leave town). Thus a scene has its own dramatic curve, which follows the same rules of drama as does its big brother, the movie itself. But while a movie should be dramatically self-contained, the resolution of a scene should create a new problem and thus a new scene (the sheriff's decision to leave town forces his moral anguish, which causes him to turn around). And the resolution of this second problem should, in turn, create yet a third problem and thus a third scene (the return to town causes the sheriff to seek help and worry over his wife's growing estrangement). Thus each scene should be tied to what comes before; were the scene to be dropped, the film would lose coherence. This narrative inevitability comprises the skeletal vertebrae of film structure, the through-line, the frame upon which the story hangs:

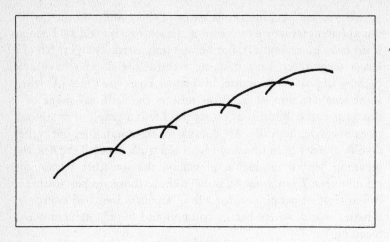

Theory Chart #4

The days of five-page scenes are largely past, a victim of TV-trained audiences faster on the upbeat and with reduced attention spans. Nonetheless, the same principles of dramatic structure still hold, often in the form of numerous miniscenes stitched together into one conglomerate scene. Dialogue is faster, and narrative connections are frequently internalized or implied rather than stated openly. Scenes often begin as late as possible, with the beginning and even the middle implied rather than shown. But however scenes are set up, ideally the internal and external problems they contain should dance together, one creating the other, where action catalyzes character, and character in turn creates action, in a complex ballet of structure and personality. It is the weaving together of character and action that makes the tapestry of drama.

There are exceptions to these guidelines, but they're exceptions that prove the guideline's power. In *Psycho,* for example, director Alfred Hitchcock was worried audiences subconsciously knew that a first act would lead inevitably into a second and then a third and that it all would come to a happy ending at the climax. It was because of this fear that the audience might leap ahead of the filmmakers that he created the false first act in *Psycho,* where the Janet Leigh character is in an affair (internal problem), absconds with money (external problem), buys a car, and escapes, only to make a really big mistake when she stops at the Bates Motel. But her death not only ends the first act, it also effectively ends the story. With Leigh dead, where do we go, and what more can we resolve about the initial problems of the film? Hitchcock's answer was to start a whole new movie, whose completely new problem is how Norman Bates deals with his nutty mother (internal problem) and how he disposes of Janet Leigh's body (external problem). Complications arise (investigators arrive and start snooping around, followed by others, and so forth) that constitute the second act, all of which find resolution in the third act, where a final confrontation reveals who Norman really is. Thus Hitchcock created this:

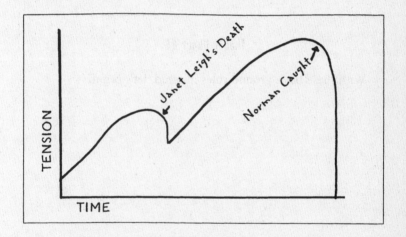

Theory Chart #5

Hitchcock went to all this trouble just so he could throw his audience a curve and make them think the rules of drama didn't apply. They did apply, but he hid them behind a false first act.

A false second act can often be found in a caper film or in a film such as *The Jewel of the Nile,* where phony obstacles and complications appear that in no way affect the first act setup and that are resolved in the third act. Such a false second act might look like this:

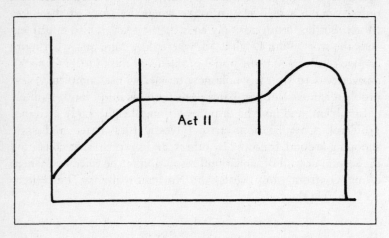

Theory Chart #6

With these basic ground rules in mind, let's begin.

PART ONE
STRUCTURE

1. THE ABYSS

The Narrative Spine Needs

a Chiropractor

▬ ▬ ▬ ▬ ▬

The Abyss is a disaster of a disaster movie. That's a cheap joke, but the movie wasn't cheap at all, weighing in at $70 million and involving mammoth special effects, including the first use of computer morphing. Since much of the movie takes place in a submerged oil rig, an immense pool of water was used to film the exteriors, making it one of the most difficult shoots in history. Whole days were taken to make one brief shot. By the time filming ended, the crew was at each other's throats, and the final result was one of the most incoherent action films ever made.

To summarize briefly, *The Abyss* begins when a nuclear attack submarine encounters a mysterious "something" near the immensely deep "Abyss" and crashes into an undersea mountain, killing the crew. The navy requisitions a submerged oil rig, run by Bud, to serve as the base of operations to retrieve the nuclear warheads and investigate the cause of the crash. Lindsey, Bud's ex-wife and the designer of the rig, is furious at Bud for allowing the navy to temporarily take over "her" undersea rig. Coffey, the navy SEAL in charge of the investigation, is increasingly paranoid and suspicious of Bud's civilian crew. As Coffey explores the wrecked sub, Lindsey sees a mysterious flying saucer–like being near the rig; but no one believes her. Overcome by paranoia, Coffey decides to use a nuclear warhead to destroy the sub, thereby keeping it out of Russian hands. He is stopped by Bud and killed. Bud and Lindsey become trapped in a rapidly filling minisub, and with only one oxygen mask between them, Lindsey lets herself "drown," allowing her heart to stop in order to help Bud get her lifeless body back on board the rig. Once there, Bud brings her back to life. But the A-bomb is set to blow. Bud dives down into the "Abyss" to deactivate the A-bomb and is saved from certain death by the mysterious creatures who live on the ocean floor and look like six-foot-tall floating butterflies with Keane eyes. These butterfly people let their art deco underwater city rise to the surface, which saves everybody, while Bud is reconciled with Lindsey.

Let's take a look at the first act scene breakdown:

- The submarine sinks after encountering "something."
- Bud is told he and his crew must help in the rescue.
- Lindsey is mad at Bud for letting the navy use "her" rig.
- Lindsey enters the undersea rig along with Coffey and his SEALs.

So far, so good. An external problem is introduced, followed by the internal problem of Bud's estrangement from Lindsey. True, Lindsey's anger seems contrived, but we've met the major characters and learned about their setting and relationships. Looming over everything is the mystery of the strange "something" that destroyed the sub. All these elements form a standard structure leading to a standard act break. Now let's look at the second act:

- The investigation of the downed sub.
- Lindsey sees a mysterious, otherworldly "something."
- Coffey gets orders to go to "phase two" (use the A-bomb).
- Lindsey says she saw "something"; Bud doesn't believe her.
- The A-bomb is removed from the sub by Coffey and his team.
- International tensions mount; the storm increases.
- The umbilicus to the outside is destroyed; they're cut off and have limited air.
- Lindsey sees the alien vehicle.
- The crew again disbelieves Lindsey; she says, "You have to look with better eyes."

- Bud defuses a fight between Coffey and Lindsey.
- Coffey and the SEALs prepare the A-bomb for detonation.
- Tensions grow between Coffey and the crew; Coffey's going nuts.
- An encounter with underwater beings—the "living water" scene; Bud sees and believes; Coffey shuts down communications.
- Coffey, now insane, resolves to handle things himself.

At this point we're about halfway through the story. Coffey has gone mad and become an irrational monster. The aliens are a growing presence, yet their nature or purpose is still unknown. But with the aliens so remote and unknowable, the narrative force of the movie hangs upon a tug-of-war between Bud and Coffey for control of the rig and of the A-bomb. The movie, in other words, which began as a story of a downed submarine and the attempt to examine it, has ignored that initial premise and become a movie about two guys fighting for control of the rig. So where do we go from here?

- Coffey pulls a gun and takes over the rig.
- Coffey locks himself away.
- Bud swims outside to do an end run around Coffey.
- Coffey and Bud fight—Coffey escapes.
- Coffey and Bud fight in minisubs; Lindsey saves Bud; Coffey dies.

Hold on there! Come again? Coffey dies? Two-thirds of the way through the movie the bad guy dies? What have we got to look forward to—thirty minutes of end titles? If the bad guy dies this soon, how can we sustain the narrative line? And, by the way, just what is the narrative line? Is this a movie about why the submarine sank, is it about the aliens, or is it about whether Coffey can take over the rig? Let's see where we go next:

- Lindsey is trapped and, in order to save herself, must "drown"; Bud saves her life.
- Bud learns the A-bomb will explode; he prepares to descend to stop it.

- Bud defuses the A-bomb and is about to die.
- The aliens save his life.
- The alien building rises to the surface; everyone lives happily ever after.

Say what? In the closing minutes of the movie Lindsey is saved, though that action is unrelated to any actions that came before or after it. Bud then defuses the A-bomb set by Coffey (which was Coffey's only reason for existing and which was the major problem of the second act). And then the sudden intervention of the aliens saves Bud. Just when all the threads of the story should be drawing together, three completely new, structurally unconnected, and narratively unrelated events are introduced, events totally unattached to anything that's come before. And as for the aliens saving Bud, that's a classic example of the deus ex machina, an old Latin term that translates as "god from a machine." During the heydays of Greece and Rome, whenever a hack playwright was stuck for an ending, he could save his hero, make true love work, stop the bad guys, or do whatever else needed doing by having Zeus literally descend from heaven and save the day (they didn't have morphing back then; it was all done with ropes and pulleys). In place of Zeus, substitute aliens. And in place of a plot, substitute this, a breakdown of the major sequences of the movie:

- The sub goes down, the navy needs Bud's base.
- The investigation of the downed sub.
- They are all cut off.
- Coffey goes crazy and dies.
- Lindsey nearly dies.
- Bud descends into the "Abyss."
- The aliens save Bud and the undersea rig.

Viewed this way, *The Abyss* isn't a complete movie, but rather a series of minimovies strung together. And each minimovie is self-contained, not dependent upon, growing from, or leading to, any other sequence. Charted on a graph, it looks like this:

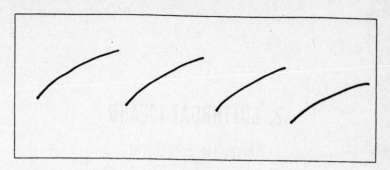

Abyss Chart #1

Much of the failure of *The Abyss* springs from this start-and-stop structure. Perhaps no other movie so clearly illustrates the need for a narrative through-line, a plot vertebra, a single major problem that powers through the film and connects all the individual scenes. For example, look at the first sequence—the sub goes down and the navy needs Bud's rig. That's a problem all right, and since that's how our movie begins, it follows that the movie should end when this problem is resolved. But the sub's going down, and the navy's needing Bud's rig is only a catalyst for a series of new problems, each unrelated to the ones that precede or follow them. Seven major sequences, seven minimovies. Only the public didn't pay to see seven minimovies; they paid to see one big one. And they got drowned in the abyss.

2. CUTTHROAT ISLAND

Shiver Me Structure!

━ ━ ━ ━ ━

Pirate queens. Evil villains. Stalwart heroes. Galleons fighting on the high seas. Hidden treasure. Secret maps. Romance. Adventure. Can't miss, you say? Then you haven't seen *Cutthroat Island,* that rare film that wrecked a studio.

Beautiful Morgan Adams is the daughter of pirate Harry Adams. When Dawg Adams, Harry's evil brother, threatens to kill Harry unless he gets Harry's third of the treasure map to Cutthroat Island that has been drawn up by their father, Morgan helps her father escape from Dawg's clutches. But during the escape Harry is fatally wounded, and as he lies dying he tells Morgan to shave off his hair; there Morgan finds, tattooed on her father's head, his third of the treasure map. Morgan scalps her dead father, buries him, and takes the map to Harry's crew, asking their help in finding the remaining sections of the map that will lead them to her grandfather's treasure. Along the way she acquires William Shaw, conniver, cheat, pickpocket, and recently created slave, to help her read her part of the map. Barely escaping another attack by Dawg, they obtain the second third of the map from Morgan's uncle, Mordechai, narrowly escaping another attack by Dawg. Shaw and Morgan acknowledge their growing attraction to each other but remain wary partners after Morgan catches Shaw secretly trying to find the fabled Cutthroat Island on a map. But then Scully, one of her father's crew, throws in with Dawg and takes over the ship.

During a violent storm, Morgan and those crewmen faithful to her are thrown into a small lifeboat and set adrift to drown. Shaw escapes after her and, unseen, flails helplessly in the immense waves. Happily, they all drift onto Cutthroat Island and begin searching for the treasure. Dawg also lands on the island and, using his third of the map, starts searching. Shaw steals Dawg's map and gives it to Morgan. Together, Morgan and Shaw find the treasure, only to have it taken from them by Dawg. Morgan, Shaw, and the crew chase after Dawg and, in a climactic battle, kill Dawg and his evil crew, sink Dawg's ship, save the treasure, and live happily ever after, robbing the high seas.

As pirate stories go, *Cutthroat Island* is serviceable enough, filled with plenty of action and over-the-top characters. But the story of its making contains just as much action, with characters even more outrageous. It seems Mario Kassar, president of Carolco Pictures, had owned a pirate script named *Cutthroat Island* for several years but was unable to get it off the ground until Renny Harlin, hot off the successful *Cliffhanger* and *Die Hard 2,* expressed an interest in it. Harlin was dating Geena Davis at the time and saw the script as the perfect vehicle for her to move from her traditional light comedies into the riskier, more lucrative world of action flicks. Geena came on board, and the hunt for a leading man commenced. Kassar was worried that Geena might not have the appeal to draw a large enough audience to justify the inevitably high costs of a pirate movie and became convinced that she should share pirate chores with a man. Michael Douglas agreed to costar with Geena on two simple conditions: first, shooting needed to start right away, because his window of availability was limited; second, his role would have to be rewritten to give him screen time equal to Geena's character. Douglas also recommended that the well-known rewrite expert Susan Shaliday start work immediately.

Based on Douglas's assurance that he would commit to the project if the new script was acceptable, and fearful of losing Douglas because of his time constraints, Kassar began selling off foreign distribution rights to *Cutthroat Island.* Also, familiar with the long lead time necessary to mount a costume movie, Kassar began building the pirate ships, sets, and costumes and started scouting locations. Malta, with its mix of exotic-looking locales, sparkling blue green waters, and proximity to first-rate hotels, was the perfect spot to make the movie. Regardless of the fact that this meant shooting the entire film in a difficult location, Malta became home central for the huge undertaking.

Everything seemed perfect until Shaliday delivered her rewrite, which everyone hated. Filled with bad characters, dialogue, and plot, the script prompted Michael Douglas to jump ship, leaving Kassar with half-built sets, immense financial commitments, and no workable script for a pirate movie starring a woman whose proven strength lay in light comedy. By now, Kassar was so financially committed that his entire company's survival hung upon turning *Cutthroat Island* into a hit. He contacted every "A"-list actor possible to offer the plum role of costarring with Geena Davis in a pirate film, and oddly enough, every single one of them turned Kassar down.

Finally they were able to recruit Matthew Modine, that household word, to climb on board. The trouble was that Modine, while a pleasant actor, has neither the reputation nor the charisma to carry a pirate film, let alone go mano a mano with Davis, who's a far more formidable film presence. Yet Harlin was confident that he could find just the writer to scribble the production out of this hole, and he hired Robert King to amp up Geena's role and amp down Modine's. Harlin, however, was busy supervising the millions of details of preproducing a major motion picture, and he didn't have enough time to spend with King, who labored alone without adequate supervision and gave birth to what was generally considered a totally unshootable script. By now they were just weeks away from shooting, and Kassar was so financially committed that he simply could not turn back; *Cutthroat Island* was going forward, with or without a script.

And shoot they did, though under circumstances that could hardly be called auspicious. Harlin commissioned another script, which was written in a maddened fever by his friend Marc Norman, an accomplished script doctor, who was supplying script pages the night before the scenes were shot. Inevitably, many of the scenes were, to say the least, shark bait.

With this tale of horrors in mind, it's little surprise that *Cut-*

throat Island ended up being not so much an action film as a disaster movie. Twenty-twenty hindsight might suggest that Kassar shouldn't have committed his company to building sets and selling off foreign territories until he had Michael Douglas firmly on board. But Douglas's limited window of availability derailed that possibility and forced Kassar to proceed. As for the three failed scripts, Renny Harlin perhaps should have kept a tighter grip on his writers by breathing down their necks and making sure their scripts were working. But Harlin was occupied with the minutiae of overseeing a major motion picture and simply didn't have the time to play wet nurse to three one-million-dollar-a-year writers who were supposed to be able to script coherent scenes without someone holding their hands.

This said, it's a little like beating a dead horse to isolate and analyze the multitude of script mistakes in *Cutthroat Island*. But even given the crisis atmosphere under which the entire production labored, there are a number of moments that should have and could have been spotted and changed. Taken separately, they aren't fatal, but together they're a litany of foreseeable and avoidable errors. These are troubles the filmmakers could reasonably have seen coming and cured before they were frozen forever on celluloid. For example, let's take a look at the action in the first act:

- Morgan leaves her lover, who is about to arrest her.
- Morgan saves her father from Dawg; her father dies, leaving her with his third of the map.
- Shaw is captured stealing jewels and made a slave.
- Morgan takes charge of the ship without challenge and resolves to find the other parts of the map; she needs a Latin expert to translate her part of the map.
- Morgan buys Shaw, who speaks Latin, and escapes with him.
- Morgan and Shaw realize the map is not in Latin, but simply written backward.

Who's this lover Morgan leaves at the beginning? Why is she leaving him? And why did she get involved with him in the first place? You'll find no answers in the movie. Nor will this lover pay off in a later scene or become a continuing character as Morgan's nemesis or savior, which would have justified his existence. Now you see him, now you don't.

Morgan's taking over the ship is also a puzzle. The fact that there's no challenge from anyone is particularly curious, considering that Scully will later on become a traitor. Why does the crew trust Morgan to captain a ship? What job experience does she have? Why isn't there a scene where she mourns the death of her father? As for Shaw, if Morgan buys him because he speaks Latin, then why have it that the map was written not in Latin, but backward? Why, in other words, throw out the one reason that justifies Shaw's presence in the movie? As far as that's concerned, once the map is translated, why does Morgan keep Shaw at all—why not resell him? No answers are available.

What we do learn is that Morgan, in the spirit of all good traditional male action heroes, is without any character arc or conflict; she's a macho action hero at the start of the film and stays that way until the end. That's probably okay in itself, but by avoiding any internal conflict, the film is relying completely upon external conflict—which means action scenes—to carry the ball. With nothing to fall back on, the failure of a coherent plot guarantees the failure of the action, which in turn guarantees the failure of the film (which would translate into the failure of Carolco).

Let's try the second act:

- Morgan at Uncle Mordechai's, where a fight with Dawg lets Shaw get the second third of the map; Dawg pursues them.
- Shaw and Morgan become attracted to each other.
- Morgan finds Shaw is secretly looking for Cutthroat Island on a map; she throws him in irons.
- Storm at sea; mutiny; Morgan and her loyal crew are set adrift; Shaw escapes and swims helplessly after her.
- They find Cutthroat Island and start looking for the treasure.
- Scully is revealed to be a traitor; he leads Dawg to Cutthroat Island.
- Shaw steals Dawg's third of the map.
- Morgan saves Shaw from quicksand, and they join forces.
- Morgan and Shaw find the treasure.

- Morgan runs from Dawg, who gets the treasure.
- A second traitor turns Shaw over to Dawg as Morgan watches; Dawg sails off in the treasure ship while other baddies follow in Morgan's old ship.
- Morgan takes over her old ship.

This is a little better. Two clear narrative lines have been established: Morgan and the bad guys are both after the treasure, while Morgan and Shaw go through the ups and downs of a relationship. There's action, intrigue, mutiny, storms, and a treasure hunt. In fact, with so much going on, it would seem the filmmakers were hoping that little questions arising in this section would be ignored by the audience in the headlong rush to a second act break. But these questions can't be ignored, and in fact become festering wounds, infecting and finally killing the script. For example, there are no explanations of why Cutthroat Island remained uncharted in the middle of an otherwise well-charted sea. Nor do we learn how Shaw got in the quicksand, or why Shaw and Morgan separate once they find the treasure. And the appearance of a second traitor means reusing the same plot device with yet another character, this time with one we haven't had time to get to know; it's hard to think of a better example of creative bankruptcy.

I won't outline the rest of the script, which deals with Morgan's pursuit of Dawg, her inevitable big fight scene where she takes over Dawg's ship, kills Dawg, saves Shaw (first leads always save second leads), regains the treasure, and sails off happily into the pirate sunset. It's nonstop fireworks, helped along by the completely unmotivated start of the big battle, where Morgan's loyal first mate suddenly decides to start the fight, knowing he's risking his life and the lives of all he cares for (not to mention a movie studio) by doing so. Well, someone had to start things rolling.

The tragedy of *Cutthroat Island* isn't that it's so bad, but that it didn't have to be so bad, that its mistakes could have been avoided had the filmmakers possessed the creative will to foresee and overcome them. Bad movies will always be made, and mistakes will always happen, but when fear is at the helm, with financial disaster blowing the sails, then intelligence walks the plank.

3. INHERIT THE WIND

The Play's the First Thing,

the Screenplay's the Second

▬▬ ▬▬ ▬▬ ▬▬

In 1925, John Scopes, an unknown biology teacher from Dayton, Tennessee, accepted an invitation from the American Civil Liberties Union to make himself into a test case; he would fight the famous Tennessee Evolution Law, which prohibited the teaching of any theory of the descent of man that differed from that told in the Bible. The case became the first in a long line of this country's "Trials of the Century" as the recently invented radio allowed the world to keep track of every motion and testimony. Clarence Darrow, the most famous liberal lawyer in America, agreed to represent Scopes, while William Jennings Bryan, who had failed three times in his bid for the presidency and was the archetypal fundamentalist interpreter of the Bible, acted as prosecutor. By the time the dust had cleared, Darrow had put Bryan on the stand and humiliated him. Even though the deeply prejudiced judge and jury held against Scopes, within six days Bryan was dead of a broken heart, Darrow was the de facto victor, and evolutionary biology was on its way to supplanting creation science as the explanation for the history of natural life.

It's a tremendous story, filled with unexpected twists and turns and larger-than-life characters and issues. In fact, the biggest surprise is that it took thirty years before a play about the "Monkey Trial" reached Broadway. *Inherit the Wind* was written by Jerome

Lawrence and Robert E. Lee, two Ohio residents who had met while writing and directing radio programs. During World War II, they first spoke of turning the Scopes trial into a play, but it wasn't until 1950 that they completed their first draft of *Inherit the Wind*. However, unlike Carl Foreman, who was writing his first draft of the screenplay for *High Noon* at about the same time and forged ahead with his indictment of McCarthyism, Lawrence and Lee were worried that "the intellectual climate was not right" for their liberal play. Five years later, with McCarthy defeated, they felt the times had changed enough for them to bring their first draft out of the drawer. They gave the play to Margo Jones, who produced it in her Dallas Theater. There the theatrical producer Herman Shumlin, always on the lookout for socially significant plays, acquired *Inherit* and took it to Broadway. The play was a success, and it was perhaps inevitable that Stanley Kramer, who seven years before had produced *High Noon*, acquired the play and turned it into the esteemed film starring Spencer Tracy and Fredric March.

To be frank, neither the play nor the movie of *Inherit the Wind* is good enough to be included as a pure example of a good script, nor is either bad enough to be used as an example of a bad script. While the dialogue in both is at times riveting, at other times it is overly simplistic. The characters are largely stock villains and cardboard heroes, and the antagonist is a paper tiger, existing only to provide a suitable target for the liberal homilies the protagonist fires at him. Simply put, it is a classic example of preaching to the converted.

Why, then, are we examining it? Because despite its flaws as a drama, I can think of no better example of the craft of adaptation from stage to screen. The choices made by the screenwriters, Nedrick Young (a victim of the blacklist who wrote under the pseudonym Nathan E. Douglas) and Harold Jacob Smith, in turning a second-rate play into a better-than-average screenplay illustrate how much plays differ from scripts. Indeed, many of their choices are simply brilliant, and the structure that they took from the play, and completely reinvented for the movie, is a wonder of the screenwriter's craft.

The stories in both the play and screenplay are similar: Bert Cates, a humble schoolteacher in Hillsboro, Tennessee, has begun teaching Darwin's theory of the evolution of man. He is arrested and tried for breaking the law. Matthew Harrison Brady and Henry Drummond agree to serve respectively as prosecutor and defense attorney. Thrown into the mix are Rachel, Bert's fiancée and the daughter of Reverend Jeremiah Brown, the religious firebrand who has instigated the public crucifixion of Cates. Writing about the proceedings with a pen dipped in purple poison is E. K. Hornbeck, the brilliantly acerbic columnist for the *Baltimore Sun*. Preparations for the trial proceed quickly, with jury selection, press conferences, and spiritual meetings lending a witch-hunt atmosphere to the town. The trial itself begins well for Brady, as the judge bars Drummond's request for expert scientific testimony to support his position. Even Rachel is forced to testify, tricked by Brady into making Bert look vindictive and small. Finally, with no other recourse, Drummond calls Brady to the stand. There, under a brilliant and withering examination, Brady is at last exposed as an unthinking, sinister clown. While the jury votes against Cates, it is seen as a moral victory for Drummond and the cause of intellectual freedom.

Let's begin by listing the scenes as they lie in the play, with a sequential letter placed after each scene:

ACT ONE, Scene One

- Kids talk about evolution. (A)
- Bert in jail; Sarah visits, says Brady is coming; Bert refuses to quit. (B)
- Preparations for Brady's arrival. (C)
- Hornbeck arrives. (D)
- Brady arrives, is made a colonel, hears a song, and makes a speech. (E)
- Brady goes off to talk with Rachel. (F)
- Hornbeck announces Henry Drummond is coming; Brady welcomes the idea. (G)
- Hornbeck tells Rachel time is passing Brady by. (H)
- Drummond arrives. (I)

ACT ONE, Scene Two

- Jury selection; Drummond made a colonel; he asks for "no commercial messages." (J)
- Rachel asks Bert to quit; Bert wants Rachel not to testify. (K)

ACT TWO, Scene One

- Brady gives a press conference. (L)
- The prayer meeting. (M)
- Brady with Drummond: "All motion is relative." (N)

ACT TWO, Scene Two

- The trial:
  Howard testifies. (O)
  Rachel testifies. (P)
  Scientists are refused permission to testify. (Q)
  Drummond calls Brady to the stand. (R)
  Brady is led off: "Baby, Baby . . ." (S)

ACT THREE

- Waiting for the jury to come in; Cates and Drummond discuss Golden Dancer. (T)
- A guilty verdict; Brady makes a radio speech and collapses. (U)
- Cates, Drummond, and Rachel sum up; they hear Brady is dead. (V)
- Hornbeck and Drummond discuss Brady. (W)
- Drummond and Cates discuss appeal. (X)

At first glance the play's three-act structure seems very similar to the three-act structure we find in movies. A problem is introduced in the first act, is made more complex in the second, and is resolved in the third. However, there are many differences. Let's look at the screenplay's structure, using the same lettering to show

how scenes have been moved around for the movie. After each movie scene for which there is no equivalent scene in the play, I'll place a number:

ACT ONE

- Bert is arrested for teaching evolution. (1)
- The city fathers are worried until they hear Brady is coming. (2)
- Bert in jail; Rachel asks him to give up. (B)
- Hornbeck says a lawyer is coming to defend Bert. (D)
- Brady arrives, gives a speech, and is made a colonel. (E)
- Rachel protests Brady's speech against Bert. (3)
- Hornbeck announces Drummond is coming, and Brady welcomes the idea. (G)
- Brady tells Sarah, his wife, that all will be well. (4)
- Rachel and her father, Reverend Brown, argue over Bert. (5)
- Drummond arrives. (I)
- Drummond sees the carnival atmosphere; meets Hornbeck and Howard and heads to his hotel. (6)
- Drummond meets Sarah, Brady, the mayor, Davenport, and the rest. (7)

ACT TWO

- Jury selection; Drummond is made a colonel; he asks for "no commercial messages." (J)
- Rachel wants Bert to stop. (B)
- Drummond says it's Bert's choice; Bert decides to stay despite Rachel's protests. (8)
- Dinner; Brady prays for Drummond. (9)
- Drummond with Sarah; they talk of Brady, who invites them to a prayer meeting. (10)
- The prayer meeting. (M)
- Brady comforts Rachel, who mentions the Stebbins boy; they go off together. (11 and F)
- Brady and Drummond discuss Golden Dancer. (12 and T)

- The trial, part one:
  Howard testifies. (O)
  Rachel testifies. (P)
  Bert won't let Drummond cross-examine. (13)
  Drummond's scientists are rejected. (Q)
  Drummond withdraws from the case and is held in
    contempt. (14)
- Mob demonstration against Bert. (15)
- Brady tells Sarah he can control the mob. (16)
- Brady is led off: "Baby, Baby . . . " (S)
- Drummond tells Hornbeck he needs a miracle. (17)

ACT THREE

- The trial, part two:
  Drummond apologizes to the judge. (18)
  Drummond calls Brady to the stand; Brady's testimony is
    the same as in the play. (R)
- Rachel says Brady is evil; Sarah defends Brady. (19)
- The verdict; Brady makes a radio speech and collapses. (U)
- Drummond confronts Hornbeck. (20)

Even a quick glance shows that a great deal has been changed from play to script. Twenty completely new scenes have been added to the script, and nine scenes (A, C, H, K, L, N, V, W, X) have been subtracted from the play. Why, in a play that was so successful on the stage and seems so straightforward, should so many changes have been made in its transition to the screen? Let's examine it beat by beat:

THE BEGINNING

The movie begins two scenes earlier than the play, first with Bert's arrest and second with a scene in which the city fathers worry that the town will be turned into a laughingstock, then learn that Brady is on his way to save them. The scene where Bert is arrested was put in for the simple reason that Aristotle and logic demanded it: a movie (or any drama) begins when a problem begins, and the problem of *Inherit the Wind* begins when Bert teaches evolution and is arrested. Not only does this allow us briefly to see Bert teaching evolution (something the play can talk about only vicariously, thus diluting the dramatic potential), it also directly shows us the problem to be overcome. I suspect the playwrights ignored Aristotle and didn't place this obviously needed scene into their play for logistic reasons: it would have involved a classroom scene, complete with schoolchildren, and the production costs of carrying that many actors would have gone through the roof. The scene with the city fathers humanizes the townspeople of Hillsboro and also examines the economic and cultural forces that motivate their actions, forces that the play largely ignores. Without this scene the people of Hillsboro are demonized in a manner that works in the simpler play but would have backfired in a more complex and realistic movie.

Thus the third scene of the movie is the second scene of the play: Bert speaks to Rachel about the ambiguity of truth, describing the twilight that lasts six months at the top of the world. It's a good line and a good point, but in the movie it's given to Henry Drummond, who speaks the line about halfway through the film, just after jury selection. Why the change? Because not only does it strengthen the protagonist, lending him the wisdom we expect from an ancient dragon slayer, but it was also probably a political necessity. Spencer Tracy was one of the greatest American film actors, but he was also a great egoist. (According to the story, when he was acting with his beloved Katharine Hepburn and her agent asked for Hepburn's billing above his in the credits, he refused, arguing, "This isn't the *Titanic,* with women and children first; this is a goddamn movie.") If there's one transcendent political truth in Hollywood, it's that the top dog gets the best bones and the top actor gets the best lines.

PREPARATIONS FOR THE TRIAL

At this point the play shifts to Brady's arrival in Hillsboro; the movie, on the other hand, goes to Bert in jail, visited first by Rachel and then by Hornbeck. Why the change? Because while the play has already established Bert and Rachel in its opening scene, the movie now has to play catch-up. Not only that, but the movie gives Brady a speech upon his arrival in Hillsboro that isn't in the play ("We did not seek this struggle . . ."). While this speech sets up the trial to come, it would have been a mistake in the play, which wanted to hoard its ammunition for the one climactic trial scene at the end. The filmmakers, however, knowing they'd be dividing the trial in two and letting the sections run through much of the length of the film, had less reason to stockpile their sentiments; besides, knowing an audience in general can't retain major ideas for more than twenty minutes, they wanted to tell the audience what they were going to tell them long before they told them.

There's another major difference in this sequence between the play and movie versions. In the play, Brady meets Rachel and goes off with her (to learn Bert's secret thoughts, which Brady will use against Bert in the trial). But this same scene in the movie is placed far later, after the prayer meeting. Why the shift? First, because movies rely much more upon realism than do plays, and it's far more realistic that Rachel wouldn't tell those deep secrets to a total stranger upon first meeting him—as she does in the play—but would wait until she had grown to trust him. Also, moved to a later point, this sequence doesn't take as long to pay off at the trial and doesn't demand so much of the audience's always untrustworthy memory. But the play, using fewer scenes (because of the problem of the time it takes to scene-shift), had to cram in the Brady/Rachel moment where it was expedient and thus was forced to portray an unrealistic situation.

AFTER BRADY'S ARRIVAL

The movie now adds two scenes that aren't in the play. First, Brady assures his wife, Sarah, that all will be well and that he can control the people of Hillsboro. Second, Rachel is confronted and trapped by her fanatically religious father. There are several reasons for these additions. First, the greater need for realism in movies dictated these scenes. Second, these additions allow the audience to make an emotional leap, letting us look deeper into our characters. In fact, while quick, jumpy little scenes like these (especially Brady's brief talk with his wife) can work in films, they are often too abrupt for a theater audience. These two scenes also heighten tension by making us wait for the trial. And they permit us emotional breathing room before jumping into the tensions to come. The more interesting of these new scenes is the tense confrontation between Rachel and her father. In the play Rachel speaks about her father, whereas in the movie she speaks directly to him. This sharper collision could have worked in the play, and was, I think, a simple mistake by the playwrights, who missed their chance for heightened drama. Like the second draft that corrects the mistakes of the first, the play makes a mistake that the movie fixes.

DRUMMOND AND BRADY SPEAK

A minor moment in the play, set just after the prayer meeting, becomes a major scene in the movie. Drummond sits on a porch with Brady and speaks movingly of his Golden Dancer, a toy he had craved as a boy that turned out to be made of cheapjack material and that broke immediately upon his sitting on it. But in the play Drummond discusses Golden Dancer with Bert. Thus we have a change not only in scene location, but also in the people within the scene. The ability to jump location quickly is one of the great freedoms of the movies: the play places this scene after the prayer meeting because it would have been too difficult to switch sets. But in the movie we can jump to the two adversaries sitting on a porch without losing a beat. The porch setting also allows Brady and Drummond to talk privately, lending a much needed intimacy to the drama. And by switching the characters in the scene from Drummond/Cates to Drummond/Brady, the screenwriters are showcasing what the playwrights should have known: It's always best to include a strong dramatic moment between your principal characters—without such a moment or series of moments, the characters become passive and their power diminishes. The play, by staging the Golden Dancer scene between Drummond and Bert, not only reduces the moment by limiting the emotional stakes between the characters, it also is preaching to the converted (a continuing mistake of the play) rather than turning the moment into a dialogue between Brady and Drummond. A cannon has been aimed not at Brady, the villain, but at Bert, an innocent bystander. Not only that, but the Golden Dancer scene serves as an emotional place holder, telling us ahead of time that the upcoming verdict is irrelevant. This may have been dramatically necessary for the play, but it's weaker than the Drummond/Brady confrontation.

THE TRIAL

While the play runs the trial as one long third act, the movie breaks it up into two major sequences running through the second and third acts. There are many reasons for this change. First, movies almost always work better with shorter scenes. Audiences, schooled by television and bombarded by image after fleeting image, have become impatient, demanding that scenes begin at an emotional high and end as quickly as possible. (Quentin Tarantino, Kevin Smith, and a few other young screenwriters have fought this general trend.) Second, it's simply more realistic to break up the trial into several days. Third, it heightens tension, as we're forced to wait for the inevitable confrontation between Brady and Drummond. Fourth, it allows for an act break to come between the two sequences, creating a low point—a moment when all seems lost—that the protagonist is forced to resolve in order to power through into the third act. It is this decision to break up the trial into two sequences that is not only one of the most brilliant decisions of the screenwriters, but one that absolutely dictates the structure for the entire film.

RACHEL TESTIFIES

The scene where Bert begs Rachel not to testify is perhaps the one instance where the play is more realistic than the movie. The play sets the scene at the beginning of the film, as Rachel visits Bert in jail. But the movie places the scene right in the middle of the trial, with hundreds of people all around the two lovers. Perhaps the screenwriters felt that forcing them to speak so intimately in front of all those people would heighten the drama; but the more likely explanation is that they were trapped and couldn't write themselves out of an unrealistic situation. However, this does let Bert stop Drummond from cross-examining Rachel (a moment that is ignored in the play but is correctly milked for its dramatic content in the movie). It also makes Bert a stronger figure, the only character who stands up to Drummond and wins. As for Brady's interrogation of Rachel, while it intensifies the drama, it also demonizes Brady (and requires the "Baby, Baby . . ." scene, where Brady collapses emotionally and is comforted by his wife, placed here to "undemonize" him). The film, which needs every ounce of realism it can find, diminishes its realism at a critical point and permits its antagonist to turn into a bogeyman.

THE STEBBINS BOY

The Stebbins boy died in an accidental drowning, and the Reverend Brown told his congregation that he was damned to hell because he hadn't been baptized. However, the play only "talks about" the Stebbins boy, whereas the movie actually shows Mr. Stebbins (which personalizes the story) and also has him post bail for Drummond when he's cited for contempt. Not only does this allow one dramatic situation to pay off another, it also shows us that not everyone in Heavenly Hillsboro is a religious fanatic. Indeed, the town banker, whom we've earlier seen as a voice of reason and temperance, allows Stebbins's farm to serve as collateral in the posting of bail for Drummond. The town has been humanized and the drama increased and made more specific, and all with the brilliant simple addition of less than a page of script.

DRUMMOND'S CONTEMPT CHARGE

Faced with the need to bring the protagonist to as low a point as possible as the end of the second act approached, the screenwriters (not surprisingly) had the judge throw a contempt charge at Drummond. In fact, the real surprise may be that the playwrights didn't do the same thing. True, they weren't faced with a second act break or with the need to divide the trial into two sequences, so they didn't need to bring Drummond so low. But it is an electric moment in the film that personalizes the collision between Drummond and the judge, serves to enunciate Drummond's passion for the law, and sets up Brady as nearly unbeatable. Not only that, it does the one thing any dramatist must always do to an audience: it makes them wait. Will Drummond get out of the contempt charge? How can he beat Brady with this new albatross around his neck? Tune in to the third act.

THE BREAK INTO THE THIRD ACT

Although the contempt charge is the last and lowest blow, it's been preceded by the judge's refusal to allow expert witnesses to testify against the biblical interpretation of evolution, by Rachel's damning testimony, and by Brady's grand speeches. At his lowest point, Drummond lies in his hotel room with Hornbeck and realizes that he needs a miracle—and finds the Bible. This moment of epiphany powers us into the third act, where Drummond brings Brady to the stand and demolishes him. But the play has no such break. Instead Drummond is brought low by the refusal to allow expert witnesses and immediately plays his ace by summoning Brady. No break. No moment of despair. No epiphany. Just a smooth (and largely unbelievable) transition from the depths to the heights.

"BABY, BABY . . ."

This scene between Brady and his wife, Sarah, comes after the trial in the play and between the two trial sequences in the movie. There are considerable reasons for this seemingly simple change. In the play this scene is used as a break between the second and third acts. Brady's sudden frailty is poignant and makes us want to see the final confrontation between him and Drummond. But in the movie there has already been a (much more powerful) break between the second and third acts, using not an antagonist as the narrative glue, but rather the more conventional (and much stronger) protagonist. Since the scene was no longer necessary where the playwrights had placed it, the screenwriters positioned it in the more realistic, but less dramatic, location right after Brady's interrogation of Rachel. This is one of the very few places where the movie opts for a lower dramatic moment than does the play. But in both cases the scene serves its purpose: in the play it's an effective act break, while in the movie it helps to humanize a man the film has so far demonized.

HORNBECK

The intriguing character of E. K. Hornbeck is never "explained" in the play; there are no moments where his inner soul is explored or even brought to the surface for a look. What you see with Hornbeck is what you get: an acerbic prankster, sprinkling a fairy dust of witty put-downs on the proceedings. But in the movie there's a final coda where Drummond, who up to this moment has used Hornbeck as his right-hand man, now turns his incisive mind on the ultimate cynic:

> DRUMMOND
>
> What touches you? What warms you? Every man has a dream—what do you dream about? . . . You're alone. . . . And when you go to your grave there'll be no one to pull the grass up over you. . . . You'll be what you've always been—alone.

> HORNBECK
>
> You're wrong, Drummond. You'll be there—you're the type. Who else would defend my right to be lonely?

It's more than just a simple dramatic moment that explains Hornbeck. It also explains Drummond, revealing some of the humanity that elevates him above the Hornbecks of the world. And at the denouement in both the play and the movie, when Drummond grabs both the Bible and Darwin's theory of evolution—finding that they weigh about the same—and carries them together out of the courtroom, it is a moment that, in the movie, has been earned. But lacking this final clash between Hornbeck and Drummond, the play ends without Drummond's having earned the right to carry those two books together. In the play Drummond hasn't staked out the middle ground and thereby hasn't paid his dues for his humanity.

4. SINGIN' IN THE RAIN

The Perfect Film That Shouldn't Work

Singin' in the Rain may be the only film that is, without question, the best of its kind. Debates rage over the best western (is it *High Noon? The Searchers? Shane? The Wild Bunch?*), the best detective film *(The Big Sleep? Chinatown?)*, the best comedy (*Bringing Up Baby?* and any film by the Marx Brothers?), and so on. But of *Singin' in the Rain* there's no doubt: it's simply the finest musical ever made. Its vivacity, humor, brilliantly crafted characters, and perfect integration of story with song make any other musical pale in comparison. It is also deceptively complex in its structure and shatters many of the standard rules for act breaks and narrative through-lines.

It all began with an impossible assignment. In 1950 a prominent producer and lyricist named Arthur Freed owned a number of old songs from the twenties and thirties. Not wanting to lose his investment, he asked Betty Comden and Adolph Green, an up-and-coming comedy writing team, to take these songs and weave a story around them. Which, if you think about it, is ass-backward. If they wanted a love scene, a funny story, or a sad moment, but couldn't find a song on Freed's list to express it, they'd have to twist their plot to fit the songs rather than create a song to fit the story. It's a narrative bed of Procrustes. Not only that, but these were outdated songs, twenty and thirty years behind the times, which further restricted the sort of material that Comden and Green could write. It's difficult to imagine a more unlikely launching point for a film classic.

Comden and Green began by making the obvious choice to set the movie during the time in which the songs were written. Since these songs had a real razzmatazz feeling, the writers decided to employ a showbiz background and set the movie in the world of Hollywood. As movie buffs, Comden and Green loved that fragile period between 1927 and 1930 when silent pictures died and talkies began, when one empire fell and a new empire arose.

For the crucial first scene, which would create the overarching feeling and tone for the rest of the movie, they came up with three possible beginnings. The first was an interview with a gossip columnist, a Louella Parsons or Hedda Hopper, one of the formidable matrons who ruled Hollywood in those golden days. The second was a big Hollywood premiere. The third was to begin with a hero who had to struggle with the transition from silent films to talkies. Comden and Green spent a confused month fruitlessly trying to decide which of these three beginnings to use.

As Betty Comden tells it, she was sitting at home telling her husband how she was stuck when he gave her the advice that has since served every screenwriting student in good stead: When in doubt, combine. They tried it and began the film with a gossip columnist at a Hollywood premiere interviewing a movie actor who's about to make the jump into the unknown waters of the talkies. Once the brilliant decision was made to combine three scenes into one, the rest of the writing went quickly.

The Gene Kelly character, Don Lockwood, is loosely based upon John Gilbert, a silent-screen lover who, legend has it, never made the transition to sound because of a squeaky, high-pitched voice. But Comden and Green didn't want to end the film with a wrecked career, so they wisely decided to make Don Lockwood into an ex-song-and-dance man who'd left his vaudeville roots to remake himself into a silent-screen lover. This decision not only made for a potentially complex character, it allowed for the songs that were the raison d'être of the film. After all, they were writing for Gene Kelly and had to find a character to accommodate his abilities; again, their choice was brilliantly right.

An American in Paris, a film now largely forgotten except to film historians, had won the Best Picture Oscar in 1951 and was hailed as an instant classic, potentially casting a long shadow over *Singin' in the Rain*. Especially daunting was *American*'s knock-you-on-your-ass finale, seventeen minutes of pull-out-the-stops dancing and singing. This tour de force created for Comden and Green a problem as great as Freed's initial assignment: audiences had loved *American*'s finale, and the clamor made Comden and Green feel they had to put an equivalent showstopping number into *Singin' in the Rain,* something that could outshowstop *An American in Paris*. And this showstopper had to be inserted whether or not it had anything to do with the narrative line or the characters.

The casting of Debbie Reynolds was another problem. Although a fine singer with a perky, attractive personality, she had had little dancing experience. In fact, she had had little film experience, though she had stood out in a few minor roles; but MGM had tagged her for stardom and insisted she serve as the love interest for Kelly. Whether they wanted her or not, Comden and Green had to write a singing-and-dancing movie where the leading actress could sing but not dance. This created what now seems the inevitable decision to create a buddy for Gene Kelly, someone who could perform the physical gymnastics Debbie couldn't. Thus, Debbie Reynolds's inadequacies necessitated the extraordinary creation of Cosmo, Don Lockwood's best friend.

Of course, this is all twenty-twenty hindsight. The seeming inevitability of those choices wasn't so inevitable at the time. Comden and Green weren't even writing at this point, just shooting ideas around, and it's those story conference moments that make or break a film when it's at its most vulnerable. Any one of these decisions—the choice of period, of style, of opening, of leading and supporting characters—could have been different. There are damned few ideas that can't sound good after a few hours of being trapped in a room, trying to come up with a story. The very act of collaborative creation is a desperate, often atavistic fight, where the muse tries to make the writer choose bad ideas, and his only defense is his professional shit detector. That Comden and Green made such astonishingly right decisions is as miraculous a part of the creation of *Singin' in the Rain* as any other part. In fact, the very limitations imposed upon Comden and Green—having to work from songs before story, the need for a showstopping number to compete with *An American in Paris,* and Debbie Reynolds's inability to dance—were problems that liberated the writers from easy choices and forced decisions upon them that made for a more complex and sophisticated film. Necessity is the mother of invention. Or, in this case, of a great film.

A further note: Comden and Green, as amateur film historians, knew instinctively that truth is stranger, and more interesting, than fiction. Rather than create the world of Hollywood as it moved from silents to talkies, they re-created it. Most of the funny anecdotes in the film spring from real Hollywood history. The cameras, booms, costumes, lights, microphones—all are authentic. Still, at the same time *Singin' in the Rain* is imbued with the sensitivities of the fifties. So this film is, as much as anything else, a historical document. In fact, as we in the nineties watch a film made in the fifties about events in the twenties, we're watching a document of a document.

We'll look at the structure of *Singin' in the Rain* in three different ways: first in the choice of songs, next in scene structure, and last in terms of theme. Let's begin where Comden and Green were forced to begin, with the songs Freed imposed upon them. "Imposed" may sound a bit strong, since the songs are delightful, but the imposition was real enough. The songs in the film fall in this order:

"Fit As a Fiddle"
"All I Do Is Dream of You"
"Make 'Em Laugh"
A montage of songs ending with "Beautiful Girl"
"You Were Meant for Me"
"Moses Supposes"
"Good Mornin'"
"Singin' in the Rain"
"Would You?"
"Broadway Rhythm" leading into "Broadway Melody"
"Singin' in the Rain"

All right, we know why these songs, but why this order? "Fit As a Fiddle" and "All I Do Is Dream of You" start the film for two reasons. First, they're both upbeat audience grabbers, a perfect way to begin a movie. Second, both leads, Don and Kathy, are, without knowing it, singing to the true love they haven't met. The songs, in other words, set up a thematic resonance, an emotional readiness to fall in love. They state a problem to be solved and, in so stating it, advance the narrative line.

"Make 'Em Laugh" serves a political purpose. Since it's a show-biz tradition that the second lead has to have his own song, it was necessary for Comden and Green to create a song for Donald O'Connor as Cosmo. Besides, anyone strong enough and talented enough to play against Kelly would demand his moment in the spotlight. Cosmo has no traditional "B" love story, however, which would normally serve as a narrative cutaway in a musical. (Think of the Ado Annie/Will "B" love story in *Oklahoma!*, or the Lieutenant Cable/Liat "B" love story in *South Pacific*.) This "B" story is probably missing because Comden and Green simply didn't have the room. Knowing they'd have to put in a very long show-stopper number to compete with that invisible eight-hundred-pound gorilla *An American in Paris*, they didn't have the time to develop a fourth character as a love interest for Cosmo. Consequently, since they couldn't give O'Connor a song to complicate his emotional arc, Comden and Green chose to augment Don Lockwood's. "Make 'Em Laugh" is the only song actually written for the film (and created, the story goes, from bits of clowning O'Connor did between takes). The song does nothing for Cosmo, but it advances Don's emotional arc and thus advances the narrative line.

The song montage springs from the embarrassment of riches Arthur Freed laid on Comden and Green. Because they didn't want to abandon these marvelous songs, but could not use them to advance the narrative, the writers placed them at the break between acts one and two. Thus they end a narrative line and begin a new one—something that is extremely dangerous, because anything that stops the story, even for a few beats, can be a movie killer. But this montage succeeds in part because the songs are so great and the staging so brilliant. Also, it begins with a new problem, that of the coming of talkies, and ends with the resumption of the narrative line through "Beautiful Girl"—in which Don has once again found Kathy, and our story line begins again, as seamlessly as possible.

"Moses Supposes" is another political choice. With Debbie Reynolds unable to perform a true showstopping dance number alone with Gene Kelly, something every musical "had" to have, that task was given to Donald O'Connor, a dancer as fluid as, and perhaps even more athletic than, Kelly. "Moses" also solves the problem of Don Lockwood's transition to talkies, since it proves he can sing and dance with the best of 'em. This works in contrast with the problem in the second part of the movie, where Lina becomes a triple threat ("Can't sing, can't dance, can't act").

"Good Mornin'" comes right after the failure of the preview of *The Duelling Cavalier* and is used to enunciate and resolve that external problem by turning *The Duelling Cavalier* into a musical. This leads directly into "Singin' in the Rain," which resolves Gene Kelly's internal problem of whether he dares resurrect his career as a song-and-dance man. The resolution of these two integrated problems marks the end of the second act. From there we go into the obligatory "Broadway Melody" numbers, and we end with a reprise of "Singin' in the Rain."

Thus all of the songs in *Singin' in the Rain* set up or resolve either internal or external problems of the film. These problems, taken together, make up the structure. (See "Singin' Chart #1" on page 33.)

It's surprising how complicated *Singin' in the Rain* actually turns out to be, since it seems so effortless and simple. A musical, packed with songs, has less time to create a complex plot, especially with that immense thirteen-minute brick wall of a showstopper at the end. Allowing three or four minutes per song, and assuming an hour-and-forty-five-minute film, a musical typically has an hour of pure narrative time. How, then, do you tell a story, let alone a complicated story, in just an hour?

To answer that question, musical-comedy writers were born, writers gifted in the quick sketching of character and plot, writers able to integrate story with song as seamlessly as possible. This whole wheezing, cumbersome, unnatural bastard child, neither

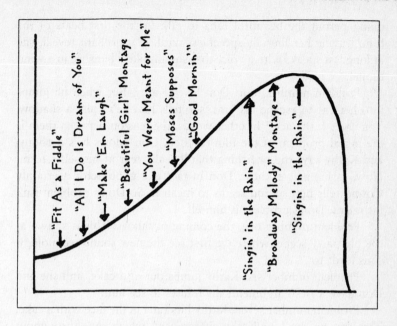

Singin' Chart #1

pure story nor pure music, neither drama nor comedy, has to seem as beautiful, as simple, and as inevitable as any story. It's an art form made up of patches, but unlike other art forms, it can't show one hemstitch or seam—a particular challenge, given the almost impossible assignment Freed handed Comden and Green.

With all these problems in mind, let's examine the first act of *Singin' in the Rain,* an act that itself exists largely to lay out a series of problems.

Problem number one: Don is interviewed by the gossip columnist and tells how he became a star. But while he talks about "Dignity, always dignity" and brags about what a refined, highbrow performer he is, we see he's actually a third-rate song-and-dance man. The first problem of the film, therefore, is that Don's a phony, and a liar to boot.

Problem number two: Don hates Lina. This is brought out during his flashback interview.

Problem number three: Lina has a terrible voice. The writers didn't permit the beautiful Lina to talk for the first beats of the film, leaving her literally speechless until, in a brilliant reveal, she at long last speaks with a voice that sounds like a banshee in a wind tunnel.

Problem number four: Don loves Kathy. But when he jumps into her car to escape his fans, she tells him he's "just a shadow. You can't really act." In other words, the tension between them is the initial problem of the film restated. Don knows he's a phony, and Kathy says the one thing that'll really tear at his self-esteem. Now, as far as we know, Don in fact is a good actor. Certainly Cosmo tells him so and seems to mean it. So Don's problem isn't his talent; Don's problem is himself.

Problem number five: the coming of talkies. This is shown at the big party scene, where we first see the new sound technology. This leads to . . .

Problem number six: Kathy jumps out of a cake, and she and Don have a fresh argument; she refuses to see him.

Problem number seven: Kathy hits Lina in the face with a cake. This sets up the Lina/Kathy antagonism, which runs throughout the entire film.

Problem number eight: Kathy runs off, and Don can't find her.

Problem number nine: Lina gets Kathy fired. Problem seven is reintroduced and strengthened.

Problem number ten: Simpson, the studio head, stops Don and Lina's new picture. The talkies are a sensation. This reprises and strengthens problem number five.

Problem number eleven: Lina can't talk properly. This was presented as a casual joke in problem number three. But here, combined with the coming of talkies, it's a time bomb waiting to explode.

Thus each scene in the first act either creates a new problem or augments an existing problem and makes it more complex. (See the chapter on *Network* for another example of this.) And what appears to be an effortless first act is, in fact, immensely complicated yet told with astounding elegance and grace. The gears are there, the machinery is working, but all is camouflaged as to be almost invisible.

Still, so far this is a standard film structure. It is more beautiful than most, more witty, more creative, but it uses regular dramatic guidelines. The internal problems of Don's insecurities and his love for Kathy are wonderfully meshed with the external problems of the coming of talkies, Lina's grating voice, and whether Don can make the transition to talkies. Normally, after setting up the characters and their problems, the first act would end and the second act begin with the complication of those initial problems. But Comden and Green don't do that; having masterfully used standard dramatic structure for the first act, they then stop the movie dead with the "Beautiful Girl" montage.

This is bold and tricky. It stops the narrative flow and sets a new tone for the film. It shouldn't work because it loses our main characters, yet it does work because the montage is so delightful that it creates an alternative film complete in itself. And it also works because the first act, by being so deceptively dense in the problems it layers on us, fairly begs for digestion time. That is, an audience has to "swallow" a lot of information and relationships, and they need time to take it all in. The montage gives us this needed time by acting as a narrative place maker, the demarcation between the first and second acts, so that when the movie resumes, we can pick up where we left off. It all sounds very simple; it's not. But it works, and that's the cardinal rule of screenwriting (of any art): Follow no rules except the one that works.

Comden and Green also took out an insurance policy on their script by planting the seeds for the second act within this montage, which ends with Kathy Selden in a chorus line. As the camera pulls back to reveal a camera crew filming the montage, someone asks, "Who's that girl?" "That's Kathy Selden." "Great. Let's give her a chance in a movie." "Lina won't like it." "Don't worry about Lina." The montage then ends, and we're off and running into the second act, piggybacking on one of the problems brought up in the first act: the jealous hatred Lina feels for Kathy and how she's already tried to sabotage her career.

Now begins one of the most extraordinary structural choices of the film, and one of its greatest risks. The central problem of the first act is the Don/Kathy relationship, tied up as it is with Don's insecurities, Kathy's ambitions, her disappearance, and her calling Don a walking shadow. In fact, a relationship as laden as this

35

would normally sustain an entire film before it was resolved—and certainly for the length of a musical, whose narrative is abbreviated by the songs. The old structural workhorse of boy meets girl (first act), boy loses girl (second act), and boy finds girl (third act) would commonly be used here. But rather than use Kathy and Don as the center of the film, Comden and Green immediately resolve that relationship. Don meets Kathy, sings "You Were Meant for Me," and they're in love, without complication or problem, for the rest of the film (except for a passing beat at the very end). So the question becomes: Now what?

Having stopped the film after the first act, and then jump-started it into the second act, Comden and Green again bring things to a grinding halt by solving Don and Kathy's relationship, the central internal problem of the film. But they immediately jump-start things again, this time by reintroducing another of the problems they set up in the first act: the coming of the talkies and what to do about *The Duelling Cavalier*. This external problem now takes over the film and is complicated by the voice-lesson scenes. This leads into "Moses Supposes," which functions as a narrative segue reintroducing the fact that Don began his career as a song-and-dance man. From there we move into the various problems that occur in the making of *The Duelling Cavalier*, and from there into the test screening and resulting disaster. All of this material is tied together, with disaster leading to disaster, chaos giving birth to chaos; ultimately it serves as proof that the strongest narrative strategy is to build upon existing problems and make things steadily worse: heightened tension is the flip side of heightened narrative drive. As Hitchcock said, "Pile on the terror."

This escalating list of problems forms a standard second act structure. The only trick is, since the screenwriters have resolved the internal Don/Kathy problem, they're playing with half a deck. But the film's astounding vivacity, its pell-mell pace, and its genuine humor keep things rolling. The only internal problem still remaining from the first act is Don's continuing insecurity as an actor, and even this is submerged in the bravura rhythms of watching the ongoing train wreck called *The Duelling Cavalier*. Again, it's risky filmmaking. And again it works. Don't try this at home, kids!

Finally the decision to turn *The Duelling Cavalier* into a

musical is followed, in a thematic one-two punch, with "Good Mornin'" and "Singin' in the Rain." The resolution of the external problem accompanies the resolution of Don's internal insecurities in his realization that he can make the transition to the talkies. And, again, Comden and Green have broken a narrative rule: just at the end of the second act, where we should be powering toward the third act conclusion, they stop the movie by resolving the entire second act. And they punctuate that almost certain calamity just as they did in the juncture between the first and second acts, by stopping everything cold, this time with a thirteen-minute montage (the obligatory homage to *An American in Paris*). Again, they are ending the movie, telling us they're ending the movie, and then daring us to sit through the montage before settling in for the beginning of the third act—an act, as far as we can tell, without a problem to solve.

Now what? With amazing audacity, Comden and Green create a whole new film, which we'll call the third act, and give it a new problem. Up to now we've had Lina as dope, clown, and terminal twerp. But whatever she's been, she's never been evil. Even when she kicked Kathy out of a job, she did it off camera (and the expression "Out of sight, out of mind" was never more true than in movies). But beginning in this third act, Lina is reborn as a monster, and the third act revolves around her; that is, a secondary character, used largely for laughs in the first two acts, becomes the motive antagonist in the third act. It is, again, the most audacious of filmmaking.

Just as it's Cosmo who is the narrative catalyst in the second act (he suggests they lip-synch Kathy for Lina's voice, that they make *The Duelling Cavalier* into a musical, and that Don "Make 'Em Laugh"), it's Don who is the narrative catalyst for the third act, coming up with the idea to literally raise the curtain on Lina at the climax. And it's Don who shouts out, "Stop that girl!" as Kathy runs up the aisle, an emotional gesture that reveals a genuine, resolved character, a man who can no longer be accused of being a phony. Thus the resolution of the narrative problem of the third act (giving Lina her comeuppance) is also the moment in which Don's internal problem finds visual resolution. Pretty damned nifty. It falls together like this:

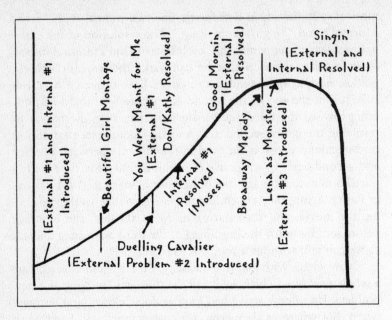

Singin' Chart #2

But there's more. Besides the external and internal problems, all of which are resolved by the end, there's also a thematic through-line. In fact, there are four separate movies in *Singin' in the Rain*, each connected to the theme "How I became a star." The first film is shown at the Hollywood premiere, where we see Don's version of how he became a star versus the more sordid reality of how he really made it big. Then there's the "Broadway Melody" sequence, which is the story of how a young hoofer goes to Broadway and becomes a star. The third sequence is how Don, already a silent star, remakes himself into a talkies star by turning from a Lothario into a song-and-dance man. And the fourth story is how Kathy becomes a star. Four different stories of becoming a star run through the film. And it's this thematic glue that holds the story together when it stops and starts at the second and third act breaks. In fact, without this thematic glue, the film would have fallen apart and become another *Abyss*, where a series of minimovies never gel into a coherent whole. So we have this:

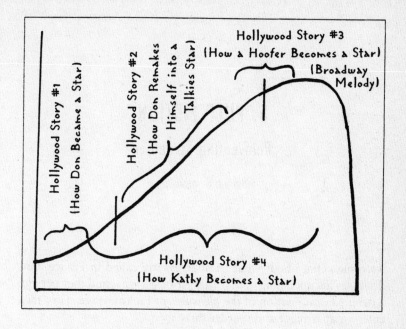

Singin' Chart #3

No doubt this structural sophistication was the result of who knows how many drafts and false starts. Much of the complication was dictated to Comden and Green by the songs they had to use, by the killer *American in Paris* piece that had to go at the end, and by a few simple decisions regarding the creation of decisive act breaks. But the result was one of the most complex films ever created. And one of the best.

5. PULP FICTION

Reinventing Structure

▬ ▬ ▬ ▬

Two men chat about what hamburgers are called in France. One discusses his upcoming date with their boss's wife, and they get into a detailed examination of the pleasures of foot massage. They then enter an apartment and murder three men.

This is the world of *Pulp Fiction,* where stickup thieves are named Honey Bunny and Pumpkin, girlfriends go out for blueberry pancakes while their lovers are nearly sodomized, and professional killers win a twist contest and then plunge an adrenaline needle into the heart of a woman who has overdosed on heroin. It is this mad mixing of the mundane with the brutal that, along with an uncanny ear for dialogue and a daring use of structure, has come to distinguish the amazing work of Quentin Tarantino. *Pulp Fiction* burst upon the movie scene like a thunderclap, and its reverberations will be heard for a long time to come.

Pulp Fiction is, as Tarantino says on his title page, three stories about one story. It is bracketed by the shorter tale of Honey Bunny and Pumpkin, two lowlife thieves who plan and execute a stickup of a coffee shop. It's followed by the gangland execution by Vincent and Jules of two young hoodlums who have stolen a briefcase from their boss, Marsellus Wallace, the local crime lord. This garish scene is followed by the first tale, entitled "Vincent Vega and Marsellus Wallace's Wife," where Vincent has his date with Mia,

Marsellus's wild wife. After dinner at a fifties-style restaurant, Mia mistakes a bag of heroin for cocaine and overdoses. Vincent rushes the comatose Mia to his dealer, where, after a Laurel and Hardy search for an adrenaline syringe, Vincent plunges the needle into Mia's heart, reviving her and ending their date.

The second tale, entitled "The Gold Watch," tells of Butch, an aging boxer, who has been ordered by Marsellus to throw his upcoming fight. Butch instead wins the fight, accidentally killing his opponent in the process, and prepares to leave town before Marsellus finds and kills him. But Fabienne, his girlfriend, has left Butch's heirloom wristwatch in their old apartment, and Butch is forced to retrieve it. However, Vincent is waiting for Butch, who happens upon the killer as he's leaving the toilet. Butch accidentally kills Vincent and runs out of his apartment with his watch, only to bump into Marsellus. The two fight and wind up in a pawnshop, where they are captured by Maynard and Zed, two hillbilly sociopathic homosexual rapists. As Marsellus is being raped, Butch escapes, only to return and save Marsellus, killing Maynard in the process. Marsellus forgives Butch for not throwing the fight and lets him leave Los Angeles a free man.

The third tale, entitled "The Bonnie Situation," picks up where the earlier Vincent and Jules episode ended, with the two killers experiencing what may be a miracle when they impossibly survive a fusillade of bullets from the third of the young hoodlums. They kill the hoodlum and take off with Marvin, their informant, whom Vincent accidentally kills by blowing his head off. They hurry to the house of a friend of Jules named Jimmie, who tells them they must get out before his wife, Bonnie, returns home, finds a headless corpse in her garage, and divorces Jimmie. Jules calls Marsellus, who in turn has a super Mr. Fixit named Mr. Wolf tell them how to clean up the bloody mess. Jules and Vincent then go to a coffee shop, where they see Honey Bunny and Pumpkin start their stickup. Jules gives Pumpkin his money but refuses to give him Marsellus's briefcase. Jules then explains why he is no longer interested in killing Pumpkin, or in killing anyone ever again, and, after letting Honey Bunny and Pumpkin go, walks out with Vincent. We know that Vincent is unknowingly headed toward his own execution because we have already seen Vincent killed by Butch, while Jules, by abandoning the career of a professional killer, is walking into a new life.

It's a baroque tale, to say the least, punctuated by its revolutionary use of movie time. When all the dust has settled, it is Tarantino's unique method of structure that will remain, a genuine landmark in the history of motion pictures. Let's list the scenes as they appear in the movie and lay out how this jibes with their unveiling in actual time. I've placed the linear time equivalents after each scene, running from the first scene as it actually occurred (1) up to the last (5). The letters signify how each scene breaks down into smaller sequences.

- Honey Bunny and Pumpkin plan to rob a coffee shop. (2F)
- Vincent and Jules drive to and prepare to enter an apartment, meanwhile talking of Big Macs and foot massage. (2A)
- Vincent and Jules enter the young hoodlums' apartment, get the briefcase, and kill two hoodlums. (2B)
- Marsellus tells Butch to take a dive. (3)
- Vincent buys heroin from Lance and shoots up. (4A)
- Vincent's date with Mia: dinner and dancing, followed by shooting her with adrenaline. (4B)
- The boy Butch in 1972 receives his dead father's watch and learns it is a family heirloom. (1)
- Butch goes to his boxing match, then escapes into a taxi, where Esmarelda asks him what it's like to kill a man. (5A)
- Butch with Fabienne; Butch can't find his watch. (5B)
- Butch returns to his old apartment and kills Vincent. (5C)
- Butch runs into Marsellus, is captured by Maynard and Zed. Butch kills Maynard and saves Marsellus, who lets Butch go. (5D)
- Butch leaves Los Angeles with Fabienne. (5E)
- Jules and Vincent are saved by a miracle and kill the third hoodlum. (2C)
- Vincent accidentally kills Marvin in a car. (2D)
- Jimmie's house: Mr. Wolf cleans up the bloody mess. (2E)
- Vincent and Jules at the coffee shop. (2G)

That's basically the entire list of scenes. It's amazing that such a short list produces such a long movie (it runs well over two hours). In general, only filmed plays, or perhaps the work of Billy Wilder (such as his astounding *Some Like It Hot*), contain so few scenes. Part of this comes from the unusual use of run-on dialogue that Tarantino employs, rejoicing as he does in its unexpected verbal riffs. Where any other screenwriter might end a scene after a page of plot-advancing dialogue, Tarantino will typically go on for five or even ten pages, celebrating the sheer loquacious ebullience of his characters.

However, take a look at the order of scenes as they would have unrolled in real time, beginning with the brief scene in 1972 where the boy Butch receives the watch and ending five major sequences later with Butch driving out of Los Angeles with Fabienne. Sequence two, involving both the Honey Bunny stickup and Vincent and Jules's assassination of the three hoodlums, breaks down into four smaller units that lie like bookends at the beginning and end of the story. Beneath those sequences are placed sequences three, four, and five, all in their actual time progression. Looked at that way, except for the flashback, scene 1, the only real jumping around is in 2C through 2E, and in 2F and 2G, all of which are shown after their occurrence in real time. Yet this simple shift of a few scenes absolutely defines and magnifies the story.

Let's take a look at how the movie would have played out without the shift of 2C through 2E, 2F, and 2G. If these scenes had been moved to where they actually happened, then a graph showing the major characters against time would look like "Pulp Chart #1" on page 44.

Looked at this way, the two major characters, Jules and Vincent, drop out of the story halfway through, with the action then taken up by Marsellus and Butch, two lesser characters. In other words, if the movie were shown the way events really unfolded, the drama would have been diminished. Now, let's look at how the simple shifting of 2C through 2E, 2F, and 2G changes our graph ("Pulp Chart #2" on page 44).

Jules and Vincent, our major players, run from beginning to end, with the debate between Jules and Vincent whether to embrace or ignore the miracle at the apartment now coming right before the

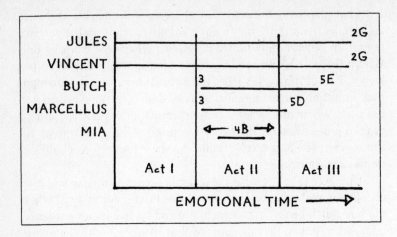

Pulp Chart #1

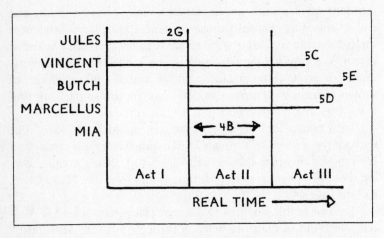

Pulp Chart #2

climactic moment at the coffee shop. Thus, the scenes with the greatest emotional weight come at the end, while lesser scenes, entailing lesser characters and less weighty life decisions, come earlier. Tarantino is ignoring time and placing a rising line of pure emotion as the glue that attaches scenes together. Conventional drama, on the other hand, places tension against time like this:

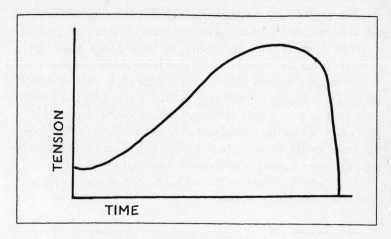

Pulp Chart #3

Tension against time usually works. The only real break from this practice began in the 1950s in France, where filmmakers, distrustful of the artificiality of this structure, tried to make a cinema that, at least on the surface, more closely reflected the way real life unfolds in a series of seemingly unconnected events, like this:

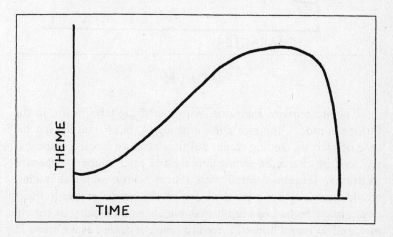

Pulp Chart #4

The truth is that this method, with theme acting as the narrative cement rather than causal events, is just as artificial as the traditional American method. Still, it formed the basis for a countercinema for several decades and filled art houses with some very wonderful movies. Here dramatic theory lay, with moviemakers having to choose whether they wanted to adopt the usual American approach to movie writing, with its occasionally rigid or predictable structure, or embrace the Europeans, with their looser but more lifelike structure, which often risked losing its drive and urgency under a series of narratively unrelated scenes.

But Quentin Tarantino throws both approaches out the window and instead gives us this:

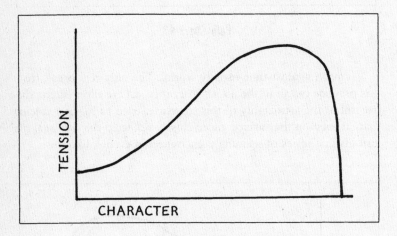

Pulp Chart #5

The arc remains the same, with increasing tension (or, in the European model, the escalating urgency of the theme) upping the ante of each succeeding scene. But now time no longer exists; it is replaced by character, an astounding and revolutionary approach to drama. Tarantino, faced with a story whose major characters would normally have checked out of the movie at the halfway point, knew he had to keep his people alive and kicking at the climax and so found himself forced to reinvent drama as we know it. Once again, necessity was the mother of invention.

But *Pulp Fiction* is a structural tour de force in other ways as well. For example, notice how scenes constantly change tone and texture, usually moving from soft to suddenly violent, continually throwing us off and surprising us with their shifting rhythms. The opening scene, where Vincent and Jules discuss hamburgers and foot massage only moments before they murder three men, is just one example of this.

Or notice how the three major sequences of Vincent's date with Mia, Butch's terrible journey to retrieve his wristwatch, and Jules and Vincent's comic antics to clean up their blood-soaked car are all given a standard three-act structure. Vincent's date with Mia begins its "first act" when he picks her up at her home, proceeds into a "second act" as they eat and dance, and shifts into a "third act" when he saves her from her heroin overdose. Similarly, Butch's tough morning begins its "first act" when Butch talks with Fabienne and discovers his watch is still back at his apartment. "Act two" entails Butch's trip to his apartment, the killing of Vincent, and the run-in with Marsellus and the two hillbillies. "Act three" begins when Butch decides to return to the sadomasochistic basement and save Marsellus. The "first act" of Jules and Vincent's morning begins when they kill the third hoodlum and turns into a "second act" when Vincent accidentally kills Marvin, forcing them to clean up the car. "Act three" takes place in the coffee shop, where Jules saves Honey Bunny and Pumpkin. In other words, all three major stories are told in a traditional form that gives a narrative coherency to what would otherwise be an entirely discontinuous script.

In addition to its structural bravura, *Pulp Fiction* offers a rich and complex treatment of the themes of rescue, of miracles, and of salvation. The rescue motif runs through virtually every sequence, beginning with the rescue of the briefcase from the young hoodlums, proceeding through Vincent's rescue of Mia and Butch's rescue of Marsellus, and ending with Jules's rescue of Honey Bunny and Pumpkin. This theme parallels the continuing presence of miracles, the most obvious being the bullets that miraculously miss Vincent and Jules. But it's really just as much of a miracle that Vincent is able to resurrect Mia from the dead, or that Butch is able to magically pull loose from his ropes and save Marsellus from rape.

Pulp Fiction masterfully integrates the ideas of rescue and miracles with the theme of salvation, where moral choices are constantly presented to our major characters, choices they reject at the risk not only of their souls, but of their lives. Butch saves Marsellus and thereby, without knowing it, saves himself from Marsellus's wrath. And the decision placed before Vincent and Jules whether to accept or reject as a miracle being saved from the bullets that impossibly miss them absolutely determines their destiny: Jules saves himself by accepting the bullets as a miracle, while Vincent damns himself spiritually and physically by rejecting the miracle and thereby refusing to save himself. In fact, *Pulp Fiction* asks a similar question of us, whether to accept or reject its lowlifes, thugs, and killers; the script clearly says that everyone is worthy not only of notice, but of salvation.

Finally, let's examine the major characters and see what thematic and narrative functions they perform:

Honey Bunny and Pumpkin—are saved by Jules.
Vincent—remains "the tyranny of evil men" by denying the
    miracle; he does save Mia but remains unsaved himself.
Jules—changes from murderer to would-be saint, taking lives
    in the beginning and saving lives in the end.
Butch—changes from a corrupt boxer to an honest man to an
    accidental killer to Marsellus's savior—"shepherding the
    weak."
Marsellus—even though he extends mercy to Butch, he
    remains the "tyranny of evil men."
Mia—is saved by Vincent.
Mr. Wolf—saves Jules and Vincent.

So everyone in *Pulp Fiction* accepts or rejects the moral choice to save or be saved. It is ironic that a film dealing with lowlifes and killers should remain one of the most ethical films of the decade.

Finally, no examination of *Pulp Fiction* would be complete without looking at an example of Tarantino's celebrated verbal riffs. Other writers, such as Kevin Smith with his wonderful *Clerks,* have adapted and even expanded the almost theatrically ornate verbal gymnastics that Tarantino employs. In a sense, the world of film dialogue has come full circle; the early talkies used a theatrically complex dialogue that suddenly became telegraphic and poetically dense with the rise of Jimmy Cagney and his hard-bitten gangster films. With a few exceptions this new tradition of tough, abbreviated dialogue held sway in American filmmaking until the nineties, when Tarantino charged onto the scene. This is the scene where Jules and Vincent chat with the hoodlums who stole a briefcase from Marsellus. Like so much of Tarantino's work, it begins slowly, almost comically, lulling us into a false sense of complacency before zapping us at the end.

JULES

How you boys doin'?

(to Brett)

Am I trippin', or did I just ask you a question?

BRETT

We're doin' okay.

JULES

Do you know who we are?

BRETT *shakes his head "no."*

JULES

We're associates of your business partner, Marsellus Wallace. You remember your business partner, don't ya?

(to Brett)

Now I'm gonna take a wild guess here: You're Brett, right?

BRETT

I'm Brett.

> JULES
>
> I thought so. Well, you remember your busi-
> ness partner, Marsellus Wallace, don't ya,
> Brett?

> BRETT
>
> I remember him.

> JULES
>
> Good for you. Looks like me and Vincent
> caught you at breakfast, sorry 'bout that.
> What'cha eatin'?

> BRETT
>
> Hamburgers.

> JULES
>
> Hamburgers. The cornerstone of any nutri-
> tious breakfast. What kinda hamburgers?

> BRETT
>
> Cheeseburgers.

> JULES
>
> No, I mean where did you get 'em? McDon-
> ald's, Wendy's, Jack in the Box, where?

> BRETT
>
> Big Kahuna Burger.

*(Jules asks for a bite of Brett's burger, which he washes down with
Brett's Sprite. He then learns where they have Marcellus's
briefcase, which Vincent retrieves. Jules then shoots Brett's friend
and scares Brett into a petrified terror.)*

> JULES
>
> You ever read the Bible, Brett?

BRETT

Yes.

JULES

There's a passage I got memorized, seems appropriate for this situation: Ezekiel 25:17. "The path of the righteous man is beset on all sides by the inequities of the selfish and the tyranny of evil men. Blessed is he who, in the name of charity and good will, shepherds the weak through the valley of darkness, for he is truly his brother's keeper and the finder of lost children. And I will strike down upon thee with great vengeance and furious anger those who attempt to poison and destroy my brothers. And you will know my name is the Lord when I lay my vengeance upon you."

The two men empty their guns at the same time on the sitting Brett.

When they are finished, the bullet-ridden carcass just sits there for a moment, then topples over.

The comic becomes the horrific, the verbal fireworks destroyed in a hail of bullets. And punctuating it all are the themes of salvation and vengeance, declaimed by a professional killer just moments before he earns his keep.

6. THE USUAL SUSPECTS

The Great Script That Could Have Been Greater

■ ■ ■ ■

The greatest trick the devil ever pulled was convincing the world he didn't exist.

But the devil does exist, and his name is Keyser Sose. In Christopher McQuarrie's brilliant screenplay the mysterious Keyser begins as a misty image, seen in shadow, puffing calmly on a cigarette as he murders a man who looks up at him with a love that transcends fear. We next hear of him through the words of others, words spoken in terror. Later we hear of his legend, of a man who would kill his wife and children rather than let them live in shame. Still later we see the results of his actions: a guilty man freed by high-powered emissaries, a man murdered on a beach, a boat filled with desperate, murdered men, left burning in a harbor. Finally, at the end, we see him for the last time: a man who, all along, hid from us in plain sight—the devil himself, slipping away, never to appear again.

Keyser Sose is one of the most compelling villains in film history, and the structure that McQuarrie created to reveal him serves as his perfect frame. The story of the six murderous weeks that lead up to the final deadly climax on the boat is told by Verbal Kint, a tiny, frightened man stricken with cerebral palsy. He tells his tale to Agent Kujan, a U.S. Customs agent investigating not only the harbor deaths, but also the supposed death of Dean Keaton, a brilliant cop-turned-bad who has been Kujan's nemesis for years. Kujan badgers, cajoles, and sweet-talks Verbal into telling all he knows.

Using a system of flashbacks that gradually brings us up to the present, Verbal unfolds his story. It is a tale of five men, Keaton, McManus, Fenster, Hockney, and Verbal, who meet in a police lineup and decide to plan an emerald robbery. The heist succeeds and leads to yet another robbery, again successful, where a heroin smuggler named Saul is killed. But then the mysterious Mr. Kobayashi appears and announces that he works for the nefarious Keyser Sose. He says Keyser Sose demands that the five thieves attack a boat docked in San Pedro Harbor; it is a suicidal mission, but for those who survive, a great fortune is promised. Fenster refuses to participate and is found murdered. When the rest threaten to kill Kobayashi, he nevertheless forces them to proceed with the attack on the boat. The attack is successful, but the thieves are killed by Keyser Sose, except for Verbal, who is picked up the next morning by the police and forced to talk to Agent Kujan.

As Verbal finishes his tale, Kujan convinces him that it was Keaton all along who masterminded the entire scam, that Keaton is still alive and is, in fact, Keyser Sose. Verbal bursts into tears, convinced by Kujan that Keaton was the secret hand behind everything that has happened. But as Verbal gets up and leaves the police office, Kujan looks at a bulletin board and sees that major elements of Verbal's story have been stolen from scraps and scribbles posted on the board. Not only that, but a fax comes in showing a picture of Keyser Sose, a picture that looks alarmingly like Verbal. Meanwhile Verbal, his cerebral palsy miraculously cured, has gotten into a car driven by the man who in Verbal's tale called himself Kobayashi and drives away just moments before Kujan runs outside looking for him. Kujan realizes too late that Verbal Kint is really Keyser Sose, who, like a puff of wind, will never appear again.

Thus, the entire story is told by the villain, the one man we never meet in the movie itself, the one man who knows the truth and yet refuses to tell it. Like Kujan, we are duped and learn belatedly what little Keyser Sose condescends to let us know. The script is practically unique not only for its use of a hidden villain as narrator, but also for its mind-rattling play with a truth that remains always veiled from us, forever unreachable, a truth that, finally, is itself a character in the drama as elusive as Keyser Sose himself.

Perhaps only Akira Kurosawa's *Rashomon*—a film that also tells its tale in flashbacks—approaches *The Usual Suspects* as an examination of the final futility of seeking the truth.

At the same time, *The Usual Suspects* is riddled with problems and is the most flawed of the "good" scripts that this book examines. It is the extraordinary collision of the brilliant with the ill conceived, the bold with the amateurish, that animates the script. *The Usual Suspects* is a great script that could have been greater, and the tragedy is that McQuarrie's wonderful invention of a narrator who toys with the very nature of truth itself obscured the many mistakes that finally inhibited his writing.

I've separated the main beats of the structure into two headings: those scenes taking place in the present and marked with a number and those scenes that happened in the past and are marked with a letter. The order of letters and numbers reflects in which order they occurred in real time. Thus A happened first and was followed by B, and so on.

ACT ONE

- Last night: the unseen Keyser Sose kills Keaton on the boat, then burns it. (H)
- Six weeks ago: the five suspects meet in lineup, talk in lockup, discuss their next robbery. (A)
- The present: Verbal starts talking to Kujan. (1)

ACT TWO

- Six weeks ago: the emerald heist. (B)
- The present: Verbal mentions Kobayashi. (2)
- Five weeks ago: Redfoot the fence buys the emeralds, tells of a new job; the five suspects kill Saul and get his heroin and money. (C)
- The present: Kujan learns about Keyser Sose. (3)
- Two weeks ago: Kobayashi gives the suspects their boat assignment. (D)
- The present: Verbal tells Kujan about Keyser Sose. (4)
- Two weeks ago: the four suspects find Fenster murdered. (E)

- The present: Verbal says Keaton wanted to kill Kobayashi. (5)
- Two weeks ago: the four suspects threaten to kill Kobayashi, who nevertheless makes them go forward with the boat assignment. (F)

ACT THREE

- Two weeks ago: the four suspects hold up the boat, kill the crew, and are themselves all killed except for Verbal, who hides. (G & H)
- The present: Kujan insists Keaton is alive and is Keyser Sose; Verbal agrees and walks out; Kujan realizes too late that Verbal is Keyser Sose. (6)

As you can see, the structure moves along two separate tracks, each told in linear time, creating a sort of footprint approach, like this:

PRESENT ____   ____   ____   ____

PAST   ____   ____   ____

TIME

Suspects Chart #1

This footprint approach is the most common way to structure flashbacks. Anything more complex than this—for example, *Last Year at Marienbad,* where past events are not revealed in a linear order—can often become too confusing to follow. Billy Wilder's *The Spirit of St. Louis* is a good example of this footprint structure, where, as Charles Lindbergh flies across the Atlantic in one story line, he thinks back on his past life in a second story line. The only twist McQuarrie adds is to begin and end his structure with the attack on the boat, showing Keyser's murder of Keaton twice, first as an ambiguous action where he can't be identified and second in greater detail, although we still can't tell who kills Keaton. This device, known as a "bookend," serves to hold the rest of the story together, herding it like a cowboy keeping his cattle tightly packed in line. On the simplest level this "bookend" serves to ask the external question of the movie: Who is this man (Keaton) who lies dying on a burning ship, and who is this unseen stranger who kills him? In other words, what possible series of events could have led to this extraordinary confrontation on the boat? Once that external problem is voiced in the first scene, the movie soon introduces its internal problem, that of slowly revealing the identity of Verbal Kint and then of Keyser Sose. The movie ends with a double climax, first showing us the continuation of the "bookend," where we again see what happened on the boat, and then taking us up to the present, where we finally resolve the internal problem of Verbal/Keyser's identity.

Although *The Usual Suspects* is really two movies (the present, in which Verbal is interrogated by Kujan, and the past, in which Verbal's tale is revealed to us), its act structure breaks down conventionally. Act one consists of the first three scenes and ends when Verbal finally begins to talk about the emerald heist. The plot grows more complex during the second act and reaches a low point for the four surviving suspects when their attempt to threaten Kobayashi fails and they realize they have no choice but to accept Keyser Sose's suicide mission against the boat. Act three deals with the boat attack, reaches its double climax, and ends as Keyser Sose drives away, never to be seen again. McQuarrie probably employed this relatively simple act structure because he knew his use of flashbacks, coupled with his surprise reveal of the villain as the narrator, would already sufficiently challenge the audience; enough was enough, and a simple narrative spine gave support to a film that otherwise would have been too much to handle.

It's impossible to think about *The Usual Suspects* without first wondering which parts of what we've heard are true, which might be true, and which are merely lies. In laying out the parts (and this list is by no means complete), we might start with this:

THINGS WE KNOW TO BE TRUE

- Keyser Sose has an assistant.
- Edie is dead.
- Fenster is dead.
- All of the suspects are dead (except Verbal).
- There was a lineup.
- There was a hijacking.
- The suspects were somehow made to attack the boat.
- The Saul robbery happened.
- Keaton starts the boat fire, but Keyser pisses on the flames.
- There are no drugs on the boat.

THINGS THAT MIGHT BE TRUE

- There is a fence in California who buys the emeralds.
- The idea of the emerald heist came from McManus.
- Keyser Sose murdered his own family and rose to power.
- Verbal and Keaton first met six months before the movie began (highly unlikely but possible).
- Verbal killed Saul.

THINGS WE KNOW ARE LIES

- Keyser's assistant's name is Kobayashi.
- The fence's name is Redfoot.
- Verbal is a cripple.
- Verbal was in a barbershop quartet in Skokie, Illinois.
- Verbal hid during the attack on the ship.

Other questions remain forever unanswered. Why did Keyser allow himself to be captured by the police after the attack on the boat? Why didn't he just kill Keaton and the rest, destroy the boat, and leave? Why, if on the boat Keyser kills the one person who can finger him, do we find yet another man, badly burned, who survives to describe what Keyser looks like? Is this a second man of whom Keyser had no knowledge, and will Keyser kill him? Why did Keyser let a physical description of himself get around? Why did Verbal admit to Kujan that he killed Saul, when by so doing, he would face a murder charge? Why did Kujan let Verbal go after he admitted to killing Saul? Put simply, these questions have no answers because the screenwriter didn't consider them.

There are other problems with the script, problems dealing primarily with McQuarrie's overdependence upon words to describe actions. For example, when Kujan discusses Keaton's history with Verbal, we never see shots of Keaton throwing people down elevator shafts, being killed in prison, and so on—instead we get the talking head of Kujan. We are told that Kobayashi calls the suspects to say where they can find Fenster's body, but we don't see the scene where Kobayashi makes this call. Nor do we see Fenster, a character whom we've come to know and care about, being killed; we see only his dead body, a far less powerful visual and one not adequate enough to compensate for the time and emotion we've invested in him. It would have been a wonderfully horrifying and mysterious scene to show Verbal/Keyser, masked in shadow or seen from Fenster's point of view, killing Fenster as he suddenly, too late, realizes Verbal's true identity. We never see Keaton deciding that he and the other suspects must kill Kobayashi, nor do we see them beginning to make plans—instead we get a pale description of the decision being made. We never see Edie being shot, nor do we ever see her dead body, something that would have nailed home the fact of her death. And while we do see a fleeting image of Keaton dressed as Keyser Sose, the whole scene of Kujan browbeating Verbal into believing Kujan's pet theory that Keaton is really Keyser Sose would have been far more powerful if we had seen Keaton/Keyser killing Hockney, McManus, and the man in the bathrobe. By depriving us of these visuals, McQuarrie relied too much upon a number of talking heads to fill not only the screen, but the drama as well; this reliance on words rather than actions lessens the film's otherwise extraordinary impact and makes it more obscure than necessary.

Not only that, but the two love stories in the movie—those of Keaton and Verbal and of Keaton and Edie—are given little development and are handled with none of the sophistication that marks the rest of the script. Keaton, presented as the alternative identity for Keyser, is said to love Edie so much that he is tempted to give up his life of crime and devote himself to her. But precious little time is devoted to his relationship with Edie, and what we see is a paint-by-the-numbers scene, without insight or depth.

Similarly, we are asked to believe that Keaton returns to a life of crime in part out of concern for Verbal, who begs for Keaton's help in the emerald heist. Later, as Keaton lies dying, Keyser gives him the greatest gift an elusive devil can give: he lets Keaton look him in the face before his execution. But these acts of love aren't sufficiently supported in the script, which avoids deep emotional attachment while fearlessly confronting so many other problems.

Nonetheless, the audacity of the plot, the vividness of the characters, and the cutting-edge immediacy and sharpness of the dialogue overcome most of these shortcomings. *The Usual Suspects* remains an extraordinary film, eerie and resonant, rich with its theme that truth is elusive, always receding before us, never attainable, and that the very nature of life is to reach for the unreachable. While Keyser Sose may disappear in a puff of breath, *The Usual Suspects* stays behind, haunting us forever not only for the great script it is, but for the greater script it could have been.

7. HIGH NOON

Aristotle Goes Out West

━━ ━━ ━━ ━━

A man stands in the middle of a dusty street. He is alone, the street deserted, the sun high overhead. He scans the buildings one last time, vainly searching for someone, anyone, to join him; but no one appears. He wipes a drop of sweat off his brow, gulps down his fear, and as the camera booms up until the man is a tiny dot, he walks away from us toward certain death.

We are in the land of the western, that mythic creation where brave men face impossible odds battling terrible villains, all for law and honor and the women they love. But in the case of *High Noon* there's something missing from that classic fairy tale: this time our hero is alone, abandoned by the town he has fought to civilize. Will Kane has seen everything in which he believes—all his friends, everyone he respects, even the love of the woman he has just married—come crumbling down before his eyes. The world will never be the same again for Will Kane, and the movie western will never be the same after *High Noon*.

The great myth of the western was born in the period when the boundaries of America began pressing past the Mississippi, in a brief, wild, romantic era, when rustlers and Indians, gold miners and cattlemen, settlers and ranchers, vied for the conquest of a continent. Though supplanted briefly by the gangster myths of the thirties, and the science fiction mythology of George Lucas in the seventies, the western myth still remains with us, constantly defining and redefining where we stand and what we dream. The simplistic Wild West morality tales of the thirties and forties described the sentiments of those decades, where good conquered evil and hard work paid off. The sixties was a time of moral intervention and found its keynote in *The Magnificent Seven,* where first-world gunfighters saved third-world farmers. The seventies was a time of moral reappraisal, which *Butch Cassidy and the Sundance Kid* or *McCabe and Mrs. Miller* aptly captured. The eighties created *Silverado,* a pale retread of a western hearkening back to simpler times. The nineties brought us *Unforgiven,* a morally ambiguous tale born of a morally ambiguous era. Each movie describes and defines the decade in which it was created.

Which brings us to the fifties, a period in which a Commie lay behind every door and no one could trust his neighbor not to be a spy or a traitor. It was during these paranoid times that the young screenwriter Carl Foreman in 1947 first conceived of a western that would reflect his strong feelings in favor of the United Nations. But as the evil of McCarthyism spread, and as Foreman and his liberal friends began to be investigated by the House Un-American Activities Committee (HUAC), Foreman in 1948 began to refocus his story around the Communist witch-hunts. He worked with Stanley Kramer's small film company, writing the first treatment of *High Noon* in 1949. But the idea lay dormant for several years while Kramer produced *Home of the Brave, The Men,* and *Cyrano de Bergerac.* Finally, in 1951 *High Noon* was reactivated and Foreman went to work on the script. It was the height of the HUAC hearings, with Hollywood stars naming fellow artists as subversives, and the paranoia and backstabbing that haunted Foreman's personal life began to populate his script. The famous scene where Gary Cooper goes to church only to be abandoned by everyone sprang from personal experiences Foreman went through as his friends debated whether to turn on their fellow filmmakers for the sake of keeping their own jobs. In fact, Foreman found himself writing at a fever pitch simply because he knew it was only a matter of time before he himself would be called before HUAC and asked to name names. He knew in advance that he'd refuse, and this resolution helped power the equally haunted resolution of his hero in the script. As Carl Foreman later said, "I became the Gary Cooper character."

He also became Aristotle, using many of the ancient philosopher's prescriptions for drama. Like *The Clock, 12 Angry Men, Cleo From 5 to 7, Dr. Strangelove,* and the last half of *Crimson Tide, High Noon* is told in real time, with the eighty-five-minute running time of the movie corresponding almost exactly to the running time of the actual story. And, more Aristotelian in setting than any of those other films except *12 Angry Men,* which takes place in one room, *High Noon* is confined to the one claustrophobic town of Hadleyville, an intellectual proscenium where the drama begins when three bad guys ride into town and ends as the hero rides out.

After the script was completed, Kramer went first to Fred Zinnemann, a rising young Austrian director whose *The Men,* starring Marlon Brando in his first screen role, had been one of Kramer's first productions. Zinnemann, an expatriate European who knew nothing about westerns, agreed to direct the script not because he cared about the period, or about Foreman's deft skewering of the McCarthy era, but because Zinnemann was attracted to the moral crisis faced by the marshal, a universal situation that resonates even now, almost half a century after the HUAC witch-hunts.

Kramer next approached Gary Cooper, whose career was running on empty after a few failed movies. Cooper liked the script and agreed to cut his $275,000-per-picture price to $60,000 plus a percentage of the profits. For the role of Helen Ramirez, the marshal's ex-lover, a rising Mexican actress named Katy Jurado was chosen; gossip around the set ran that she was on her way to becoming a big star and would bury the model turned actress who was to play Cooper's wife, an unknown in virtually her first film named Grace Kelly.

After the film had been completed, Kramer and Foreman were devastated to find the first test screening was a disaster. The audience didn't "get it." Elmo Williams reedited the film, cutting out sequences, rearranging others, and adding, throughout the movie, excerpts from "Do Not Forsake Me, Oh My Darlin'," Dimitri Tiomkin's extraordinarily haunting song with lyrics by

Ned Washington. Shots that had earlier been edited out, of Cooper flinching in pain as his duodenal ulcer acted up, were reedited back in because his grimaces of pain looked exactly like the anguish of a man stricken with fear. But test screenings still weren't very good, and it was with absolute surprise that Kramer, Zinnemann, and Foreman found when the film came out that they had created an instant classic. Cooper won his second Best Actor Oscar, Grace Kelly began her meteoric rise to stardom, Fred Zinnemann cemented his claim as one of the rising young directors of the fifties, Stanley Kramer established himself as one of the finest producers in Hollywood; Carl Foreman, however, soon found himself marooned in Europe, where he would live for much of the next decade, a victim of the Communist witch-hunts, a refugee from the paranoiac accusations and fears that he had fought and written about.

High Noon is the story of Will Kane, who has just married the beautiful Amy when he learns that Frank Miller, a psychopathic killer who swore to kill Will just before he was sent to jail, has been released and is returning on the noon train; three of Miller's old gunmen wait for Miller at the station; in less than two hours, four men will be setting out to kill Will. Will's friends and Amy tell him to leave town, which he does, with Amy beside him. But once out of town Will tells Amy that he must return, that he can't run from a threat; besides, he and Amy would be more vulnerable alone on the prairie than in town with a posse of locals backing him up. Back in town, Will finds that Amy, a committed Quaker, is against violence and tells Will that if he stays, she's leaving him forever. Will tells her that he can't leave, and Amy goes to wait for the noon train. Will starts hunting for help. He first goes to his friend the judge, who, certain that Will will be killed and fearful of Miller's violence, leaves town. Harvey, Will's deputy, will help only if Will appoints him the new marshal; when Will refuses Harvey storms off. Men in the bar, liking the lawlessness that Miller represents, refuse to help. Will seeks out some of the better citizens as they worship in church and finds that the minister is morally paralyzed and can offer no help. Worse, Will's best friend persuades the churchgoers that a gunfight would be bad for business and urges Will to leave. Will's mentor, an aging sheriff, is too old, arthritic, and embittered to help. The one man who had earlier volunteered backs out when he sees Will can't assemble a posse. Even Helen Ramirez, Will's ex-lover, not only refuses to lend her assistant, Sam, to help Will, but prepares to leave town, abandoning Will to certain death. After trying and failing everywhere to find help, Will writes his last will and testament, convinced he is about to be killed. The noon train arrives, and Will, all alone, goes off to face four killers. But in a running gun battle surging through town, Will kills two of the men, only to have the third killed by Amy, who has returned. Will shoots Frank Miller and embraces Amy as the townspeople, unwilling to help Will in his hour of need, now come out from hiding and congratulate him on his bravery. Will stares at them and, in a final gesture of contempt, throws his badge into the dirt. He then rides off with Amy.

The structure of *High Noon* is absolutely classic, textbook Aristotle, containing one of the most concise and perfect examples in film of a first act:

- Under opening credits, three bad guys meet and ride into town.
- Will Kane marries Amy with his friends in attendance; the three bad guys ask the stationmaster about the noon train; the stationmaster receives a telegram and runs into town.
- Will gives up his badge and learns Frank Miller is arriving on the noon train; Will's friends tell him to leave; Will and Amy ride out of town.
- Helen Ramirez and Harvey watch Will and Amy ride out of town.
- Will says he must go back: "I have to, that's the whole thing."

The whole first act runs just ten minutes, far shorter than a typical first act, yet it contains everything necessary to propel us into a second act. The external problem has been personified by the three bad guys riding malevolently into town and asking about the noon train. The internal conflict between Will's duty to protect the town and his desire to honor his wife's wishes to leave is resolved when Will decides he must go back and fight Frank Miller.

Between the beginning and Will's decision to return, we've met many of the townspeople with whom we'll be dealing throughout the rest of the story. In a remarkably concise ten minutes an entire world's been created, fully populated with well-realized characters, heavy with crisis, and locked down by the protagonist's decision to engage the enemy. From here we move swiftly into the second act:

- Will and Amy argue; she says he must leave with her or she'll leave alone; Will says he must stay and fight.
- The judge packs and leaves; he calls Will a fool for staying.
- Helen and Harvey talk; Harvey gets an idea and runs out.
- Harvey tells Will: "Appoint me the new marshal and I'll fight with you"; Will refuses and Harvey leaves.
- Helen tells Sam not to help Will.
- Herb tells Will he'll be back "loaded for bear."
- Will and Amy talk; they cannot reconcile.
- Will asks for help in the saloon; he is rejected and jeered at.
- Will with Mart the sheriff, who is too old and crippled to help.
- A drunk asks Will for a chance to help; Will declines.
- Helen sells her store; she prepares to leave town.
- Sam Fuller hides while Will asks for him.
- Harvey and Helen fight; they break up.
- Will asks for help in church; he is rejected by all, including his best friend.
- Harvey and Will fight in the livery stable.
- Herb sees Will is alone; Herb backs out of the fight.
- A young teenager asks Will's permission to help; Will declines.
- Will writes his last will and testament as the noon-train whistle blows.

It is hard to imagine a second act more relentless in its progression. Since the little town is in fact a microcosm of the world, everyone in it represents a part of humanity. When first Amy, then the judge, and then Harvey reject Will, literally love, law, and order have left the town. Normally symbolism this obvious would be intrusive and clichéd, but as in Hemingway's *The Old Man and the*

Sea, where the symbolism is there to be observed or ignored as the reader chooses, and where the story functions perfectly well on its narrative logic, the heavier meaning doesn't distract from the story and its own insistent realism. When the judge takes down the scales of justice and folds up the American flag, the objects are simply the things a judge would logically throw into his saddlebag before he rode out of town; the audience can infer more if they like, but the story doesn't hang upon it. While the other people Will meets obviously symbolize differing elements of society, they also are simply what they are: the people Will would logically seek out for help. In exact proportion, the tension rises with each new setback for the protagonist, creating a narrative urgency that is relentless. As for the act break, it comes at the classic low point for the protagonist when Will, completely without help or hope, abandoned by everyone, writes out his last will and testament as he hears the train whistle announcing the arrival of men sworn to kill him. Will stands, readies his guns, and steps forth to embrace his destiny by walking into the third act:

- In a running gun battle Will kills the first killer.
- Amy, about to leave on the train, hears the shot and runs back into town; Helen leaves town forever.
- Will runs into a barn, where he kills a second killer; he rides a horse out of the burning barn and holes up in a building; Miller and another shoot it out with Will.
- Amy enters a building where she kills a third killer; she is captured by Frank Miller, who holds her hostage.
- Will steps outside; Amy breaks free, and Will kills Miller.
- Will and Amy are greeted by the townspeople; Will throws down his badge and rides out of town with Amy.

Just as it's difficult to think of a more demoralizing act than the second, it's hard to think of a more glorious act than the third. Not only does Will defeat four-to-one odds, but he does it with the help of his wife, who lets her love for him overcome her religious scruples. The climax, classic in its form, involves Will's killing of his nemesis (the external threat defeated), followed almost immediately by his embrace of his wife and his rejection of the townspeople who turned on him (his internal fears defeated). His riding out of town is the perfect denouement: quick, decisive, and final.

The only question that the film begs is the central issue of how all the events of the past hour and a half have changed Will. Has he forever and completely lost his faith in humanity? Is there room for Will (and us) to hope? Is there any chance that mankind can act in its own best self-interests, or are we forever relegated to excuses for why we decline moral challenges and allow evil to flourish? The film doesn't give any answers, but Will's riding away into the distance casts a dim light on his—and, for that matter, our—hopes for the human race.

For a film as taut as this, with a plot as simple and insistent, it's remarkable how many connective tissues Carl Foreman invented to keep the narrative moving along. Besides the central problem of the danger posed to Will and the steps he takes to fight that danger, Elmo Williams also uses the motif of the dirgelike "Do Not Forsake Me, Oh My Darlin'" to remind us again and again of what's at stake. Similarly, the visual motifs of clocks, counting out the minutes and seconds until noon, continually tell us time is running out. (In fact, Zinnemann "overcranked" his shots of the many clocks in the movie, shooting a few more than the standard twenty-four frames per second, so that their hands and pendulums move slower and more ominously than they would in real life.) Last, Foreman from time to time puts in characters (the judge, the old sheriff, Helen, and others) who discuss the theme and keep it powering forward. Like the old debater's trick, Foreman tells us what he's going to tell us, tells us, then tells us what he told us.

As if this weren't enough to keep the story on rails, Foreman also created three alternate stories to use as cutaways. This was necessitated in part by having to show some other narrative line while Will was walking from place to place; rather than show Will walking across the street, Foreman would cut to alternate stories. Normally a "B" story would be more than enough to do the job, but Foreman, with less time to play with but vastly greater ambition, created not just a "B" story (Amy and her anguish over leaving Will), but also a "C" story (Helen's methodical preparations to leave town) and a "D" story (Harvey's internal journey through greed and self-pity to shame). Each of these lesser stories finds its own rising line of tension and its own resolution; and, rather beautifully, all revolve around the mutually shared themes of loyalty and self-preservation.

Nor does the complexity end there. Foreman intended to have the town represent the body politic for all humanity, so he populated it with people who corresponded to as many of the varying aspects of mankind as he could. Each has his own separate reason for turning on Will:

> The judge—fears reprisals from Miller.
> Harvey—wants more power.
> The men in the bar—are attracted to Miller's lawlessness.
> Mart the ex-sheriff—is too old and embittered to help.
> Sam Fuller—is afraid to make his wife a widow.
> Herb—doesn't want to die.
> The church people—are afraid of losing money.
> Amy—thinks killing is wrong.
> Helen—her pride is hurt by Will's leaving her.

But not everyone turns on Will:

> Sam, Helen's assistant—only follows her orders in not helping Will.
> The drunk—is too old and alcoholic to help.
> The teenager—is too young to help.

All of these reasons for not helping Will are real and believable. Nor has Foreman completely stacked his deck with cowards, mercenaries, and misguided idealists. There are brave men in town, but some are too young, too sick, or too old—Foreman doesn't discount or deny bravery, but he also says that luck and timing have just as much to do with salvation. In fact, in a sequence in the script that was shot but later edited out, Foreman even invented a cutaway "E" story of a brave deputy who, hauling a criminal into jail, is simply out of town when the shooting starts.

A last note on this extraordinary film. *High Noon* follows two broad progressions: Will begins his internal journey as an idealistic lawman who believes in the moral mechanism of civil probity to finally safeguard society; in other words, Will believes that we are our brother's keeper, that all the fine platitudes about civic obligations really work, that the ethical fabric that binds society protects us all. But by the end Will feels that he has lived a lie, that he can finally count on no one but himself (and Amy), and that each individual creates his own moral universe. As the town shifts from the trappings of civilization to the depths of barbarism, Will moves from idealism to bitter realism. In one sense Will Kane is Rick from *Casablanca* just after he was dumped by Ilsa and before he regains his hope for mankind. The two characters together form a whole, beginning with Will's initial idealism and ending with Rick reclaiming his. We pray that in time Will might regain his faith in humanity (and that humanity will deserve that faith); but at the end of *High Noon,* Will, with his dreams and hopes gone, walks away from a world that lied to him that civilization works.

8. CITIZEN KANE

Flashback As Narrative

He talked like a college professor at two. At three he looked like Dr. Fu Manchu and spouted Shakespeare like a veteran. At eight he started making his own highballs. He was leading man for Katharine Cornell at eighteen. Today, at twenty-four, he has the most amazing contract ever signed in Hollywood.

—Alva Johnson and Fred Smith,
writing about Orson Welles for the *Saturday Evening Post*

And that was just the half of it. Orson Welles was a legend by the time he was twenty. His radio broadcast of H. G. Wells's *The War of the Worlds* terrified the country and had hundreds jumping into jalopies and tearing off into the hills to escape the Martian invasion. His *Macbeth* was the first all-black production of Shakespeare on Broadway. His production of Marc Blitzstein's pro-union opera, *The Cradle Will Rock,* was so controversial that it was shuttered by an act of Congress. His *Julius Caesar* was a modern-dress version that drew parallels between power politics in the Roman Empire and the rise of fascism in Europe; it galvanized Broadway and created the core of actors who would work with Welles throughout his career, including Joseph Cotten, Agnes Moorehead, Everett Sloane, George Coulouris, Ray Collins, and Paul Stewart. Leaving Broadway, he broke new ground in radio drama with his Mercury Theatre on the Air, reinventing the use of narration and the narrator's voice.

But it was his movie contract with RKO Studio in July of 1939 that had the world talking. Welles, at the age of twenty-four, was granted complete artistic control over any movie he chose to make. Hollywood, insanely jealous of the power this Broadway upstart had been granted, sniped at him left and right, calling him Little Orson Annie and praying for his comeuppance.

And at first it looked as though they'd get their wish. Welles first wanted to make Joseph Conrad's *Heart of Darkness,* which he had already done as a radio drama. He planned to play both Marlow and Kurtz and even shot long test sequences. But the proposed budget was too high, and the project was finally dropped. Next Welles tried *The Smiler with the Knife,* a political thriller based on the novel by Nicholas Blake. Welles says he wrote the script "in seven days," but the project was abandoned when he and the studio people couldn't agree on casting (Welles wanted a relatively unknown actress named Lucille Ball, but the studio declined, saying she couldn't carry a film; just as well: twenty years later she owned the studio). Knowing he was becoming the laughingstock of Hollywood, Welles picked a fight with his brilliant producer, John Houseman, who promptly quit. Without an idea, and barely hanging on to his studio deal, Welles happened upon a brilliant but alcoholic and erratic screenwriter named Herman Mankiewicz, who suggested they make a "prismatic" film about the life of a man seen from several points of view. At first John Dillinger was suggested, then the evangelist Aimee Semple McPherson. When Welles turned down these names (as he was bound to do, since he couldn't have played either lead), Mankiewicz "innocently" suggested William Randolph Hearst, the newspaper tycoon, about whom he "happened" to have just written a first draft. Welles saw he'd been maneuvered by Mankiewicz, but he also saw the possibilities and jumped at the idea.

Mankiewicz's first draft was entitled *American.* There had been other flashback movies before—Mankiewicz was friends with Preston Sturges, who wrote *The Power and the Glory,* an account of a railroad tycoon as recalled by his friends and enemies at his funeral. But this new film of Mankiewicz's would deal with one of the most famous and powerful living Americans and would face inevitable political pressure if it ever came out, let alone if it were ever made—something RKO was reluctant to let happen. They fought Welles at every turn, insisting that he make something more politically correct.

But even if Welles could grease *American* past the studio, he had another problem: Mankiewicz had a reputation as not only the most witty and brilliant screenwriter in the world, but also as the most impossible; he had been kicked out of nearly every studio in town for insulting whoever stood in his way, and he was virtually unemployable. Shamelessly erratic, Mankiewicz was known for getting drunk and wandering off in the middle of writing a script to play the ponies or bet on which fly would go to a cube of sugar. But then fate stepped in: Mankiewicz broke his leg in a drunken fall at Chasen's. Entombed in a huge cast, he was, at least temporarily, incapacitated, a situation that, in Mankiewicz's case, meant sober. To see that he'd stay that way, Houseman, who had patched things up with Welles, packed Mankiewicz off to a guest ranch in a small town named Victorville. It was there, watched over by both Welles and Houseman, that Mankiewicz crafted one of the greatest screenplays ever written.

At first Welles wanted to grab full credit for what he knew was a brilliant screenplay. But Mankiewicz had labored too long in the greedy fields of Hollywood not to know how that game was played; he had ample proof that he was the primary author of what had now become *Citizen Kane* and forced Welles to give him cocredit. In a way, there was a rough-and-ready justice in Welles's unfair grab for a credit he really didn't deserve: Welles didn't win the Academy Award in 1941 for either best actor or for best director—the two awards he probably did deserve—and instead walked away with the Oscar for best original screenplay, an award he shared with Mankiewicz.

Citizen Kane was Welles's greatest triumph and greatest tragedy. It has been voted the best film of all time by poll after poll and resonates in our collective unconscious unlike almost any other movie. But its financial failure (or, more exactly, its failure to succeed), due in part to Hearst's efforts to stop and then limit its release, and in part to the difficulty of the subject matter, turned Welles from a genius with a blank check into merely a genius. He was never again given the creative control to make the movies that were in his fantastic brain, and the rest of his life is a sad tale of abandoned projects or of films that hint at the brilliance that budget constraints and ham-handed moneymen castrated. Always in need of money, either to finance his projects or simply to support himself, Welles was finally relegated to selling cheap wine on TV and hoping to complete the films he had begun and never had the time or the finances to finish. As Welles said until the day he died, "I drag my myth around with me."

Considering its reputation as a complex movie, the structure of *Citizen Kane* is fairly simple. Part of this reputation springs from the confusion its plot evoked when it first appeared. Its structure, based on a series of flashbacks, was something new and challenging to the audience of the forties. And some of its complicated reputation springs from the extraordinary visual style that confuses some viewers before they can even begin to understand the plot. Finally, *Citizen Kane* is a movie that must be carefully watched. Turn aside for just a moment and you'll miss what happened to the first Mrs. Kane. Grab for your popcorn and Kane's son is dead. Cough and ten years have passed. Pauline Kael is right: *Kane* is a shallow masterpiece, lacking the profound psychological insights of other great films, but it's one masterpiece that demands our complete attention.

It is the structure of *Citizen Kane* upon which this chapter will concentrate. The brilliant choices as to who tells the story, in what order they tell it, and which memories are recounted are textbook examples of the use of flashback. The very simplicity of the approach, and the easily comprehensible MacGuffin of Rosebud, allow for a greater thematic and narrative resonance than would be possible in a straight plot. Like the flashback structure employed in *The Usual Suspects, Citizen Kane* is a Pandora's box whose outer simplicity reveals surprises and wonders without end.

Let's take a look at the extraordinary first act, which begins with one of the most famous openings in movie history:

- 1941—We approach Xanadu and enter Kane's bedroom; he lets go of a snow globe, says, "Rosebud," and dies.
- *News on the March*—Kane's life is told, newsreel style.
- Projection room; Thompson is told to find Rosebud.

That's it, three scenes. The first, beginning with the famous shot of a series of walls and barriers topped with a NO TRESPASSING sign alerts us to the theme, that we are venturing into territory to which we really have no right to go, that we are trespassers, and that whatever we learn is finally none of our damn business. The snowy scene captured in a child's toy, as we'll later learn, is a clue to the mystery of Charles Foster Kane. But it's Kane's last word, "Rosebud," that presents us with the first and overarching problem of the movie. Who is this man? How does he—how can anyone—live as he does? And why is he saying "Rosebud" as he dies? The scene is filled with questions that propel and define the rest of the movie. Critics have charged that the whole MacGuffin of Rosebud is simplistic and that no single event can explain a life; Welles himself said the psychology of the movie is "dollar-book Freud." All of this is probably true. But if the final explanation of Kane's life is unsatisfying, it is also deeply powerful—an image and an explanation that resonate and move us profoundly even as we rebel against their simplicity. But then, who's to say that even if the final truth of anyone's life is ultimately unknowable, a great truth nevertheless lies within the seemingly simplistic answer of Rosebud?

Ostensibly many of these questions are answered in the second scene, which tells the official version of Kane's life and gives us the biographical vertebrae upon which the rest of the movie will hang. Like the old debater's trick, we're told up front what the rest of the movie will go on to tell. This newsreel anchors us and places the events to follow in a context; it tells us where we're going and leaves us less disoriented and better able to see how events fit together. In another sense, while the newsreel scene answers many of the questions posed in the first scene, it implies just as many new questions, which are posed directly in the third scene, where newsmen sit in the brilliantly photographed screening room and wonder whether the heart and substance of any life can be laid out and tied up with a ribbon. Just as the movie began with the NO TRESPASSING sign, the third scene implies that the truth, which the second scene makes seem so easily definable, is in fact finally unknowable. Still, a possible solution is offered: Kane's dying word, "Rosebud," may hold the key to his life, the clue that explains everything he did. Thus Thompson, our reporter-guide, is assigned to find Rosebud.

The first act ends with that assignment: in a brilliant three scenes we've met all of our major characters (the newsreel did that for us) and had the movie's central problem posed to us, first indirectly by our witnessing of Kane's death as he utters "Rosebud," then directly by Thompson's boss. If the boss had let the question of Rosebud go unasked, there would have been no movement into the second act and no movie; the boss, by accepting the challenge and mystery of Rosebud, powers Thompson and us into the second act:

- Thompson meets Susan; she refuses to talk.
- Thompson at the Thatcher Library, where he reads Thatcher's diary:
    - 1871—Thatcher takes charge of Kane, five, from his mother, against her husband's wishes.
    - 1898—Kane, thirty-three, tells Thatcher he will defend the poor with his newspaper.
    - 1930—Kane, bankrupt, tells Thatcher he wishes he'd become everything Thatcher hates.
- Thompson meets Bernstein:
    - 1890—Kane moves in, starts running a newspaper, writes his "Declaration of Principles" to help the people.
    - 1898—Kane buys away reporters from a rival newspaper; he and his people celebrate.
    - 1899—Leland and Bernstein look at the statues Kane has bought.
    - 1900—Kane returns from Europe with his first wife.
- Thompson meets Jed Leland:
    - 1900–1909—Kane's marriage to his first wife disintegrates; Leland says Kane loved only himself and his mother.
    - 1915—Kane meets Susan: "I run a couple of newspapers, what do you do?"
    - 1916—Kane at a political rally to stop Gettys; Kane is about to become governor; Kane and his first wife go to Susan's house; Gettys confronts Kane; Kane's political career is ruined: "Fraud at Polls!";

          Leland argues with Kane: "You want love on your terms."

      1919—Susan "sings" at the opera; Leland writes a bad review; Kane finishes the review and fires Leland.

- Thompson visits Susan:

      1917—Kane forces Susan to take voice lessons.

      1919—Susan "sings" at the opera; Kane claps; Susan argues with Kane after Leland sends back the "Declaration of Principles."

      1920—Susan attempts suicide; Kane agrees to let her stop singing.

      1929–1932—Susan does jigsaw puzzles in Xanadu.

      1932—Susan and Kane at the "picnic"; Susan threatens to leave, and Kane begs her to stay; she leaves.

There it is—one of the most famous second acts in movie history. Notice that Thompson's search for Rosebud begins with Susan, Kane's second wife, who refuses to talk to him. Why put this scene in, when it doesn't reveal anything about Kane (except, obliquely, how Kane, even in death, casts a shadow over Susan's life)? The reason is that if Susan weren't inserted here, she'd be lost to the story until Jed Leland speaks of her halfway through the second act. Placing Susan up front prepares us for her later entrance and ensures that she doesn't end up an intrusive new character introduced too late into the story for us to care about her.

The decision to begin the flashbacks with the Thatcher material was made for two reasons. First, Thatcher knew Kane the least and saw him only between long periods of separation. Second, Thatcher gives us a sweeping overview of Kane's life that prepares us for the closer glimpses to come. Like an astronomer looking at a star first through a wide-angle lens and then narrowing down to increasingly more powerful lenses, we begin our observation of Kane from a distance. This Thatcher sequence is also a minimovie in its own right, beginning when Kane is torn from his mother, proceeding through Kane's idealistic young manhood as a crusading newspaperman, and ending with Kane's financial ruin—a unifying device that lends a coherency to all the flashbacks to come, much as Quentin Tarantino in *Pulp Fiction* told a series of minimovies that are connected through characters and theme.

Bernstein, the unquestioning gofer, is next in line to tell his version of Kane's life. If Thatcher perceived Kane through a veil of hate, then Bernstein remembers him with blithe incomprehension: Bernstein sees all, understands little, remains forever loyal, and grows rich. But while Thatcher saw Kane through the sweep of years, Bernstein chooses to remember only the idealistic early years. Like Thatcher, Bernstein tells a minimovie, a story complete in itself, beginning with Kane as a single young man taking charge of a newspaper, continuing through his rise to power and the birth of his corruption when he hires away rival reporters and forces them to sing his song, and ending with his first wife: the idealist has been tainted, the bachelor has married, the weak has become strong. Like the Thatcher wide-angle overview, this finer lens is presented in chronological order so as to be less confusing to the audience. In fact, there's very little overlap throughout the entire film—with the exception of Thatcher's remembrance, one character leaves off his or her memory of Kane just where another's begins—a necessary device, or the movie, already challenging, would have become too difficult to comprehend.

The third section is still more intimate. Jed Leland begins where Bernstein left off, with Kane's marriage to his first wife. Leland's version of the marriage is a high point of the movie and one of the great scenes in all film, brilliantly distilling a marriage into a series of overlapping breakfast conversations—it is screenwriting at its very best: quick, creative, and fluid, using the rapid progression of time with the grace of a choreographer. Leland's minimovie, beginning with the problem of the breakup of Kane's marriage, now proceeds to solve that problem by introducing us to Susan. Thematically Susan is the personification of the "little people" about whom Kane has spoken so passionately but of whom he has so little direct knowledge. His growing love for Susan runs parallel with his rise to political power. These two narrative lines collide when Kane's affair with Susan is exposed and Kane's political future is destroyed. The screenwriters are adroit in noting the irony that it is Kane's love for a little person that destroys his chance to help the "little people." They're just as adroit in sliding by the irony that Kane is on his way to a warehouse to revisit his past (that is, to glimpse his beloved sled) when he meets Susan, who represents the same innocence he'd once found in his past. The minimovie moves into its second act when it's complicated by Kane's scandal, which ruins his hopes for the governor's office, and advances into its third act when Kane pushes Susan's career much as he had planned to push his own and forces her to sing opera. This brilliant opera sequence climaxes with the destruction of Kane's friendship with Leland. A minimovie that begins with the breakup of a marriage ends with the breakup of a friendship.

The fourth sequence lets us glimpse Kane from the most intimate perspective yet, that of his second wife, Susan. But while Leland paints a largely idyllic romance between Kane and Susan, she sees things far differently. Browbeaten by Kane into singing opera, she turns shrewish and bitter, berating Kane for his egomania, attempting suicide, and, when that fails, leaving Kane, as Paddy Chayefsky would say in *Network,* to his "glacial isolation." In fact, it's significant that every sequence ends with a loss: the Thatcher sequence begins with Kane being stripped from his parents' side and ends with him bankrupt; Kane loses his innocence in the Bernstein sequence; in Leland's minimovie Kane loses his first marriage, his hopes, and his friendship; and in Susan's minimovie Kane first loses his ability to control political events, then suffers a growing inability to control the people's tastes, and finally is unable to keep his wife. Through the entire second act Kane's life is one loss or defeat after another, in an unending line that, inevitably, leaves Kane old, embittered, and alone. The extraordinary surprise is that this litany of loss is balanced by a visual and narrative style that is so fast, so unexpected, and so ironically joyful that the viewer leaves it not depressed, but exhilarated.

When Susan leaves Kane the movie is at its low point: Kane has lost his empire, his dreams, his youth, and his love. He is alone, abandoned by everyone and everything except for the slender hope that he just might learn from his mistakes, gain greater self-knowledge, and build afresh as he proceeds into the third act of his life:

- Thompson at Xanadu with Raymond, the butler:

    1932—After Susan leaves, Kane destroys Susan's
    room; he finds a snow globe and says,
    "Rosebud."

    1941—Kane's things are cataloged; the "valuables"
    are kept, the "worthless" items are burned; only
    we see that a sled named Rosebud is burned with
    the other "trash."

So Kane, given a last chance to remake himself, instead destroys Susan's room in a defensive rage, only to confront his past unexpectedly when he happens upon the little snow globe and remembers his last moment of unadulterated joy, when he was a little boy sledding with his beloved Rosebud. This is the internal climax of the film, the moment that seals Kane's fate, dooming him to his cynical, embittered isolation, from which he will escape only by his death. The external climax of the film follows immediately, when the question with which the film began—and the task to which Thompson was assigned—is answered: Rosebud was Kane's sled, a symbol of the innocence and unencumbered love that characterized his young life before his mother forced him to leave her and his idyllic childhood forever.

9. THE BONFIRE OF THE VANITIES

Third Act Suicide

▬ ▬ ▬ ▬

In the fifteenth century in Florence a religious fanatic named Girolamo Savonarola led a crusade against the crass materialism of his age. He ordered his followers to storm through the homes of the wealthy, collecting the jewels, gold, pictures, wigs, furniture, and books that symbolized the extravagance of that extravagant age. These "vanities" were burned in a great bonfire in the town square. Soon a carnival atmosphere pervaded the proceedings, and as the trappings of wealth were set afire, Savonarola's cult followers sang hymns and danced wildly around the flames. But it was all too good to last. In time, Savonarola's rivals denounced his fierce asceticism, and his followers eventually grew tired of the endless bonfires. Finally, soon after the last "vanities" were thrown onto the fire of purification, Savonarola himself was publicly burned.

It was with this grotesque tale in mind, and with Ronald Reagan still firmly ensconced in the White House, that Tom Wolfe in 1987 wrote *The Bonfire of the Vanities*. It is a fierce denunciation of the crass materialism and "me first, last, and always" philosophy of the Reagan years, written with the pizzazz and style of Henry James on acid. It is the picaresque tale of Sherman McCoy, born with a silver spoon stuck firmly in his mouth, who at thirty-eight calls himself a "Master of the Universe" because he makes a million dollars a year selling bonds on Wall Street. He possesses all the trappings of success: a six-million-dollar mansion on Park

Avenue, a socialite wife (with whom he rarely speaks), a lovely daughter, a "cottage" in the Hamptons, a Mercedes, and a mistress named Maria Ruskin. But his dazzling success is shattered one fine night when he and Maria take a wrong turn on the way back from the airport and wind up in the South Bronx. There, amid the squalor of drug dealers, pimps, and whores, they encounter two black teenagers who may (or may not) be trying to rob them. They panic at the sight of these symbols of third world resentment, and Maria steps on the gas to escape, accidentally hitting one of the teenagers. She and Sherman escape back to Manhattan, where they make love and decide to forget about the "disagreeable incident" in the Bronx.

But the powers who run New York won't let them forget. Abe Weiss, the district attorney, looking for an issue that can give him the minority vote and propel him into the mayor's office, seizes upon the now comatose black teenager as a symbol of white racism and orders that the "hit-and-run would-be killer" be found and arrested. Peter Fallow, a British reporter down on his luck, grabs the story and runs with it, making Sherman the most loathed man in all five boroughs. Reverend Bacon, a black leader of the down-trodden and a political force in his own right, denounces Sherman as proof of a racist system. Soon Sherman is arrested and turned into a cause célèbre, reviled by the hoi polloi and ostracized by his own beloved Park Avenue aristocrats. His wife leaves him, his mistress deserts him, he is fired from his job and cast down into the pitiless public glare of fifteen minutes of fame. In the ensuing trial Sherman saves himself by illegally producing a tape recording of himself talking with Maria, in which she admits to driving his Mercedes when it hit the teenager. Sherman is set free, but . . . to what? He finds himself without a job, a family, or any hope for the future; on the other hand, he's become the one thing he's spent the last thirty-eight years trying to avoid—a man.

The novel became an instant best-seller. In a world where "little" novels dealing with small, personalized problems were the rage, Tom Wolfe had the audacity and talent to take on the greatest city in the world at the apex of the twentieth century. His characters range from the poorest drug addict to the richest Yale-educated WASP, from shyster lawyers to welfare moms, from yellow journalists to "X-ray" Park Avenue women, starved to near perfection. As an indictment of the Reagan era it stands unparalleled in its wit, exuberance, and perception.

Needless to say, Hollywood gobbled it up in one gulp. The fact that it contained not one unrepellent character didn't deter them, nor did the fact that Sherman McCoy, the only protagonist in sight and the only character for whom we can reasonably care, is a greedy, shallow, philandering little money-grubber who becomes only mildly sympathetic as the novel draws to a close. Not to worry: the book was going through the roof. Peter Guber and Jon Peters, a prominent producing team officed out of Warner Bros., where they had just produced the megahit *Batman,* bought the film rights for $750,000. Guber then hired Michael Cristopher, whose *The Witches of Eastwick,* while a disastrous production, had been distinguished by Cristopher's ability to rewrite endless drafts as new conceptions of the film were thrown at him almost daily. The facts that his final script for *Eastwick* had been nothing special, and that his script of *Falling in Love* had fallen on its face largely because of his characterless writing, were happily ignored in the euphoria of paying him $600,000 to turn the novel of this year into what everyone was convinced would be the film of next year. To direct this blockbuster in the making, the executives at Warner Bros. chose Brian De Palma, a brilliant pictorial conceptionist whose best work, such as *Carrie* and *The Untouchables,* had been wonderfully observant social satires. No one doubted De Palma's talent, but he had never before worked in the high-stakes arena of blockbusters, a special sort of filmmaking whose product is normally targeted for a pretty low common denominator.

Cristopher's first draft was a disaster, straying too far from the original conception. De Palma worked with Cristopher, crafting succeeding drafts of the script to his vision of a satire along the lines of the wonderful *Dr. Strangelove,* one of the very few movies ever made without one redeeming character. To capture the spirit of Wolfe's exuberant prose, Cristopher turned the secondary character of Peter Fallow, the lowlife British journalist who publicizes Sherman's tragedy, into a primary character next in importance only to Sherman himself. Because actor Bruce Willis, then atop the slippery pole of Hollywood success, wanted to take part in the bonfire, the character of Peter Fallow was reborn as an American. In itself, this wasn't a significant change; what was significant was that De Palma and Cristopher soon discovered that Willis's limitations as an actor forced them into oversimplifying Fallow's character, thereby taking out much of the satiric punch. The possibility that Willis might hurt the film, and should be replaced by a better actor, wasn't seriously considered—Willis was, after all, a star.

Wolfe's explosive prose, it was felt, needed a cinematic equivalent, and Fallow's voice-over commentary was chosen, describing every social nuance and plot twist, whether or not the audience could figure it out for themselves. That Dickens, Melville, and many other brilliant prose stylists had successful films made from their work without resorting to a voice-over didn't persuade the filmmakers; a voice-over would give the audience the special flavor that their visuals and story could not. As an initial (and unnecessary) admission of storytelling failure by the filmmakers before the cameras had even rolled, it was devastating.

As to who should portray Sherman McCoy, who spends most of the novel as a loathsome, greedy toad, Guber decided that Tom Hanks, just emerging into the rarefied ranks of top-flight movie stars, was the perfect candidate. Hanks was the most purely likable star in Hollywood, and it was felt that his Everyman amiability would turn McCoy . . . well, if not into a good guy, then at least into the least unlikable of the bad guys. In fact, if there is one mantra in Hollywood, it is that every movie must have at least one character for whom we can "root." That Shakespeare wrote *King Lear, Macbeth,* and numerous other plays whose central characters were less than candidates for the Good Citizenship Award was ignored—antihero movies have always been deemed too "special" for mass audiences. Ignored was *The Treasure of the Sierra Madre,* whose major character, Fred C. Dobbs, as performed by Humphrey Bogart, becomes increasingly paranoid and unlikable as the drama progresses. Ignored was *Hud,* with Paul Newman's astounding portrayal of one of the most unlikable characters in movie history—a film that, by the way, turned a tidy profit. Ignored, too, was *The Day of the Jackal,* whose antagonist-as-protagonist professional assassin galvanized the movie and made it special. Ignored even was *Dr. Strangelove,* De Palma's original stylistic template, whose every character was an idiot or unredeemed. So the defining characteristic of *The Bonfire of the Vanities*—that it was a hilarious social satire in which every character is deserving of our contempt—was changed. Sherman McCoy was the de facto hero; therefore Sherman McCoy must be transformed into someone for whom we could root.

The structure of *Bonfire* is simple enough. Let's take a look at the first act:

- Peter Fallow, a drunk reporter, is feted as the famous author of a book about Sherman McCoy—he tells the rest of the movie in flashback.
- Sherman takes out the dog as an excuse to call Maria; he accidentally calls his own home, and his wife answers.
- Judy, Sherman's wife, is sure Sherman's having an affair but is willing to put up with it.
- A South Bronx judge knows the district attorney needs a white fall guy to get elected mayor.
- The district attorney needs a white fall guy to get elected mayor.
- Sherman takes his daughter, Campbell, to school and goes to work, where he is a master of the universe working on a $600 million deal.
- Maria arrives at the airport; Sherman picks her up; they take a wrong turn and end up in the South Bronx.
- In the South Bronx Maria accidentally hits a black teenager as they escape and drive back toward Manhattan. Maria and Sherman decide to forget about hitting the black teenager.

Notice that the first character we see is Peter Fallow, an appearance that implies that this whole movie is going to be Peter's story; this implication is strengthened when we see what a crass, cynical SOB Fallow is and that he'll be the voice-over through whom all narrative connections will be made. De Palma's decision to shoot this opening scene in one continuous five-minute take—a technical tour de force, but one that only cements in the audience's mind the conviction that no moviemaker would go to so much trouble for a secondary character—also shouts to us that this is Fallow's story. But if we're to assume the real problem of the movie is how Peter became the crass idiot we first see him to be, then what are we to make of the second major character we see, Sherman McCoy? We might then assume that it's his story, except that the third character we see is the judge, a symbol of moral rectitude in an immoral world and an equally attractive candidate to be our hero. Or how about the fourth major character we see, Abe Weiss, desperate to find a white fall guy who'll help him get elected mayor? (Incidentally, the judge tells us that the district attorney is looking for a white fall guy, and in the very next scene, the district attorney tells us he's looking for a white fall guy; why give us the same information twice? The filmmakers should have been aware of this redundancy and cut or rewritten one of the scenes.)

Or is the real problem of the movie the world that these four characters represent, New York City during the Reagan years, a city hell-bent on money-grubbing selfishness? If that's the real problem of the movie, then we're in for a bit of a surprise in the sixth scene, when Sherman McCoy takes his daughter to school and we finally realize that he is our hero after all—a settling-down of the main story line that takes place way too late to avoid initially confusing an audience.

However, once Sherman finally shows up, things move along nicely. The bit about Sherman accidentally calling his own home was a brilliant invention by Wolfe and shows us how affairs on Park Avenue are winked at. There is one surprising change from the novel, which depicts Judy McCoy as a bright, cold, social-climbing aristocrat: in the movie she's a featherhead, a cruel joke of a woman, incapable of conversation. One can't help wondering whether a more realistic characterization might not only have added to Sherman's problems, but broadened our perspective on his upper-crust world. From here Sherman's $600 million deal moves along smoothly into his horror scene in the South Bronx. The teenager's collision with the rear bumper of Sherman's Mercedes leads to a classic first act break because it presents the protagonist with the classic first act question: whether to accept or refuse the challenge posed to him (in this case, whether to admit or ignore the accidental hitting of the black teenager). Sherman's answer to that question leads us into the second act:

- The Reverend Bacon wants justice for the black teenager, now in a coma.
- Sherman and Judy visit Sherman's parents; Judy says Sherman accepts "crumbs" to make his living.
- Peter Fallow desperately needs a story to resurrect his floundering career.
- Fallow learns of the black teenager and starts to investigate.
- Sherman reads the newspaper; Fallow's story tells of a search for the hit-and-run driver who hit the black teenager.
- Sherman with Maria—he's worried; she placates him.
- Fallow talks with Reverend Bacon.
- Abe Weiss wants the driver of the hit-and-run to be found.
- Lawyers tell the black teenager's mother she can make a lot of money; she cynically goes off to buy clothes.
- Cops question Sherman; he looks nervous and guilty.
- Cops tell Weiss they found the hit-and-run driver; but they're stymied at getting a conviction until they find a corroborating witness.
- Sherman's lawyer tells him not to worry.
- Cops find a black teenager willing to testify against Sherman.
- Sherman's lawyer tells Sherman he'll be arrested in the morning.
- Sherman at the opera, which sings of guilt and redemption.
- After the opera Sherman tells Maria he'll be arrested in the morning; there's more talk of repentance.
- As Sherman's arrested he learns Maria has left the country.
- Sherman is humiliated as he's arrested and arraigned.
- Sherman, distraught and laid low, talks with Fallow on the subway.
- At a party at Sherman's house Judy tells Sherman she's leaving him, then hurries off to be the perfect hostess; Sherman also learns he's been fired and, seeing his crass "friends," throws them out by shooting off a shotgun.

- Sherman's lawyer plays a tape of Sherman with Maria, proving Sherman is innocent; however, the tape is inadmissible as evidence.
- Caroline, who is mad at Maria for making love to her boyfriend, photocopies her genitals as she tells Fallow the woman in the car with Sherman was Maria.
- Fallow interviews Maria's husband, who dies talking about Arabs.
- Maria refuses to talk to Fallow.
- Abe Weiss agrees to make a deal with Maria to make her testify against Sherman.
- Sherman tries to secretly tape Maria into admitting her guilt, but he fails.
- Sherman, alone, abandoned, talks with his father, who says Sherman should save himself by lying.

Not a bad second act. In fact, although *Bonfire* was savaged by the critics, it's filled with many wonderful scenes and packed with sharp social satire and funny observations. It moves along at a good clip and takes Sherman McCoy steadily lower: Sherman finds himself without job, wife, daughter, mistress, or hope. If the film had simply continued along like this, with its okay plotting and not bad social satire, it might not have been only a success—it might have been a considerable success. The tragedy of *Bonfire* isn't that it failed, but rather that it so nearly succeeded. This entire second act runs like a clock, with only a few problematic scenes (though their faults are glaring). What, for example, is the need of the opera scene, which simply spells out Sherman's crisis for the audience? It's a sign either of the filmmaker's insecurities about their ability to tell a clear story or of their contempt for the audience's intelligence; either way, they felt the need to "tell" their audience something that their movie should have already made clear.

As for Caroline, who supplies a crucial plot point, why are we being introduced to a completely new character two-thirds of the way through the movie? Why couldn't she have been brought in earlier, so we'd have gotten to know her, or at least seen her again later, so that her character is resolved? Instead she's simply a plot device, supplying crucial plot information and then dropping out of existence. There's probably no surer proof of a screenwriter's failure to tell a story successfully than these two lapses: having to spell out the theme for us (in the opera scene) and resorting to a "now you see her now you don't" character to propel the plot.

And what about Maria's husband, who dies telling a story about Arabs on planes that has nothing to do with the plot? Mr. Ruskin's only reason for existing is to allow Fallow to obtain Maria's phone number, which in turn allows Fallow to interview Maria. Aside from that, Ruskin doesn't advance the plot or embroider the satire. In fact, as a character who basically appears in only one scene, he's another Caroline, appearing for a quickie plot advancement and then disappearing. Once again the filmmakers gave birth to a character only to kill him off after he moves the plot along.

As for Fallow, we see him first as a drunken loser, then as an opportunist cashing in on Sherman's bad luck, then as a man helping Sherman to the subway and being moved by Sherman's unending tale of woe, then as a reporter passively observing the trial, and finally as a cynical drunk cashing in on Sherman's tragedy. Which Fallow are we to believe: the buffoon who destroys Sherman's life, the drunk accepting the plaudits of the paparazzi, or the compassionate man lending a sympathetic ear to Sherman's troubles? These scenes aren't necessarily irreconcilable, but it is disconcerting for an audience if the film doesn't at least comment upon the seeming contradictions.

There are also a few scenes in the second act that we miss in their absence: Judy merely tells Sherman she's leaving him and then whisks off, leaving both us and Sherman with the desire to talk to her, to argue for her to stay, and to let Sherman unload his feelings on her. The movie, by avoiding this scene, skims the emotional surface, avoiding a deeper resonance that would have made the satire more effective. And where's the scene where Campbell leaves her daddy to move out with Mommy? One of the most poignant bits in the novel is that Sherman, for all his shallow greed, absolutely loves his daughter; it's the one humanizing element in Sherman's Reaganesque soul and the one facet in Sherman's character that the filmmakers avoided.

We power into the third act on the heels of the scene in which Sherman's father tells Sherman that he must save himself any way he can, even if it means lying. Too bad the story couldn't have ended here, because the third act promptly commits movie suicide:

- The trial:
    Maria testifies against Sherman.
    Sherman plays the tape proving Maria drove the car.
    Sherman lies, saying the tape is his.
    The judge dismisses the case; Sherman is free.
    The judge tells the court that they should all be decent.
- Out of the flashback, Peter Fallow receives the plaudits of the crowd, including all the characters (except Sherman) whom we've seen throughout the movie.

Since the second act ended with Sherman's father telling him to lie, why do the filmmakers proceed to do precisely what we've been told they're going to do? Where's the surprise? The reversal? Why tell an audience what's going to happen before it happens? The answer to these questions is simple: By telling the audience what's going to happen, the filmmakers are destroying any chances for third act suspense, and in so doing, they have driven a knife into the film's climax.

But this raises a new question: Where exactly is our climax? The most likely answer is that it occurs when the judge dismisses the case, making Sherman a free man. But if that's the climax, why does the judge then proceed to give a long speech telling us all to be decent? Is this our second climax? And if it is, what was the point of Sherman's saving himself by lying? Is the film saying that Sherman was wrong to lie, that he wasn't being decent? Or does decency sometimes include lying? For whom are we asked to root—for Sherman, who's been our main character and who saves himself through a lie, or for the judge, another incidental character like Caroline or Maria's husband, who mouths a sentiment that insults either Sherman for his lie or the audience who's been asked to applaud his lie? The answer to all these questions is that the filmmakers created two consecutive climaxes that totally contradict each other. Perhaps the filmmakers thought they were being clever in their contradictions, but they were simply being confusing. Film doesn't allow for the ambiguous complexities of two conflicting conclusions. The film and the filmmakers have to make up their minds.

But the film doesn't end there; instead it gives us yet a third climax, where the drunken Peter Fallow accepts the applause of the same miscreants we've come to hate. Since a film should end when the greatest problem is solved, are we to believe that all along Peter Fallow was the film's primary problem? Are we to believe that Fallow's success is justified at any price, even if it means the destruction of Sherman McCoy's career and life? These questions have no easy answers. Having resolved Sherman's problem, the filmmakers should have ended the film as quickly as possible, rather than giving us yet another ending. If they insisted upon resolving Peter Fallow, then that resolution should have occurred as part of Sherman's larger resolution, not as a separate, add-on scene.

Besides, Fallow's last scene contradicts the earlier two climaxes. Assuming the importance of the opera scene, which cries out for the moral necessity of guilt and redemption—a scene De Palma insisted upon filming despite the opposition of the Warner Bros. executives, who were counting pennies as the production went overbudget—where is Fallow's guilt? His redemption? Are we to believe that decency is wrong and that the judge was a fool? Does Fallow learn from Sherman's lie or simply cash in on it? The filmmakers should have created a script that never allows an audience to pose these questions in the first place. They should have created a film with one coherent theme that embraces, explains, and resolves all the characters and situations it depicts. The filmmakers should have seen that they didn't have such an overarching theme and should have modified their story until they settled on such a theme.

The film can't have its cake and eat it, too—either it cynically hails the Reagan years or it decries them. Nor does the responsibility lie entirely with the muddy thinking of De Palma and Cristopher. The Warner Bros. executives should have either guided or forced De Palma and Cristopher away from their disastrous third act, never allowing them to throw in three separate and contradictory climaxes, an ending that not only destroyed the film, but destroyed its chance for the success that so many of its scenes deserve. In the end it wasn't Sherman McCoy's vanities that burned, but *Bonfire* itself, consumed in a third act that lost its mind.

10. LAST ACTION HERO
Deconstruction Self-Destructs

███ ███ ███ ███

Mark Canton, head of production at Columbia TriStar, needed a blockbuster movie for the big summer 1993 release. Steve Roth, a rising young producer, gave him a spec script his staff had come across called *Last Action Hero,* written by two unknowns, Zak Penn and Adam Leff. The script, about a teenage boy who literally enters the world of the movies, where he teams up with Jack Slater, celluloid supercop, was bouncy and fresh, filled with good action and plenty of jokes. Canton liked it and thought it could go through the roof; there was just one problem: there was really only one actor who could play Jack Slater—the one, the only, Arnold.

When you're Arnold Schwarzenegger life can be very nice. You make millions of dollars every year, you're one of the most famous people on the planet, and whole movie studios lie at your feet like puppy dogs begging for treats. You have a production office that reads and develops scripts, and you spend lots of time wondering which of those scripts you'll deign to take out of development hell and make into a real, live, actual movie. Mark Canton knew he was just one of many suitors asking for Arnold's blessing. Happily for Canton, the big guy read Penn and Leff's script and agreed to do it—joy! rapture! box office through the roof!—on one tiny proviso: he wanted the entire script rewritten. Penn and Leff's script was bought for a pittance, and Shane Black, whose brilliant and profitable action comedies *Lethal Weapon*(s) "*1*", *2,* and *3* had become a cottage industry for Warner Bros., was chosen to do the rewrite. Shane, in turn, asked to work with his buddy David Arnott. The two produced an entirely new version of *Last Action Hero,* retaining only the premise of a kid entering a movie world and partnering with a superhero cop, a scene that spoofed Hamlet, a running gag of the supercop's boss telling anal jokes, and no more than half a dozen lines of Penn and Leff's dialogue; everything else—scenes, action, dialogue, and setting—was totally rewritten. Arnold read the new script and pronounced himself pleased—joy! rapture! box office through the roof!—asking only one more tiny proviso: that the script, which was way too long, be rewritten, this time by William Goldman. Goldman was his own Hollywood cottage industry, turning out successful scripts (*Butch Cassidy and the Sundance Kid, All the President's Men, Misery, Maverick,* and others) at a tremendous rate. In little time Black and Arnott's script was whittled down to a reasonably shootable length and again handed over to Arnold, who this time pronounced himself satisfied—joy! rapture! etc.

John McTiernan, whose *Die Hard* had virtually created the movie career of Bruce Willis, was brought on as director; it was felt that his expert ability to juggle eye-poppin' action with jokey dialogue made him the perfect choice; besides, he was acceptable to Arnold. Checks were written, cameras rolled, and in due course *Last Action Hero* played before millions, becoming one of the most disliked films of 1993.

So what went wrong? How could a film costing up to $100 million (no one's saying what it really cost), written by some of the most talented and successful screenwriters in the world, starring one of the biggest stars in the world, directed by a top action director, take a long walk off a short plank?

There are two answers to that question, one easy and the other tricky. Let's start with the easy answer—the script, which was filled with unresolved characters, unexplained actions, a confusing plot, and multiple climaxes. Despite these flaws, which we'll examine, *Last Action Hero*'s structure is fairly simple, following a traditional three-act form. The first act breaks down like this:

- Jack Slater is about to save his son from a bad guy named the Ripper when the film goes out of focus and we realize we were watching a movie called *Jack Slater III*.
- Danny, our hero, is told by Nick, the projectionist, to come at midnight to see an early screening of *Jack Slater IV*.
- Danny at school watches Olivier's *Hamlet,* imagines Jack Slater as Hamlet killing everyone in sight.
- Danny at home with his overworked mom.
- Danny is held up by a burglar and humiliated by him.
- At the theater Danny gets a magic ticket from Nick; he tears it in two and places one half in the ticket box and the other in his wallet.
- Danny watches *Jack Slater IV,* seeing the bad guys, Benedict and Vivaldi, threaten Jack's cousin. The magic ticket glows, and Danny is literally blown into the movie.

Not such a bad beginning. Its snazzy trick opening fools us into thinking the movie's about Jack Slater, supercop, when in fact it's about little Danny's infatuation with the movie hero. We see a little of Danny's life: that his only friend seems to be Nick, that in school he daydreams of Jack Slater, that his loving mother has little time for him, and that he is held up and humiliated by a burglar. Danny himself, in other words, is the problem of the first act—his fears, his loneliness, his dreams of becoming an action hero like Jack Slater. And the problem is not badly set up; Danny is understood only by Nick the projectionist, and while he may be a little obsessive about Jack Slater, he's still a great kid.

Nonetheless, on closer examination the first act could use a buff and shine. The scene between Danny and his mom, designed to explain his home life, is perfunctory and rushed. There's no moment showing Danny's relationship—or lack of it—with other schoolkids or with his teacher. The *Hamlet* scene, in which in Danny's imagination Jack Slater plays the Prince and kicks butt on a totally awesome scale, is cute but uses minutes of precious screen time that could have been better used to develop Danny's relationship with his mother and people in his school. Finally, the thug who burglarizes Danny's apartment and taunts Danny to fight him is a poor choice of opponents to demonstrate Danny's wimpiness;

anyone, no matter how brave, would back down from a knife-wielding thief. Why not instead have Danny back down from, say, a schoolyard bully—as Penn and Leff had in their draft and which Black and Arnott tossed—a confrontation that Danny might conceivably win, and from which he backs down not out of wisdom, but rather from cowardice? While none of these problems in themselves is going to toast a film, and even taken together are not going to send us up in flames, we're already in a little trouble. Now let's look at the second act:

- In the movie world Danny finds himself riding with Jack in a car chase.
- Danny goes with Jack to the police station; Jack talks with his ex-wife on the phone; meets his best friend, John Practice; Danny has special knowledge of the bad guys (gained from his watching *Jack Slater IV*), and Lieutenant Dekker assigns Danny as Jack's partner.
- Danny and Jack at a video store; Jack refuses to believe he's not real but is only in a movie.
- Danny locates Vivaldi's mansion; they meet Benedict.
- Benedict with Vivaldi; Benedict wants to check into Danny, who knows too much about him.
- Jack's ex-wife's home; Danny meets Jack's daughter; Jack leaves and remembers his son's death; Benedict and thugs enter; alerted by Danny, Jack kills the thugs; Benedict escapes with Danny's wallet; Jack chases after him; Danny plays chicken with Benedict, who escapes.
- Benedict finds the magic ticket and learns its power.
- Jack's ex-wife's house blows up.
- Lieutenant Dekker takes Jack's badge.

So far, so good. We're about halfway into the movie. An uneasy alliance has formed between Danny and Jack. Danny has helped Jack stop Benedict's thugs, but Benedict holds the magic ticket. We've met Jack's lovely daughter. We've heard some jokes, seen some character progression, and had a nice action scene. It seems a shame only to talk about Jack's ex-wife, rather than show her to us, which might have led to some interesting sparks between her and Jack, especially after her house blows up. Instead the house is just a vehicle for more, largely gratuitous pyrotechnics. A movie hero dealing with his ex-wife would have been a fascinating scene, greatly enlarging Jack's character; Danny could even act as a catalytic Cupid, helping to bring them together. Short of that, why not instead blow up Jack's house, thus leaving him homeless and more prone to stress and thus to character growth? Still, all in all the plot's moving right along into the second half of the second act:

- Jack's apartment; Jack talks about his sad life.
- Jack and Danny discuss Leo the Fart's upcoming funeral; they realize it's a setup to spray poison gas on the Torelli mob.
- Leo the Fart's funeral. Jack stops Practice, who is a traitor; Danny helps Jack save the day; Jack's daughter brings Jack fresh clothes.

Wait a minute. Leo the Fart? Where did he come from? Why wasn't he introduced earlier—say, in the first scenes with Vivaldi? Why couldn't we have seen him murdered, rather than being told about it? Why, in other words, does the film show Jack and Danny talking about him, rather than letting us see the plot unfold for ourselves? "Talking about," as in *The Jewel of the Nile,* is almost always the kiss of death to a strong plotline. Also, the rather turgid scene in Jack's apartment could have used a rewrite; why not show Jack's anguish and confusion, rather than just having him talk about it? Since Danny feels alienated in his world, it would have been an unexpected symmetry to see—not just hear about—Jack's alienation in his. Ideally such alienation should have been used to advance the plot; for example, Jack could display his lost feelings as he investigates with Danny.

And where's Jack's lovely daughter, whom we met earlier and who's disappeared from the movie? Why introduce such a likable character, just to give her the deep six? The movie would have profited emotionally from Jack's getting to know his daughter, to care for her, and to experience her as a real man, not as a fictional superhero. Besides, how could the screenwriters have resisted placing her in some more jeopardy to further energize the plot? The movie, in other words, is heading south. It's possible that Bill Goldman, having to cut out so much of Black and Arnott's script, had to jettison the implied scenes and "talk about" them instead. But that's a possible explanation, not an excuse. The challenge for the screenwriters is to make all of this work within the context of a two-hour movie. This sad and hackneyed attempt at talking about plot points rather than showing them played out, and introducing characters only to have them disappear, is a sure sign of a script in an advanced state of panic.

Now to the rest of the second act:

- Benedict kills Vivaldi and plans to take over Vivaldi's operation with the magic ticket. Jack and Danny crash in, Benedict and chauffeur escape into Danny's world; Danny and Jack follow.
- Jack and Danny in Manhattan; they chase Benedict, who escapes; Jack is stunned to find himself in Manhattan.
- Danny takes Jack to Nick; Jack is depressed to learn he is fictional and trapped in Danny's world.
- Danny introduces Jack to his mother.
- Benedict explores Manhattan; sees that a bad guy can win here.
- Jack talks with Danny's mom; Jack is growing gentler, more "real"; he and Danny resolve to find Benedict.

Jack, depressed to learn his true fictional identity, fearful that he is trapped in Danny's world, desperate to find Benedict, resolves to press on. All part of a classic second act break. It's also a clever idea to move the action from Jack's world into Danny's; just as Danny has grown from his contact with Jack, Jack must now learn from Danny. And the idea of Benedict on the loose in Manhattan with a magic ticket is a nifty notion. It ups the ante for the hero by upping the power of the villain. In fact, after slipping so badly in the last sequence (all that terrible stuff with Leo the Fart, Jack talking about how depressed he is, Jack's never-seen ex-wife, and his daughter disappearing from the rest of the movie), the movie's back on track as we enter the third act:

- Benedict has brought the Ripper to Manhattan; they will act together to stop Jack and rule the world.
- Jack and Danny search for clues; they find and chase after Benedict; he escapes.
- The premiere of *Jack Slater IV*. The real Arnold Schwarzenegger appears; Jack and Danny save Arnold from the Ripper.
- A replay of the beginning; the Ripper holds Danny; Jack kills the Ripper and saves Danny.
- Jack fights Benedict, who shoots Jack; Danny saves Jack, who kills Benedict; the magic ticket is lost.
- Death (from Bergman's *The Seventh Seal*) enters the real world.
- Jack's mortally wounded in an ambulance; Danny takes over, drives to the theater to save Jack's life.
- In the theater Jack is about to die as Death appears, tells Danny how to save Jack: find the other half of the magic ticket; Danny finds the ticket stub in the ticket box.
- Jack reenters his movie world, where he now has only a flesh wound; Jack and Danny say good-bye, and Danny reenters his real world.

We're in trouble here. Benedict develops a scheme to take over the world by releasing movie villains; so far, so good. But he tells the Ripper that their first step in realizing his dastardly plan is to kill Arnold Schwarzenegger, in the belief that killing the actor will cause the death of the character he portrayed—thus, by killing Arnold, they'll be killing Jack. But the operating idea isn't explained, nor has it been tested and proved; and even if it had been, it still wouldn't make any sense. And this is no small point, since the entire third act hinges around the premiere of *Jack Slater IV* and the threat the Ripper poses to Arnold. But since it isn't explained—and probably couldn't be—we have lots of bogus suspense as the Ripper stalks Arnold, a real-life man who has nothing to do with the plot or with the Jack Slater character he portrays. The concept is clever, and with enough fleshing-out might well have worked, but without the villain's operating premise clearly spelled out and previously demonstrated to the audience, the whole reason for the third act is diminished.

Which brings us to the three—count 'em, three—climaxes of the movie. Since the screenwriters had established the Ripper and Benedict as separate villains from separate Jack Slater movies, each had to be dealt with individually. But this leaves us with two thrilling conclusions, the first, where Jack replays the beginning of the movie and, this time, is able to save the Ripper's hostage; and the second, where Jack takes care of Benedict. True, there is a character progression as Jack saves Danny after the Ripper dies, and Danny in turn saves Jack when they fight Benedict. But that character growth doesn't justify the tension-created-tension-relieved-tension-created feeling that two action climaxes produce. The screenwriters could have gotten out of the hole they dug for themselves by having Benedict be a continuing villain, appearing in both Jack Slater films; this would not only have given us more time to develop Benedict or the Ripper as the villain (you choose), but it would also have given us just one (longer, bigger) action climax. The decision to have two villains necessitated two climaxes, diminished the emotional stakes, and dragged things out.

Wait a minute, what about the third climax? That's the one where Jack, mortally wounded, is saved by Danny, who drags him back into his movie world, where heroes only have flesh wounds. Not a bad idea, but the writers bollix it up by inserting Death into the mix. Not that Death is a bad idea or a bad character; but he's someone we've never met until now, and he's stepping out of *The Seventh Seal*—a film that maybe 1 percent of the audience has even heard of, let alone seen.

This all brings us back to the *Hamlet* satire way back in the first act. Jack Slater playing Hamlet is a cute idea, but it doesn't pay off anywhere, and especially here, at the end of the movie, where the reintroduction of a movie character from the beginning of the film would make the most sense. If the screenwriters were so hot to put in Death, then it's *The Seventh Seal* that should have been satirized in Danny's English class, not *Hamlet*. That way, when Death walks down the theater aisle, at least we know who he is and what he's capable of. The only function that Death performs in the movie is to give Danny the clue that Jack can be saved by finding the other half of the magic ticket. Now that's a nice clue, but it's also a clue Danny could have easily figured out for himself. And if he had, it would have made Danny's effort to save Jack all the greater. Instead Death, a black-caped deus ex machina, tells Danny how to end the movie, thus making Danny look like a dope. *The Bonfire of the Vanities*—a film developed by the same studio under the same administration—suffers from the same problem of characters who appear, nudge along the plot, and then disappear.

So how did some of the brightest and highest-paid screenwriters in the world write a script filled with so many obvious holes, and why would a studio let such a flawed script go into production? Chances are the screenwriters were all too aware of the problems they were creating, but the very process of hiring one writer to rewrite another is too often a formula for disaster. Good ideas get mangled or bad ideas get pressed forward under the constraints of time or ego. And as for its getting a green light, when a star of Schwarzenegger's stature wants to make a movie, then anything and everything is done to accommodate him, including going with a script that isn't ready.

This said, *Last Action Hero* still might have turned a profit. The action was good, the jokes were funny, the scenes jumped right along, and the whole movie was a gas in a funky, stupid sort of way. But there is a deeper, and never discussed, problem—the trick reason I referred to earlier—which, I believe, fatally doomed *Last Action Hero* before "The End" was written on Penn and Leff's long-forgotten first draft. Put simply, *Last Action Hero* is a movie that punches a hole between the worlds of illusion and reality. It satirizes movie formulas and movie heroes. It says, "Hey, this is all a made-up con job we moviemakers have been pulling on you folks all these years, with rules and laws we follow to make sure that, come what may, by the closing credits the villain will take a fall and the hero will get the girl. But now we're going to show you how this great, ponderous beast really works. We're going to open up the mechanism and show you the insides, and then we're going to ask you to pay good money to find this out." Other movies had tried this before: but *Deathtrap* simply failed at the box office; Harold Pinter's brilliant screen adaptation of John Fowles's novel

The French Lieutenant's Woman was a small-market upscale art house film; and Woody Allen's very good *The Purple Rose of Cairo* was too special to reach a large audience. The good people at Warner Bros. weren't aiming for this selective an audience. They were swinging for the bleachers. They were aiming at the great unwashed masses.

Only the great unwashed didn't want to pay good money to watch a major summer release called *Last Action Hero* and have their illusions shattered. They wanted to keep their dreams intact. And they still do.

II. FARGO

Satire Isn't Always What Closes on Saturday Night

■ ■ ■ ■ ■

Satire is what closes on Saturday night.

—George S. Kaufman

A car, hauling another car, appears out of a snow white blizzard; it hurtles toward us, blasting through the ice-enshrouded landscape. At the wheel is a bland-looking man, his face set, his eyes bulging in fear and determination. He roars past us and continues on, headed toward Fargo, North Dakota. And so it begins, the mad, terrible, hilarious tale of *Fargo,* where killers kidnap housewives, car salesmen scheme for money, innocent people die, and the guilty are brought to justice by a pregnant police chief whose husband paints ducks.

Fargo is that rarest of films, a satire that works. Normally, satire walks a knife's edge between the childish and the overly topical. Only if it stays between those two dangers can it succeed. In fact, so threatening is the form, so delicate the treatment, that it's rare to see a satire made at all, let alone one as triumphant as *Fargo.* Written, produced, and directed by the Coen brothers, Ethan and Joel, *Fargo* delights in the prim, circumscribed world of "Minnesota nice," where any self-respecting sentence ends with the word "then." Rarely has language been used as effectively or tellingly to paint a culture. Rarely have characters been as offbeat and yet as fully realized. With the possible exceptions of *Network,*

The Great Dictator, and *Dr. Strangelove,* it is difficult to think of a satire that succeeds as well.

Fargo is the story of Jerry, a car salesman who hires two thugs named Carl and Gaear to have his wife kidnapped; Jerry will pay off Carl and Gaear with part of the ransom money he collects from his rich father-in-law, keeping the rest to pay off his mountainous debts. But the kidnappers are stopped by a highway patrolman whom Gaear kills, along with two passing motorists who witness the scene. Marge, the pregnant chief of police of Brainerd, Minnesota, investigates the triple homicide and soon tracks the killers to Minneapolis. There she meets Jerry, who barely escapes her, and also runs into Mike, an old high school classmate desperate to date her. Jerry's father-in-law tries to pay the ransom and ends up getting killed by Carl, who is himself shot and staggers back to Gaear, who has killed Jerry's wife and now kills Carl. Marge tracks down Gaear and brings him to justice, while police in North Dakota track down Jerry and bring him in. As *Fargo* ends, Marge snuggles in her husband's arms, delighted that his duck painting will be on the three-cent stamp and contentedly awaiting the birth of their first child.

The structure of *Fargo* takes a number of risks, particularly in its first act structure, its late introduction of the protagonist, and its third act break. Let's begin with the first act:

- In Fargo, North Dakota, Jerry hires Carl and Gaear to kidnap his wife.
- Back home in Minneapolis, Jerry eats dinner with his wife, son, and Wade, his father-in-law.
- Carl and Gaear drive toward Minneapolis.
- Jerry cheats a car buyer.
- Carl and Gaear have sex with prostitutes in Brainerd, Minnesota.
- Wade likes Jerry's proposed business deal; they make plans to meet.
- Realizing he may not need the ransom money, Jerry tries to call off the kidnapping but can't reach Carl or Gaear.
- Jerry falls deeper into debt; creditors are after him.
- Jerry's wife is kidnapped.

This first act starts out simply enough with a standard introduction of the external problem: Jerry wants his wife kidnapped. But from there we meander around, watching scenes that often aren't absolutely necessary for the progression of the story. In fact, it would be possible to go straight from the first scene to the actual kidnapping without missing any vital plot points. So why keep all of these scenes? First, it lets us meet the main characters and enjoy the contrast between Jerry's middle-class respectability and the kidnappers' inherent goofiness. Second, it lets us meet another character we need to know before the plot can really begin—the state of Minnesota, icebound, staid, sober, and yet with a subtle air of violence hidden beneath its bland exterior. If you're going to put in scenes that only further character or theme, it's best to place them early on, when an audience will still put up with them. Generally speaking, an audience will give you fifteen to twenty minutes to get things going at the beginning of a movie before ankling for the aisles. As for the act break, it comes naturally when the wife is kidnapped. Until then, nothing that happens is inevitable; after that, everything is inevitable. Basically, then, the structure of the first act is a simple crosscutting between Carl and Gaear on their way to the Twin Cities and Jerry blundering through his increasingly chaotic life.

The second act is unusual in that it introduces Marge, the protagonist, about half an hour into the movie. Normally this would be the kiss of death, since the late introduction of a protagonist is almost sure to leave an audience adrift, wondering for whom to root. A late-arriving protagonist also leaves the audience confused as to just what sort of a protagonist they're dealing with: who is this person who's suddenly been thrown at us, and why were we given so little time to establish his or her personality? The same situation obtains in *The Day of the Jackal*, where Police Commissioner Lebel's late arrival disrupts the audience. But the Coens were able to pull it off, partly because bringing in Marge earlier wouldn't have made any sense, and partly because her vividly written character (aided by Frances McDormand's wonderful Oscar-winning performance) helped the audience play catch-up. Other than introducing Marge later than usual, the rest of the second act contains a standard converging structure, where Jerry's increasingly desperate maneuvers to keep the kidnapping going while evading detection are crosscut against Marge's steady, methodical investigation. It looks something like this:

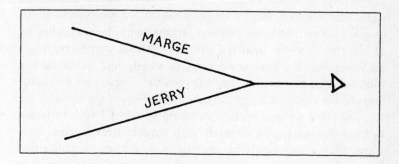

Fargo Chart #1

But there's something else going on in the second act. Whereas the first act break comes at a plot juncture (the kidnapping of the wife), the second act break comes at a thematic juncture. Some film critics have rightly rejoiced in *Fargo* because it contains superfluous scenes that aren't rolled out of some paint-by-the-numbers script-writing factory. *Fargo* is filled with scenes and moments that aren't necessary to propel the rather stark and brief plot. But they're wrong when they say the scenes serve no purpose other than to supply a comic flavor. For example, Marge's meeting with Mike, her high school classmate, seems to do nothing to advance the plot. The poor guy tells Marge his wife has just died of cancer, and, desperately lonely, he craves a few moments with Marge, who lets him down gently. But later Marge learns that Mike was lying to her, that he never married and he's had mental problems. Marge is stunned by this news, not simply because she never saw it coming, but because, on a deeper level, it ruptures her fastidiously constructed worldview in which good triumphs and the bad are brought low. Marge is more upset by Mike's lies than by the triple homicide she's investigating, because while murder has a place in her moral universe, Mike's lies do not. Traumatized by the experience, Marge forgoes heading back to Brainerd and instead finds the resolve to forge ahead on the case and talk to Jerry one last time.

In fact, Marge's trauma is paralleled with that of Jerry, who, just a scene before, sits disconsolate in his house entryway, staring bleakly into a future in which he knows sooner or later he'll be caught and in which all of the bland phrases, happy smiles, and well-decorated exteriors no longer work. It is a moment in which he glimpses the bleak and profound truths he has been avoiding all of his life. Thus the dual revelations by Marge and Jerry, where each sees into the hidden workings of society and of the human soul, serve as the dividing line between the simple plot complications of the second act and the moral collisions of the third.

The third act details the downward spiral of Jerry's fortunes, as his kidnapping plot unravels with corpses strewing the landscape. Marge forges on in her investigation, alerting the police that Jerry is a fugitive from justice and then finding Gaear shredding what's left of Carl into a wood chipper. In what is the external climax of the movie, she captures Gaear and then drives him to jail. Reflecting on the madness she's witnessed, she sums up her reaction to it all by saying simply, "I just don't understand it." But while Marge, with her isolated, Pollyannaish view of the universe, doesn't get it, Jerry certainly does. As he is captured in the very next scene and thrown on a bed to be handcuffed, he screams a primordial howl of animal rage, a primitive exclamation. He has reached the savage heart of himself, a heart from which Marge recoils in incomprehension.

It is this thematic resonance that carries *Fargo* to its deepest levels and makes it more than a simple satire. Just as *Network* grappled with the power of TV to throttle our souls, and *Dr. Strangelove* explored the madness of nuclear warfare, *Fargo* asks us to question not simply the "Minnesota nice" attitude that can confound visitors to that beautiful state, but the superficial reality that it seems to describe so perfectly. Marge and Jerry have both bought into that reality, and both pay a terrible price for it. Jerry sees his superficially constructed dreams of wealth and of a bland, smiling family life destroyed when he looks into the darkest regions of himself; Marge, on the other hand, while briefly shocked by Mike's lies, finally turns a blind eye to the savage madness they reflect and retreats into the smiling happiness that is her salvation and her curse.

It's no coincidence that Marge and Jerry speak with the same cliché-laden words and phrases. These bland phrases ("Okey-doke," "You betcha," "That's a heckuva deal") mask a deeper truth that the Coens are exploring: that the inability to articulate can lead to an inability to feel; that the blandness of speech that Jerry and Marge employ indicates a deeper blandness of thought and emotion; that we are, to a greater degree than we'd like to admit, the words we speak. The similarity of speech patterns between Jerry and Marge is contrasted with the differing speech patterns of Carl and Gaear. Carl is the most articulate person in the movie, able to describe his feelings and thoughts in credible detail—he lives in a world that more closely describes reality than does either Jerry or Marge. Gaear, on the other hand, is an inarticulate psychotic, whose very inability to speak causes his monstrous impulses to build up inside until they burst; it seems that if only Gaear could express his feelings, he might not be as insane as he is (and we wouldn't have a movie).

To an extent, the Coens are grappling with the same theme George Orwell addressed in his brilliant *1984*. In it the hero, Winston, lives in a horrifying anti-Utopia ruled by Big Brother, where words are steadily being expunged from the public vocabulary and the avowed desire of the dictatorship is to so limit the words people use that they will ultimately become incapable of expressing, and therefore feeling, any thoughts antithetical to the regime. If you can't say it, you can't feel it; if you can't feel it, it doesn't exist. That's the position in which Jerry and Marge find themselves. Jerry will escape from it only by spending the next years of his life in jail (just as Sherman McCoy in *The Bonfire of the Vanities* can escape his oblivious purgatory only by having his perfectly constructed life explode in his face). But Marge will forever believe in happy endings and smiling faces, living a life in which, in the words of Arthur Jensen in *Network,* "all necessities [are] provided, all anxieties tranquilized, all boredom amused."

12. THE JEWEL OF THE NILE

Your Subtext Is Showing: The Problem of
the False Second Act

■■ ■■ ■■ ■■

Romancing the Stone was one of the great cinematic delights of the eighties. Funny, irreverent, and bold, it set the tone for films of that time with its vibrant characters and an unpredictable and witty plot. It's the story of sheltered, introverted romance novelist Joan Wilder, who at last has a chance to live the life she writes about and, in the process, not only stops the bad guys, but falls in love with the sort of adventurer she had always written about. The film was a triumph that launched the career of director Robert Zemeckis and confirmed Michael Douglas and Kathleen Turner as rising stars. However, it begat that most sinister of bastard children: the sequel.

Michael Douglas, who had also produced Romancing the Stone, knew there'd have to be a sequel. Unfortunately, Diane Thomas, the brilliant first-time screenwriter, had died, and Douglas had to look for someone else to carry on in her footsteps. Lawrence Konner and Mark Rosenthal, two rising young screenwriters, got the assignment. According to industry scuttlebutt, Douglas was unhappy with their efforts, but faced with pressing time schedules, he was forced to proceed with their script. Kathleen Turner was also dissatisfied with the script and tried to bail on the project, but Douglas held her to her contract, forcing her to act in a film in which she had no confidence. And they were right: the script for *The Jewel of the Nile* is, simply put, a continuum of disaster and miscalculation, a movie train wreck of huge proportions.

The story is simple enough. Joan and Jack have lived together on a sailing boat for six months, cruising the Mediterranean and living a life of leisure. But now Joan's latest novel as well as her relationship with Jack are at dead ends. At this point, the sinister dictator Omar invites Joan to "write the truth" about him and his exotic African kingdom. Joan breaks up with Jack and goes off with Omar, who, it is soon learned, desperately seeks the legendary Jewel of the Nile, with which he can rule the world. Jack follows her, and in the process of reconciling with Joan, they have many adventures, including a ride in a fighter jet, a climb up cliffs as they're pursued by Omar, a native wrestling match, and much more. They also stop Omar's dastardly scheme of world conquest and save the Jewel of the Nile, which turns out to be not a jewel at all, but a holy man revered by his downtrodden people.

A serviceable enough general structure. But try this dialogue on for size:

> JACK
>
> Tough day, huh?

> JOAN
>
> But when the going gets tough, the tough . . .
> I don't know what the tough do. I don't
> know what anyone does. Jack, we've been
> on this boat half a year. I need shore leave.

> JACK
>
> I thought you wanted to sail around the
> world.

> JOAN
>
> I do, but not this week. This is all becoming
> a blur—exotic ports, sunsets—it's not
> enough.

> JACK
> Not enough! You sound like someone who
> got what they wanted, and now they don't
> want what they got.

> JOAN
> I want to do something serious. How much
> romance can one woman take?

Or:

> JOAN
> My heart isn't in it. Romance doesn't seem
> real anymore.

> PUBLISHER
> You've got to stop confusing real life with a
> romantic novel.

And so on ad nauseam. I call movie moments like these "story conference scenes." You can almost hear the conversation as the overbooked screenwriter meets with the overworked studio executive over their diet Cokes and Cobb salads. The screenwriter begins the meeting: "Okay, so Joan's bored, and she doesn't know what to do with her life. It's like she got her heart's desire, and now she doesn't know what to do with it." The studio executive, worried about missing his precious late-afternoon "callback" time, and uncomfortable about dealing with "talent" in the first place, says, "Great, sounds just great. Go write, you genius, you." The deal is made, the contracts are signed, and the writer goes to work. Only the writer didn't bother to put that story conference into dramatic terms. The idea at lunch becomes dialogue in a script, with no pit stop in between to breathe character or drama into the situation.

Technically, this sort of descriptive, nondramatic, "talk about" dialogue is called subtext. That is, it relays the emotional content of the scene but does so without any dramatic clothing—in other words, without any text. The purpose of the scene is the scene itself, rather than what we can discover from it. It describes the emotions and motivations of the characters, rather than letting us feel them. But just as a person is more interesting and provocative with his or her clothes on, so is a scene more interesting if its naked subtext is hidden. The old adage of "show, don't tell" works here. If a writer can't think up a way to show how a character feels, rather than having the character tell us, if we can't see that character revealing his or her emotions through what he or she does (or doesn't do, or says or doesn't say), then that screenwriter has failed. In a way, subtextual dialogue is the ultimate insult to the audience, because it doesn't have faith that the viewer can figure out a character's deeper emotions without explanation. *The Jewel of the Nile* starts off with these flat-footed, "your subtext is showing" scenes and never recovers.

My favorite example of effective subtext is Abbott and Costello's "Who's on First," maybe the funniest one-on-one comedy routine ever written. The text of "Who's on First" is figuring out the unusual names of the ballplayers, but the subtext reveals the feuding/loving relationship between Abbott and Costello. If Rosenthal and Konner had Jack and Joan talk about anything except their relationship—the weather, the stock market, even the names of ballplayers—and if they had done it creatively, we'd in fact have known more about what was going on between Jack and Joan, and known it in a more entertaining fashion, than through their clumsy "talking about" scenes.

Another famous example of the effective use of text to reveal subtext is the scene in *The Godfather* where the mantle of power is passed from the aging Don Corleone to his son, Michael. Francis Coppola, who with Mario Puzo had written the script, realized in the middle of shooting that there was no scene where father and son say they love each other. So Coppola hired Robert Towne (on twelve hours' notice!) to write a scene between Brando and Pacino in which anything could be said except the words "I love you." But since they never discuss their feelings for each other, it's those very feelings that become the scene's subtext.

It is not unusual for subtext to become text. Sometimes the screenwriter is simply in a hole and can't figure how to reveal some information or characterization without talking about it. Also, at times of extreme tension, subtext will legitimately percolate to the surface. For example, during the third act, when Joan and Jack are literally hanging by a thread and are about to plunge to their deaths, they say, "I love you," and it feels real because, with action denied to them and words their only outlet, the moment is sufficiently rich and intense to allow their emotions to be stripped bare. In fact, at that moment if they'd talked about anything besides their love, it would have seemed an emotional evasion, and the true subtext of the scene would have become their avoidance of deeper emotional revelation.

On the other hand, there is always a subtext, even to a scene in which subtext is the text. Thus in the scene where Joan and Jack are hanging by a thread, knowing they're about to die, and they declare their love, the subtext is their realization that this is their last chance to express their feelings. Behind every statement, no matter how soul-searching, there is another, deeper meaning—a subtext even to a subtext.

There are many other reasons why *The Jewel of the Nile* failed, not the least of which is the use of a deus ex machina (god by machine). That is, they're saved by events or circumstances for which they're not responsible and consequently can't justifiably go through internal change. For example, when Jack and Joan are in the fighter jet and about to be captured by Omar and his men, a dust storm comes along and saves them. Not only does this relieve Jack and Joan of the trouble of saving themselves, it also relieves the screenwriters of having to be creative. Or when Jack and Joan are again about to be captured and are struggling up a cliff, Omar shoots a rocket that wrecks his own vehicle and allows Jack and Joan to escape. Not only does Omar's incompetence diminish him as a villain, but whenever Jack and Joan get off the hook without having to come up with a solution of their own, they have no means by which to advance their personal relationship or reveal and develop their characters.

Another major flaw is Omar himself, a stock villain without dramatic complexity, the psychotic flavor of the week. Joan realizes by the first act break that he's a bad guy when he tells her that *Time* magazine considers him a dangerous megalomaniac—a sure giveaway if ever there was one. Nor is Omar simply a bad guy: in the scene where Omar shoots off the rocket and unwittingly allows

Joan and Jack to escape, he just looks dumb. (Tip to would-be screenwriters: The dumber you make your antagonist, the more you reduce and insult your protagonist. If St. George had killed a dragonfly instead of a dragon, no one would remember him.) How much more interesting and fun it would have been if the revelation of Omar's villainy had come out slowly, ambiguously, so that the sexual tension between Joan and Omar, a tension that is supposed to augment the rift between Joan and Jack, could have been lengthened and made more riveting. The instant we learn Omar is a bad guy—and a dumb one at that—the film loses potential tension; the longer the revelation of Omar's villainy is delayed, the more interesting and emotionally lucrative the payoff. For the sake of a quickie characterization, the screenwriters dilute dramatic tension and tell us too soon what we ought to learn too late. As Damon Runyon said, "Make 'em laugh, make 'em cry, and make 'em wait." And making 'em wait is the most important of all.

The character of Joan is another problem. In the original *Romancing the Stone,* Joan is a passive, introverted woman who gets involved with an extroverted, macho action hero, and in the course of the film she becomes a delightful action character in her own right who undergoes a profound character transformation, or catharsis. In the sequel, Joan goes through no such character-changing crisis—rather, a resolved character momentarily doubts herself and then regains her resolve (ho-hum). This failure to find some new character crisis—to reinvent our heroine in new terms— is a problem not just of this sequel, but of sequels in general. It isn't hard to find a new external crisis, but since the original movie presumably ended with the protagonist resolved and at peace with himself, it's often impossible to find some new and sufficiently powerful internal crisis to throw at him. Certainly it was impossible for the writers of *The Jewel of the Nile.*

As for the astounding passivity of Jack and Joan: in a comedy it would probably be okay if protagonists can't take care of themselves. For example, in *Dumb and Dumber,* when Jim Carrey and Jeff Daniels are inept and unable to save themselves from some screwup, we root for them. But in a romantic adventure, the characters are more responsible for their actions, actions that should reveal character and would be taken by these and only these characters.

When a character is saved by some means other than himself, he's not saved, he's doomed.

But it is the structure of *The Jewel of the Nile* that ultimately wrecks the film. The premise is that Omar needs the Jewel of the Nile in order to become dictator of his country and from there attempt to take over the world. It turns out that the Jewel is a man, not a jewel (a revelation that comes at the outset of the second act, rather than as a surprise near the end, where it would have paid off more). Jack and Joan are quickly reconciled, find the Jewel, and then are pursued by Omar and Ralphie. It all goes something like this:

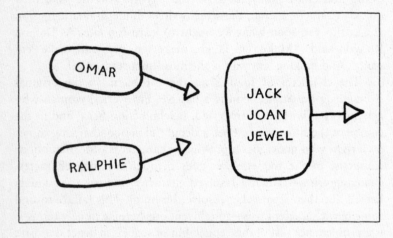

Jewel Chart #1

This structure makes for a false second act, because it demands that the screenwriters come up with a series of obstacles to keep Omar from getting to Jack and Joan. Once he's gotten to them, we're inevitably into the third act and on our way to our ending. In other words, this scenario doomed the film to a phony second act, without a narrative through-line where events propel the story forward with a sense of urgency. Instead we have a series of chases almost guaranteed to avoid character development. Still, let's play fair and not indulge in twenty-twenty hindsight. Assuming the same cast of characters—Omar, Jack, Joan, the Jewel, and Ralphie—

what structural and relationship possibilities were open to Rosenthal and Konner? The simplest structure would be this:

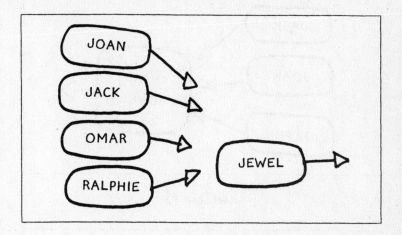

Jewel Chart #2

Here the Jewel is alone, and everyone's chasing after him. This way three separate forces are pursuing the same goal. The action would be resolved when the Jewel (the object of desire, or the MacGuffin, as Hitchcock called it) is found. This simple structure would allow differing teamings: Jack and Joan might even be competitors for the Jewel yet resolve their antagonism by being forced together against their will; Ralphie might at times join with them, only to stab them in the back, or sell them out to Omar; or maybe Omar would have to team up with them in some mutually necessary alliance of enemies. Lots of possibilities exist, all based upon a shifting array of allegiances.

Another scenario could have Omar in possession of the Jewel, so that the antagonist and the source of the pursuit are united. (See "Jewel Chart #3" on page 116.)

Now Ralphie, Jack, and Joan (antagonists and competitors, not lovers) could all be after the same object: three good guys against the bad guy and the MacGuffin.

Or how about having Ralphie in control of the Jewel, with Omar, Jack, and Joan hot after it ("Jewel Chart #4")?

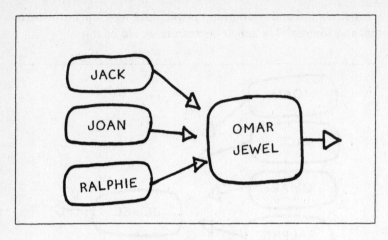

Jewel Chart #3

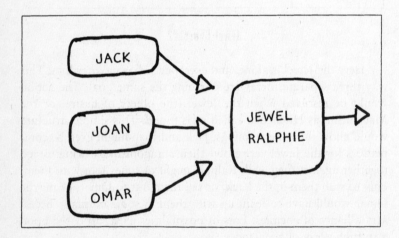

Jewel Chart #4

That way the good guys and the bad guys are after the same object, with Ralphie functioning as a wild card.

An argument could be made for any one of these structures. Personally I prefer everyone chasing after the Jewel. If Omar has the Jewel, he becomes more passive because his range of choice is limited—he's being pursued by others and can only try to avoid them. If Ralphie has the Jewel, then Omar and Jack and Joan are on equal footing—again a more interesting and dramatically richer possibility than the one Rosenthal and Konner chose.

But let's take a look at the actual film's overall structure:

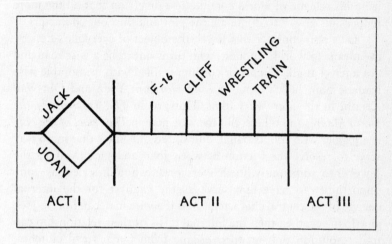

Jewel Chart #5

The first act sets up the basic situation and characters and ends with Jack and Joan rejoining each other at Omar's palace. From there, the F-16 escape leads to the cliff escape, the wrestling match, and the train scene, all second act events, all false obstacles designed as place holders until the inevitable confrontation between Omar and Jack and Joan at the third act juncture. The second act falls flat because the major action sequences are not narratively connected but are separate, interchangeable, unnecessary scenes. A false second act is a flat second act, leaving a gaping hole in a movie. The wrestling scene leads to Jack and Joan making love, thereby effectively resolving their internal first act crisis. Once that crisis is settled, the entire second half of the film becomes dependent solely upon the resolution of the external problem of whether Omar can get the Jewel and become dictator. In other words, the second act could be thrown out, and we could move straight from the first to the third acts without losing a single narrative or character beat.

Basically this structure dooms the film even if the maladroit characterizations could have been overcome. Not only that, but Omar is absent during most of the second act, all the more reducing him as a potent force in the drama. When we do see him, he is looking lamely for the famous Jewel of the Nile rather than actualizing his scheme of world conquest—a diversion that all the more reduces his power to dominate the plot and thus our characters.

Let's also consider this Jewel, the object of everyone's desires, the means to world conquest, who turns out to be a wise man and not a jewel at all. The history of film is filled with memorable wise leaders: Sam Jaffe's lama in *Lost Horizon;* Yoda and Obi-Wan Kenobi in the *Star Wars* films; Howard in *The Treasure of the Sierra Madre,* and others. But the wise man in *The Jewel of the Nile* is a juggler who spouts banal, uninspired one-liners that in no way serve to resolve the friction between Joan and Jack. Making the Jewel into someone who delivers prefab homilies destroys any opportunity to have him serve as the catalyst for the internal change of the central characters. And if a wise man can't bring Jack and Joan together, then the internal crisis of their relationship can find resolution only in their escape from Omar's evil clutches, which, as we've seen, just creates a false second act.

Okay, but if *The Jewel of the Nile* is so filled with errors, why did it make money? First, because there was such a reservoir of good feeling about *Romancing the Stone* that audiences forgave it some of its flaws. Second, the movie delivers on the action. Maybe P. T. Barnum was right: maybe nobody ever went broke betting on the stupidity of the American public. Certainly if you're going to make a stupid film, make it with plenty of action. Does this mean an intelligent, character-driven, witty *The Jewel of the Nile* would have failed? On the contrary, it would have done better than this botched sequel. The action audience still would have paid to see *Jewel,* and the broader audience, seeking a good movie, would have gone as well. Good moviemaking isn't just good craft, it's good business as well.

13. GROUNDHOG DAY

The Unexpected, Expected Structure

▬ ▬ ▬ ▬

RITA
Did you ever have déjà vu?

PHIL
Didn't you just ask me that?

Rita did ask Phil that. And she'll ask him that again and again, time after time, day after day, forever, until he finds a way out of his predicament. You see, Phil Connors, the arrogant, self-centered TV weatherman, is reliving the same day over and over again, and there's nothing he can do to stop it. The only thing he can change is how he lives each day and thereby how he affects those around him in the little town of Punxsutawney, Pennsylvania. On some days he makes love with a pretty woman, on others he gets drunk or gorges on pastries. But no matter what he does, when he wakes up in the morning it's the same day he just lived. Slowly Phil comes to love Rita, his TV producer and the only person he can't con. Stricken with despair at her dismissal of him, and of ever seeing tomorrow, Phil attempts suicide, only to realize that he can't even kill himself, that no matter whether he throws himself in front of a truck or electrocutes himself, he reawakens each morning, freshly alive, to relive the same day over and over again. Finally, as if by process of elimination, Phil tires of his egocentric behavior and finds himself learning the piano, doing a multitude of good deeds, and even saving lives. Stripped of his ego, and finally happy in his growing devotion to others, he at last gains Rita's love. They lie down together on the bed in which Phil has awakened for countless repeated Groundhog Days and drift off to sleep. Only in the morning Phil doesn't wake up alone, but rather with Rita asleep beside him. He realizes that at last today is tomorrow, that he is in love, and that he is free to make whatever life he wishes.

Danny Rubin's brilliant idea for a movie led to one of the most creative and entertaining films of the early nineties. Rubin's spec draft sold to Columbia TriStar, which gave it to Harold Ramis, who in turn brought on Bill Murray, with whom he'd worked on earlier films. Ramis and Murray were unhappy with Rubin's use of voice-overs to explain the action and with the script beginning with Phil already in multiple-day hell, so they began a rewrite—only to find themselves stuck: the ideas for changes that had sounded so good in story meetings weren't working on the page. They showed their unfinished draft to Rubin, who gave suggestions—largely interspersed with four-letter words—that they go back to his original draft. Ramis and Murray were so impressed with Rubin's passion, if not his vocabulary, that they rehired him to rewrite his own script, of which not one word now belonged to him. Finally, between Ramis's and Murray's innovations, and Rubin's sticking to his guns, a draft emerged that got a green light from the executives at TriStar.

What also emerged is a witty and largely unpredictable delight. While it employs a standard three-act structure, it takes a number of structural chances within that framework. Characters have no importance in some of Phil's "days," only to emerge as central to Phil's life in others. Scenes are reenacted, often using the same dialogue, in a daring use of structure. And though depicted with little explanation, Phil's transformation from an egocentric loser into a humble near saint is entirely believable. Rarely has a popular comedy demanded so much of a protagonist's growth or an audience's intelligence, probed so deeply into moral or philosophical questions, or left so much unexplained, yet remained so clear and entertaining.

Let's look at the structure. Danny Rubin's first draft of *Groundhog Day* began with Phil already in multiple-day hell. In other words, as Rubin saw it, Phil should be in the middle of his external crisis as the film begins. Ramis and Murray disagreed and, in effect, imposed a first act upon Rubin's second act. Thus the finished film begins like this:

- Phil reports the weather; we see he is an arrogant SOB; he meets Rita and starts out for Punxsutawney, Pennsylvania.
- Phil goes through his first day in Punxsutawney, meeting various characters in the town; he is obnoxious to one and all.

Ramis and Murray created a Phil-before to contrast with the Phil-after that Rubin had already written. This new first act does a couple of things. First, it shows us that the real problem of the movie isn't the weird circumstance into which Phil is thrown, but Phil himself, his arrogance, his egocentrism, his cold disdain for others. It tips us off that he will become the primary concern of the movie. It allows us to see how Phil lives before his world is thrown into perpetual rerun. In fact, the external problem that changes Phil begins only with the second act. When Danny Rubin first began plotting out *Groundhog Day,* he was influenced by Elisabeth Kübler-Ross's writings on people who have learned they have a terminal illness; these people go through a largely predictable emotional arc, beginning with shock and leading through fear, denial, anger, bargaining, despair, and, finally, acceptance. Rubin was struck by the terrifying inevitability of that progression and decided to use it as the vertebrae for his entire movie; Ramis and Murray, however, made it the spine of the second act:

- Phil spends his first two days in astonishment and growing fear.
- Phil tells Rita he needs help.
- On the third day Phil goes to a doctor, who sends him to a psychologist—no help.
- Phil bowls with two guys; he realizes there are no consequences to his actions; he gets drunk, gets in a car chase, gets thrown in jail.
- On the fourth through sixth days Phil does whatever he likes: picks up pretty Nancy, steals money, and acts like Clint Eastwood.

- Phil tries to date Rita, day after day perfecting their date, but no matter what he does, at the end of each date she rejects him.
- Phil is depressed and despairing; he commits suicide several times but always awakens the next day.
- Phil tells Rita he is a god; they spend a lovely day together; Phil declares his love for her "no matter what happens tomorrow."

Doesn't look like much, does it? It scans as a short second act, lacking much of the narrative complexities we've come to expect from a well-structured plot. In fact, it really breaks down into three major sections, or superscenes:

Phil's first six repeating days.
Phil's hapless dating of Rita.
Phil's attempts at suicide.

These three sequences contain all the stages of the Kübler-Ross progression Rubin was attempting to depict, ending with Phil's final acceptance of his condition. Phil has tried greed, lust, and all the other sins and found them to be empty delights, mere ashes in his mouth. With this realization comes Phil's acknowledgment that he has come to the end of himself, that he has nowhere else to go, which propels him not into death, but into the third act. Just as a traditional hero is at his lowest point when he makes the decision to move from the second to the third act, Phil, at his lowest point, makes an existential decision to move on. And on and on and on. In the same way that it traditionally is a transformed hero who enters the third act, someone who is making a final bid to over-come his obstacles, Phil has come to realize that he must reinvent himself:

- Phil helps a beggar.
- Phil starts taking piano lessons.
- Phil gives kind words to others.
- Phil tries to save the beggar's life—but can't—although he tries many times.

- Phil saves a boy from falling.
- Phil fixes a flat tire.
- Phil saves a man from choking.
- The party—Phil plays the piano, entertains, and becomes the most beloved man in town. Rita bids for him in an auction. Phil sculpts Rita's face in ice; he declares his love for her no matter what happens tomorrow as they fall asleep on his bed.
- The next day Phil awakens with Rita beside him—it is at last tomorrow; they begin a new day and a new life together.

Forgetting the unusual subject matter, the third act is fairly conventional. The hero goes through a catharsis, overcomes his initial problems (both the internal problem of his own arrogant egocentrism and the external problem of his endlessly repeating days), and gets the girl. But within that standard structural spine is a rather daring use of scenes, almost like a pointillist painting, which looks so solid from a distance but turns into a series of unrelated flecks of paint on closer examination. The beggar, barely present throughout the entire second act, becomes a central character in the third when his death becomes the final cross that Phil must bear. The two guys who early on occupy an entire night's adventures, drop out of the story entirely. The mayor, who is a pompous nonentity when we first see him, becomes Phil's relentless nemesis when Phil steals the groundhog, yet it's Phil who saves the mayor's life at the end. A man Phil passes in the hallway without a second glance later has his day, and perhaps even his life, changed by Phil's poetic subtleties.

But the philosophical questions that the script raises don't end with the observation that everyone is worthy of note, and has the potential to change their own lives, just as we have the potential to change theirs. Phil's realization that he is not God, that he can control only what is within his human powers, ultimately humbles Phil and causes him to lose his ego. It is this collision of ideas that powers the script and animates its story. And it is Phil, and his journey to greater consciousness, who represents the audience as he travels through his endlessly repeated days.

In fact, there are three major stages of realization that Phil goes though: first, that he can't control his life; second, that he can't control his love; and third, that he isn't God, able to stop death. These three insights are shown but only briefly commented on. Phil discusses his recurring existence with the two drunks, while his failure to woo Rita causes him to admit that he is at his wit's end. But the final realization that he can't stop death is simply shown, without a comment from Phil. Pretty daring writing, especially when the typical temptation is to hang up a sign in glowing letters screaming "author's message" all over the screen. Rubin's delight in showing and not telling, his trust in the intelligence of the audience to "get it" without its being explained to them, is what pushes the screenplay along so smoothly.

To be fair, Rubin's first draft did "point out" major plot and thematic issues through an obtrusive voice-over, while at the same time asking too much of an audience by beginning at what became the second act break—in effect he told too much and not enough, all at the same time. It was Ramis and Murray who insisted on making the film clearer by respecting the audience's ability to make great intuitive leaps. But it was Rubin's original concept, helped by his Kübler-Ross–inspired structure in the second act, that nevertheless powers us through the story.

A last note on the theme of *Groundhog Day*: Philosophers have debated for centuries whether mankind is innately good or bad. *Groundhog Day* suggests that while all of us are capable of great evil, when the fragile mechanisms of greed and ego are crushed under their own futility, we are, inevitably, and even against our will, drawn to the good. Phil, first seen as a thoroughly loathsome protagonist, has by the end of the film become a near saint, acutely aware of the preciousness of life and that it is best lived with love. The groundhog has merely seen his shadow, but Phil has looked into his very soul.

14. THE SEARCHERS

The Third Act Hiccup

■■■■ ■

The Searchers sprawls like a giant across the movie landscape. No western casts such a profound spell over our imagination, seems so unique and yet so quintessentially true to the genre, or is quite so timeless. It is often named not only as the greatest western ever made, but also as one of the greatest films ever made. John Wayne considered it his masterpiece; in fact, Wayne named his third son, John Ethan, after Ethan Edwards, the character he plays in the film, one of the most audacious characters ever written and one of the first and best of cinema's antiheroes. Of the nine westerns John Ford directed in Monument Valley, with the possible exception of *Stagecoach, The Searchers* best captures and immortalizes that eerie landscape, which itself has come to symbolize the American frontier. The screenplay, by Frank Nugent, creates a credible vision of a world inching toward the first glimmerings of civilization. The dialogue is fresh and masculine, the scenes often unforgettable, and the structure, while seemingly desultory, is in fact taut and inevitable. Indeed, it has only one structural flaw—a redundant third act climax involving a protagonist whose moral catharsis is not justified or foreshadowed—but it is a flaw so grievous that, in anyone's hands other than John Ford's, the movie probably would have been mortally wounded.

It is three years after the Civil War. Ethan Edwards returns alone to his brother's ranch, where he gives all of the mementos of his past to his brother's children and yearns silently for his brother's wife. He meets Martin, a neighbor, who is in love with the beautiful Laurie. Ethan and Martin, along with other men in the area, hear reports of an Indian raid on some cattle and charge off in pursuit. But the raid proves to be a ruse, and Ethan returns to see his brother and his wife murdered by Indians and their two daughters kidnapped. A posse is assembled to track down the two girls, but when the leader of the posse won't agree to Ethan's ruthless strategy of revenge, Ethan decides to go off on his own. Martin and Brad, Lucy's boyfriend, follow. They learn the eldest daughter has been raped and killed, leaving only little Debbie still alive. Brad is soon killed, and Martin continues with Ethan to find Debbie. Over the following two years Ethan and Martin travel the entire country, seeking clues to Debbie's whereabouts. Meanwhile, back at the ranch, Laurie thinks lovingly of Martin, hoping for his return and receiving a letter from him telling of his trials in search of Debbie.

Finally, after many adventures Ethan and Martin locate Debbie, now a young woman living with her Indian captors. Ethan, hating Indians and seeing that Debbie has become a part of what he despises, wants to kill her but is stopped by Martin and an Indian attack. They lose track of Debbie and the Indians holding her.

Later, Martin fights a rival for the love of Laurie while American soldiers give fresh clues to finding Debbie. Martin kills Debbie's Indian captor and is prepared to kill Ethan as well when Ethan, instead of killing Debbie, embraces her in a gesture of love. Later, Martin goes off with Laurie while Ethan is left alone just as he began, a man without a past or future.

Let's look at the structure, beginning with the first act:

- Ethan arrives, meets his brother and his family, and gives away mementos of his past.
- News arrives that Indians have attacked cattle; the posse is assembled.
- The posse learns that the cattle attack is a ruse to get them away from the now defenseless ranches.
- Attack on Ethan's brother and his family; the girls are taken.
- Ethan and Martin arrive to see the results of the massacre.
- Funeral; Ethan assembles men to catch the Indians.

A simple, clean first act. The arrival of Ethan marks the first and greatest problem—the mystery of Ethan: the man denying his past, the eternal loner. This internal problem is then followed in the second scene by the external problem of the Indian attack on the cattle. Both problems are then joined together as Ethan and Martin observe the results of the massacre: the brutality of the Indians makes Ethan even more brutal than the Indians he hates. But the posse learns too late they've been tricked, and this brings us immediately to the fourth scene, depicting the massacre of Aaron and his wife and the capture of their daughters. The script is very neatly structured so that each scene springs from the scene that preceded it and leads inevitably to the scene that follows.

The first act then rounds itself out at the funeral scene, where Ethan and the rest assemble a posse to pursue the Indians. It is the decision to go after the Indians that powers us into the second act. If Ethan had instead, for example, called on the army to punish the Indians, then the movie would have moved on without him. It is Ethan's decision to take the law into his own hands, to accept moral responsibility for revenge, that marks this as an act break.

But while the first act is pretty straightforward, the second act is quite complex. It begins with these scenes:

- The posse finds a dead Indian, whom Ethan then defiles.
- The Indians fool the posse.
- The Indians chase the posse, leading to a shoot-out by the river.
- Ethan argues tactics with the head of the posse; Ethan says he's going on alone; Brad and Martin join him.
- Ethan finds Lucy, raped and murdered.
- Brad angrily charges the Indians and is killed.
- Martin and Ethan continue on alone.

This sequence of scenes logically explains why the posse is forced to abandon the search and how only Martin and Ethan remain to continue the pursuit. It also establishes Ethan's obsessive hatred of Indians and his relationship with Martin, not dissimilar to Ishmael's relation to Ahab, or Ali's to Lawrence of Arabia—that is, Martin is a human bridge to the audience, a man in many ways morally superior to Ethan and yet swept up in Ethan's all-consuming and finally self-destructive vision. Again, while the story is brilliantly told, there is nothing unusual in the structure, which efficiently conveys a progression of events.

But at this point, having set up his characters, established the first act break, and laid out the initial complications of the second act, Frank Nugent now has to depict the passage of great stretches of time. He also has to reestablish the "home base" of Laurie's ranch, a place to which we will be returning again and again and which would cease being a factor in the story were it to drop out of the second act. It is at the ranch that the story begins and where it will end, and it is here that Martin will resolve his longings for the beautiful Laurie. Let's consider some of the narrative options that were available to Nugent. He could simply show us a number of scenes, interspersed perhaps with occasional fade-outs, which begin at the beginning and proceed to the end. He could tell the entire story from Ethan's, Martin's, or Laurie's point of view, with the "other side" of the story told through letters or gossip. Nugent could, in other words, have written a straight narrative line. Let's see what he did instead:

- Martin and Ethan return to Laurie's ranch—
    They read the Futterman letter giving clues about
        Debbie's whereabouts.
    Martin and Laurie flirt and fight.
    Martin and Ethan decide to look up Futterman.
    Martin tells Laurie he must leave her and that he fears
        Ethan will kill Debbie when he finds her—he
        must protect Debbie from him.
    Laurie tells Martin she won't be here when he
        returns.
- Futterman tells Ethan and Martin about Chief Scar, who is holding Debbie captive.
- Futterman prepares to rob Ethan; Ethan kills Futterman.
- Laurie gets a letter that describes the following events in a flashback sequence—
    Martin gets an Indian wife named Look.

Look is killed but leaves a clue about Debbie.
Ethan and Martin set out for New Mexico.
- New Mexico—Ethan meets a bartender who knows Scar is nearby.
- Ethan and Martin find Scar and Debbie.
- Ethan tries to kill Debbie, but Martin stops him.
- Scar attacks; Martin and Ethan run away.
- Enraged at Ethan's resolve to kill Debbie, Martin declares that he and Ethan are now enemies.
- Martin and Ethan return to Laurie's ranch—
    She is about to get married; Laurie and Martin flirt and fight again.
    The cavalry asks for help against Scar.

At first glance this seems to resemble the structure in *The Abyss,* where sequence after sequence tries and fails to power the story forward and in which many of the sequences could be cut out without being missed. But *The Abyss* failed because the sequences were insufficiently connected along a single narrative spine. *The Searchers* risks the same failure; it, too, is a series of seemingly unconnected adventures in which the third act solves the problem set forth in the first act, and the second act appears as a seemingly disposable series of obstacles and events. Not only that, but the action keeps jumping back and forth between Martin and Ethan's adventures on the trail and Laurie's ranch—another added risk to narrative velocity. But this back-and-forth approach doesn't hurt the narrative drive to find Debbie. Rather, it enhances it, since the use of letters and conversation at Laurie's ranch about the search for Debbie serves to continually remind us of Ethan's obsessive pursuit. In effect, no matter where we go, whether it be on the trail or to Laurie's, we can't escape the search for Debbie, which seems to fill not only the story, but the entire continent; it becomes, in other words, the narrative spine that *The Abyss* is missing and that powers us from sequence to sequence, adventure to adventure. Not only that, but the clues that Ethan and Martin find—Futterman, the Look clue, and the bartender—are all necessary to the finding of Debbie. *The Abyss* had no such narrative connections.

Notice that the Martin/Laurie relationship is the "B" story of the film, the secondary cutaway tale used whenever we need a break from the "A" story of the Martin/Ethan relationship and of the pursuit of Debbie. It's similar to *Ben-Hur*, where the Ben-Hur/Messala relationship is the "A" story while the Ben-Hur/Esther relationship is the "B." Nugent uses his Martin/Laurie "B" story as a dramatic breather to give us a rest from Ethan's mania. Just as in *Moby Dick* the Ishmael/Queequeg relationship, in being more lighthearted and loving, gave us a breather from the deadly serious Ishmael/Ahab relationship, so does Martin's love for Laurie lighten the story and keep it from bottoming out in Ethan's dark neurosis. Simply put, all work and no play would have made *The Searchers* a dull movie; Ford wisely used his broad humor (at times too broad) to lighten his tale.

Notice also how the use of Martin's letter voice-over is a brilliant device for reflecting the passage of time; it also approaches the story in a new way and keeps the movie one step ahead of the audience by creating a narrative device that is wholly unpredictable.

The exclamation point of the second act occurs when Ethan is stopped by Martin from killing Debbie. This thread of unexacted vengeance is the last and greatest issue to be resolved. When Ethan finds Debbie again, we're forced to ask, Will he kill her, and can he be stopped? This question hangs over the end of the second act like a shroud and powers us into the third act:

- The expedition after Scar.
- Martin sneaks in before the raid to grab Debbie; he kills Scar and captures Debbie.
- The raid.
- Ethan can't bring himself to kill Debbie and embraces her instead.
- Ethan and Martin return Debbie to Laurie's ranch; Debbie goes off to live with Laurie's folks while Laurie goes off with Martin; Ethan is left alone.

After the complexity of the second act, Nugent goes back to a third act as simple and clean as his first act. Debbie is found, and Ethan resolves his hatred of Indians, or at least of the Indian Debbie has partly become. Laurie goes off with Martin, and in one of the most famous endings in all of film, Ethan is left alone, the door literally closing him out from a world of peace and love.

There is, however, one problem with all of this. Ethan's first meeting with Debbie, occurring near the end of the second act, is, in fact, a third act climax that is left hanging. After all, the whole external problem of the movie is about Ethan finding Debbie, which he does with a half hour of movie still to come. The fact that we're left hanging as to whether or not he'll kill Debbie just prolongs the agony of a third act climax. In graph form it would look like this:

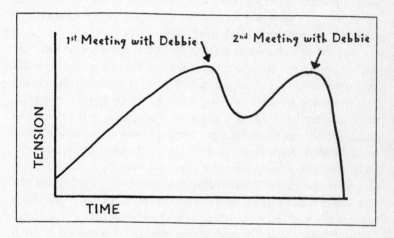

Searcher Chart #1

What we really have is two climaxes, with a pit stop in between to heighten tension. In itself, this wouldn't be so bad. *Alien, Aliens, The Terminator,* and *Terminator 2* all used a false climax to heighten tension before the film really ended. The problem here is one of motivation: Ethan was all set to kill Debbie when Martin and then the Indians stopped him. This same Ethan, with nothing to change his mind or make him feel greater compassion for Debbie, and presented with exactly the same situation, decides in the third act to embrace her. While there is some vague reference in the script—which is not in the film—to Debbie's resembling her mother or in the film, that they should go home, it all boils down to the same thing: Ethan has changed his mind without adequate setup or explanation; he has purged himself of his hate without having earned the catharsis. If he is saving Debbie because she resembles her mother, whom he loved, then can we presume Ethan would have put a bullet through her brain if she'd taken after her father, for whom he didn't care? Thus it isn't compassion, but an old memory he has always carried with him, that sparks his mercy. Ethan, then, isn't changed, particularly in his attitude toward Indians; he is all the more set in his ways. In one sense he is simply taking Debbie home to her white heritage; nonetheless, he is still unresolved about her years spent as an Indian. Ethan changes without letting us know why he has changed, how he has changed, or what he has done to deserve to change.

But Ethan's change at least allowed the audience to leave the theater happy and still liking John Wayne. Ethan's catharsis simply lets us have our cake and eat it, too—and is probably the reason that it works. Ethan Edwards is that rarest of Hollywood creatures—an antihero. He is a negative protagonist, whose neurosis and compulsions drive the story forward even as we dread where we're headed. And while it's dramatically fascinating to hitch the audience's affection to someone who may well be a villain, it also threatens one of the main reasons for any movie's existence: the box office. Macbeth, Richard III, and other classic antiheroes have never really worked well for a mass film audience. There are exceptions, of course. Paul Newman, in a wonderful portrayal in *Hud*, was so sexy and cool that audiences ignored the fact that he was a son of a bitch. But in general Hollywood is about happy heroes falling in love with happy heroines and defeating bad guys whom we can joyfully despise. Ethan Edwards, on the other hand, is a driven, neurotic loner, incapable of adequately showing love and forced into living alone until the day he dies. A fascinating, frustrating, wonderful, terrible man. But you won't see his like again, and not just because legends like his are vanishing. You won't see him again because the executives that green-light movies want happy heroes.

15. THE VERDICT

Dialogue As Litany

▬ ▬ ▬ ▬ ▬

When *The Verdict* first appeared in 1982, it seemed as fresh as a cool breeze in the desert. Its vivid characters, incisive dialogue, and quasi-documentary realism were revelations. It was a landmark in the careers of its star, Paul Newman, and of Sidney Lumet, its director. It established David Mamet, in addition to being a brilliant playwright, as an expert screenwriter. The vividly drawn characters are electric with authenticity, while the plot is a testament to classic film structure. Its dialogue bites like the best of Chayefsky while creating wholly original rhythms and cadences. Not only that but it expertly explores the worlds of the Catholic Church, of the courtroom, of the legal profession, and of a man whose greatest crusade is to save himself.

As with most Hollywood projects, the making of *The Verdict* is as much a tale of studio politics as of art. The producers, Richard Zanuck and David Brown, originally contacted Arthur Hiller to direct a movie of Barry Reed's novel *The Verdict*. Hiller liked the obscure book, since it dealt with the hot topic of medical malpractice. Not only that, but the main character, Frank Galvin, was an actor's dream: an ambulance-chasing, down-on-his-luck boozer lawyer who gets a chance to redeem himself with what may be the last case of his life. Hiller signed on the dotted line and hired David Mamet to adapt Reed's novel. Neither Hiller nor the producers were happy with Mamet's script, and Hiller bailed out on the project.

Zanuck and Brown then hired the wonderful Jay Presson Allen *(The Prime of Miss Jean Brodie, Cabaret)* to write a new script, which they loved. Enter Robert Redford, atop the slippery pole of movie stardom in 1982, who didn't like Allen's script and got James Bridges *(The China Syndrome)* to write yet another script. Nine months and two more drafts later, and Redford still wasn't happy with Bridges's script. Redford started asking his friend Sydney Pollack if he'd like to sign on as director. Pollack's answer is lost in the mists of time and moot anyway, since Redford hadn't first bothered to ask Zanuck and Brown if Pollack was acceptable to them as director. Amid much public recrimination, Redford exited, turning *The Verdict* from a "go" movie into yet another of the innumerable development projects slouching through the studios. Enter Sidney Lumet, who asked to look at the existing scripts. Zanuck and Brown sent Lumet the best of the Bridges scripts, along with Allen's draft. Lumet told them he loved the Mamet version (how he got that draft is lost in those same mists of time). Mamet was rehired, did a new ending under Lumet's supervision, and the project was off the ground. At last.

The Verdict is the tale of Frank Galvin, once a promising and brilliant lawyer, who has turned into a broke, alcoholic ambulance chaser. Deserted by everyone except his old mentor, Mickey, he is close to suicide. But Mickey gives Frank a sure thing, a case involving a woman who went brain dead in the operating room and for years has been a vegetable, kept alive by machines. Her sister has sued the hospital for malpractice. It is an open-and-shut case that will be settled out of court, with Frank getting one-third of the settlement, while everyone turns their backs on a woman transformed into a mindless husk of herself. But Frank decides to fight the case in court, attempting in the process not only to right the wrong inflicted upon the comatose girl and her family, but also to save himself from a life of similar buyoffs. He meets the beautiful Laura in a bar and begins an affair with her. Arrayed against Frank is Concannon, the most successful lawyer in the city, backed by his huge law firm and the vast resources of the Catholic hospital. As the trial proceeds, it becomes apparent that the judge is against Frank and that the case is as good as lost; witnesses disappear mysteriously or are forced by the judge to give testimony damaging to Frank's case. Frank also learns that Laura was all along a spy for Concannon. Finally, about to lose, Frank finds testimony that saves the case at the last minute. Frank wins the case, and even more to the point, he saves himself.

The subject of medical malpractice was still new cinematic territory in 1982, and the idea of a down-and-out lawyer seemed fresh and unusual. But it's the structure, so elegant and spare, brilliantly framing both theme and character, that made *The Verdict* a triumph of classic three-act theory. Here's the first act:

- Galvin visits funerals to get business, visits bars, and in despair trashes his files.
- Mickey informs Galvin that he has a "moneymaker" case for him.
- Galvin takes pictures of the brain-dead girl and talks with her family.
- Galvin finds Dr. Gruber, who is willing to testify against the girl's doctors.
- Galvin meets Laura in a bar.
- Galvin again visits the brain-dead girl and is struck by her condition.
- Galvin meets with the bishop in charge of the hospital and refuses the offered settlement money.

The internal problem that begins the film (Galvin's despair) is followed by the external problem (the "moneymaker" case). Major characters are introduced, and our hero is given the choice to fight evil or to embrace it. He refuses to take the settlement money, which forces us into the second and complicating act. Now let's look at the first half of the second act:

- Concannon and aides prepare their case; they seem unbeatable.
- Galvin and Mickey prepare their case; they seem very beatable.
- Galvin again meets Laura at the bar; they begin their affair.

- Galvin again refuses to settle the case out of court.
- Galvin's clients are furious at Galvin for refusing to settle; they threaten to ruin him.
- Galvin learns Dr. Gruber is away on vacation, unavailable to testify.
- Galvin asks the judge for an extension and is denied.
- Concannon expertly prepares witnesses for trial.
- Galvin ineffectually prepares his sole witness for trial.
- Galvin can't get the operating room nurse to testify.
- Concannon prepares for trial.
- Galvin prepares for trial.

Like many traditional second acts, this one divides into two parts, the setup and the payoff. Notice how Mamet structures his scenes so that they parallel and crosscut the preparations for the trial, contrasting the legal juggernaut Concannon is mounting against the haphazard operation Galvin's conducting. As usual, the stronger the antagonist and the weaker the protagonist, the stronger the drama and the sharper the rising line of tension. This structure of two converging dramatic lines looks something like this:

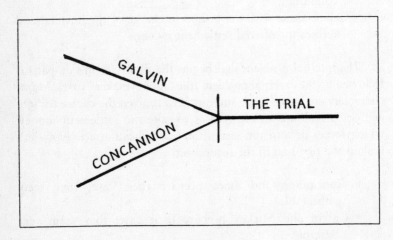

Verdict Chart #1

With the collision of these two lines at the midpoint of the script the second act proceeds into the trial:

- Galvin questions his witness; it is a fiasco.
- Galvin decides to press forward nonetheless.
- We, the audience, learn that Laura is a spy, paid by Concannon.
- Galvin and Mickey search vainly for the admitting nurse.
- Galvin tricks the operating room nurse into revealing she is shielding the admitting nurse.
- Galvin and Mickey can't find the admitting nurse anywhere.

This is the end of the second act. Things are at their lowest point. The case is as good as lost. The scenes have piled up in a ruthless, inevitable progression. The only unusual element is the revelation (which is withheld from Galvin but not from us) that Laura is a traitor. It's tricky letting the audience know more than the hero, because it risks making the hero look like a dope. But Mamet had no other place to set the scene and cleverly used it to make things seem even darker to us than they do to Galvin (in other words, if you have to let the audience know more than the hero, do it in such a way as to create sympathy for the hero, not disdain).

The third act is also traditional in its form:

- Galvin gets his phone bill; it gives him the clue that helps him track down the admitting nurse.
- Mickey discovers that Laura is Concannon's spy.
- Galvin gets the admitting nurse to agree to testify.
- Mickey tells Galvin that Laura is a spy. Galvin strikes Laura.
- The trial. Galvin presents the admitting nurse, who wins the case for him.
- Galvin is alone.

The third act begins when Galvin discovers how to find the admitting nurse. As is traditional at second act breaks, it is the hero's ability to act where another would fail that is his defining characteristic. Only Galvin could have so cleverly, so tenaciously, found how to find the admitting nurse. Only Galvin can wrench victory from the jaws of defeat. In other words, this is a perfect example of a third act.

Not only that, but there is a lovely symmetry to this act. Just as the first act began with the internal crisis of Galvin's despair and then developed the external problem of the moneymaker law case, the third act first resolves the law case and then resolves Galvin, who, in leaving Laura, is at last a whole man. He has triumphed not only over the forces of corruption, but over himself as well. Not one scene is wasted, not one scene is unnecessary—it is structure at its most concise, with each scene leading inevitably into the next with a narrative progression that is ruthless in its urgency.

But if the script is a paradigm of Aristotelian structure, it is its adroit courtroom give-and-take that bespeaks a ruthlessness that would have been more recognizable on a battlefield. No other courtroom drama in memory is as ruthless in its examination of that much-honored profession, sparing no one, not even Frank Galvin, in its revelation that the client is seen too often as an irrelevant blip on an agenda filled with ego and avarice. When Galvin turns down an opportunity to settle the case out of court, he is confronted by the husband of the plaintiff's sister:

> DONEGHY
>
> You guys, you guys, you're all the same. The doctors at the hospital, you . . . it's 'What I'm going to do for you'; but you screw up it's 'We did the best that we could. I'm dreadfully sorry . . .' And people like me live with your mistakes the rest of our lives.

Later, when Galvin interviews the nurse who knows the truth about the malpractice case, even while we see that his intentions are pure and honorable, he's still unable to unshackle himself from the lawyerly conceit that pompous bullying will win the day. The nurse attacks Galvin, accusing him of being like all the others:

MARY ROONEY

You know you guys are all the same. You
don't care who gets hurt. You're a bunch of
whores. You'll do anything for a dollar.
You've got no loyalty . . . no nothing . . .
you're a bunch of whores.

It is Galvin who recoils from this torrent of scorn, realizing
that she is right: while his intentions may be noble his methods still
define and stigmatize him. But in the end it is neither a rich doctor
who is on trial, nor the legal profession, nor even Frank Galvin
himself. The wonder of David Mamet's script is that we realize at
the end that all along it is we who were on trial. And the jury has
found us guilty.

16. TENDER MERCIES

Less Is More, Lots More

■■■ ■■■ ■■■ ■■

According to the story, Horton Foote wanted to write about a group of young country-western musicians. A producer suggested a secondary character be added to the mix, an older singer, once famous, now down on his luck, whom Foote named Mac Sledge. But the more Foote considered the character of Sledge, the more Sledge took over the film, until Foote found himself writing obsessively about Sledge and largely ignoring the younger singers. Mac Sledge became not just a down-and-out alcoholic ex-singer, but a symbol of all the down-and-outers, of all the dreams that self-destructed and all the wisdom learned almost too late. The finished script was sent to Robert Duvall, who agreed to play Sledge, but it was some time before the hunt for a director landed Bruce Beresford, a brilliant young Australian, who agreed to Foote's austere, unblinking vision of Sledge and to the radically austere fashion in which he told his tale.

It's not surprising that it took so long to get *Tender Mercies* off the ground. It is a movie that shouldn't work. The scenes are minimalist vignettes, the characters so inarticulate as to speak in clichés, grunts, and half-completed thoughts, and the plot is a series of seemingly unrelated, unconnected events. Emotions are consistently underplayed, and the few action scenes that do exist are intentionally performed off screen. Why, then, is it one of the most affecting, venturesome, and passionate films of the eighties?

Mac Sledge is a former country-western singer and songwriter whose alcoholic binges caused his marriage to singing star Dixie to disintegrate, along with his career. As the film begins he is broke, working off his motel bill by doing odd jobs around Rosa Lee's motel and gas station somewhere on the Texas prairie. Rosa Lee is a widow, raising her eight-year-old son, Sonny, by herself. Mac soon falls in love with and marries Rosa Lee, stops drinking, and begins singing and writing songs again. He also meets his estranged teenage daughter soon before she dies in a car accident. As the film ends he's hoping to begin a new life with Rosa Lee and Sonny.

Doesn't exactly keep you up at night, does it? But the emotionally urgent, passionate lives lived by *Tender Mercies*' characters shine through a minimalist plot and equally minimalist dialogue. The verbal antithesis of *Network,* the philosophical companion to *Fargo, Tender Mercies* proves that the ability to talk has nothing to do with the ability to feel. Its structure resembles an impressionist painting: it is the movie that memory retrieves, a distillation of plot that turns scenes into vignettes, fleeting glimpses of reality, without narrative arc or closure. Each scene is the result (not the cause or the process) of internal thought. Put simply, *Tender Mercies* throws its plot on its ear because it throws the concept of scenes on its ear. Thus, let's begin our discussion of *Tender Mercies* with an examination of the nature of scenes.

A movie is made up of scenes as much as a building is made up of bricks. But the comparison ends there, because while bricks can create a building of any shape or form, movie scenes build only the three-act structure, which is the basis for virtually all modern screenwriting. This structure, comprising a first act that introduces a problem, a second act that complicates the problem, and a third act that resolves the problem, finds a miniature mirror in the scenes that make it up. That is, each scene works like a condensed movie, with a beginning, a complicating middle, and a resolving end. John realizes he has to kill his nemesis; he's told how difficult that will be; he thinks of a way to overcome his difficulties and resolves to go forward, despite the risk. Beginning, middle, and end. First act, second act, third act, all contained within a simple scene. Ideally, each scene, in resolving its problem, creates a new problem that generates the next scene. Thus John's decision to proceed with the murder of his nemesis leads to his planning, which in turn leads to his attempts at murder, which leads to his escape, which leads to his being captured, and so on, each scene solving its initial problem while creating new problems and new scenes, until all are resolved in the final beat of the final scene. It is a pattern that looks something like this:

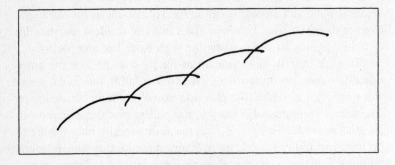

Tender Chart #1

At least that's the way it's usually done. Enter Horton Foote with his *Tender Mercies*. Instead of employing the usual structure, Foote structures his scenes something like this:

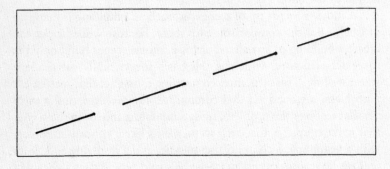

Tender Chart #2

As you can see, this approach creates huge narrative gaps, which the audience must fill in for themselves. Examples abound in

Tender Mercies, but look at the first beats of the movie, where through a series of seemingly unconnected events the script soon arrives at Mac's wholly unexpected, and completely convincing, proposal of marriage. This peripatetic approach was invented in Europe, principally by French filmmakers of the fifties and sixties like Truffaut. Tired of the old Hollywood paradigm where plot and character glued scenes together (a structure that, however elegant, can in the wrong hands seem contrived, artificial, and predictable), they tried to invent a new structure that more closely resembled real life. Things happen, one after the next, without connecting relationship or progression, a structure reflecting the belief that life cannot be reduced to a deeper, unifying meaning but is simply a random series of unconnected events. The "glue" of movies like this is thematic, rather than based on plot or character. If the truth be known, this European system of structuring is just as artificial as anything Hollywood ever churned out (which may be a reason we see less of it nowadays): after all, aligning and sequencing events in terms of theme is just as systematized, just as anticapricious, just as unreal, as the Hollywood method. Life has no natural theme, except its own lack of theme, so the imposition of a theme upon any work of art is mere artifice. But if done right, at least this way the gears and wheels are better hidden and more subtly used.

To give an idea of *Tender Mercies*' structure, let's look at the main characters as they appear in the second half of the second act, listing each of their respective scenes in the order in which they occur:

SUE ANNE: appears; Mac learns she's married; she asks for money; Mac learns she's dead.

MAC: sings for Rosa Lee; is baptized; sings; gets a new record.

DIXIE: sings; talks to Harry; is with Mac at Sue Anne's funeral.

ROSA LEE: talks to Mac about her past; dances with Mac; gives money to Sue Anne; talks with Mac.

SONNY: is baptized with Mac; talks to Rosa Lee; plays football with Mac.

As you can see, the scenes for each of these characters have little narrative connection. They're simply a string of events that, if graphed out on a timeline, would look something like this:

SUE ANNE

MAC

DIXIE

ROSA LEE

SONNY

TIME

Tender Chart #3

No character has a straight narrative line, but rather appears and disappears off the screen in a seemingly haphazard manner. The genius of this structure (and its difficulty) is that there is a method to its seeming randomness, based not upon narrative connection, but upon theme. And it's the accumulation of seemingly haphazardly selected details and moments—all thematically connected—that creates the film's emotional vibrancy.

Nor does Horton Foote help us decipher events through his dialogue, which avoids emotional confrontation, keeping so much hidden as to at times seem intentionally elusive. Here's Mac proposing to Rosa Lee (they have known each other for about five minutes of screen time and have barely talked to each other until this scene):

EXT. MOTEL VEGETABLE GARDEN—DAY

MAC *and* ROSA LEE *in the garden; he is digging with a hoe and she is weeding.*

> MAC
>
> I haven't had a drink in two months. I think
> my drinking is behind me.

> ROSA LEE
>
> Do you? I'm glad. I don't think it gets you
> anywhere.

> MAC
>
> You ever thought about marrying again?

> ROSA LEE
>
> Yes, I have. Have you?

> MAC
>
> I thought about it, lately. I guess it's no secret
> how I feel about you. A blind man could see
> that. Would you think about marrying me?

> ROSA LEE
>
> Yes, I will.

And that's it. End of scene. No wild declarations of love. No deep emotional outpourings. Almost every line is a cliché. But, unlike *Falling in Love,* which attempts the same resonance and falls on its bland face, the resonance of these words implies worlds of hurt and growth; it is perhaps one of the best examples of the "less is more" style of film dialogue. We don't even know if Rosa Lee is saying she'll think about marrying Mac or if in fact she's just accepted him.

Nor are these characters unable to speak in complex sentences and thoughts. Here's a scene toward the end of the script. Mac has just learned of the death of his teenage daughter in a car accident and tries to sum up his life to Rosa Lee.

EXT. GARDEN NEAR MOTEL—DAY

MAC *is weeding the garden rows with a hoe as* ROSA LEE *walks up to him.*

ROSA LEE
Mac, you okay?
(A pause. MAC *keeps working.)*

MAC
I was almost killed once in a car accident. I
was drunk and I ran off the side of the road
and I turned over four times. They took me
out of that car for dead, but I lived. And I
prayed last night to know why I lived and
she died, but I got no answers to my prayers.
I still don't know why she died and I lived. I
don't know the answer to nothing. Not a
blessed thing. I don't know why I wandered
out to this part of Texas drunk and you took
me in and pitied me and helped me to
straighten out and married me. Why, why
did this happen? Is there a reason that happened? And Sonny's daddy died in the war.

(pause)

My daughter killed in an automobile accident. Why? You see, I don't trust happiness.
I never did, I never will.

The words are simple, but the thoughts are profound and
deeply felt. Mac, at the film's penultimate moment, his words like
simple thunderclaps, denies his faith in happy endings. But we
sense that Mac can trust happiness, at least enough to go on with
his life with Rosa Lee and her son, Sonny. It's one of those rare
moments when the writer and his characters are so far ahead of the
audience that while no one is prepared for the scene, the audience
can nevertheless trust that the writer has placed us in his own good
and loving hands. He has.

17. SOME LIKE IT HOT

Fewer Scenes, Bigger Laughs

— — — —

JERRY
But don't you understand.
(he rips off his wig; in a male voice)
I'm a man!

OSGOOD
(oblivious)
Well—nobody's perfect.

But the movie is, or very nearly so, and if this book were retitled *Good Scripts, Great Scripts,* and if it were limited to just one film-maker, perhaps the best choice for that honor would be Billy Wilder. As brilliant as Hitchcock, as sentimental as Ford, as worldly as Huston, as comic as Sturges, Wilder has a range all his own, with a slate of films that is unmatched. Just to name a few, his *Double Indemnity* (1944) is one of the great films noir, perhaps bettered only by his brilliant *Sunset Boulevard* (1950). His *The Lost Weekend* (1945) remains perhaps the greatest film ever made about the horrors of alcoholism, while his *Stalag 17* (1953) is one of the great films about military prisoners. He followed it with *Sabrina* (1954), which still scintillates as one of the most perfect romances ever filmed. *The Spirit of St. Louis* (1957) is one of the great film biographies, while *Witness for the Prosecution* (1958) is one of the great mysteries. *The Apartment* (1960) stands as one of the great social comedies, while *One, Two, Three* (1961) is one of the great screwball comedies. It is an amazing list, filled with land-mark films, every one of which he both directed and co-wrote, usually with his collaborators, the wonderful Charles Brackett and I. A. L. Diamond. But of all his work, the one film that may last the longest, and remains the quintessential Billy Wilder movie, is his astounding *Some Like It Hot* (1959), with its perfect blend of social satire and outrageous humor.

Chicago in the Roaring Twenties. Joe and Jerry play sax and bass fiddle in a speakeasy run by Spats, a notorious gangster. After the place is raided by the cops, Joe and Jerry find themselves broke and out of a job. But the only steady work available is for a female sax and bass fiddle player in a woman's band headed to Florida. Disgruntled, they pick up a car to go to a small gig and happen upon Spats masterminding the St. Valentine's Day Massacre. Spats sees Joe and Jerry and orders the two witnesses killed. Joe and Jerry escape, with Spats and his boys right on their heels. Knowing it's only a matter of time until Spats finds them, Joe and Jerry dress up as women, call themselves Josephine and Daphne, and join the woman's band, just heading out of town on a train for the job in Florida.

On the train Joe and Jerry meet Sugar Kane, the band's beautiful singer, and both fall hard for her. Once in Florida Jerry meets Osgood, an old millionaire still on the prowl for beautiful women like "Daphne." While Jerry tries to avoid Osgood, and "Josephine" finds himself attracted to Sugar, they learn that Spats is looking for them high and low. Unable to leave the hotel, the boys hunker down. Joe steals Osgood's clothes and disguises himself as "Junior," heir to the Shell Oil fortune, and Sugar gets a crush on him. Osgood meanwhile continues to pursue "Daphne," who agrees to date the old guy since it will allow "Junior" to use Osgood's yacht to entertain Sugar. While "Daphne" dates Osgood, "Junior" dates Sugar on Osgood's yacht. At the hotel after their dates, Jerry tells Joe that Osgood proposed to him; Sugar tells them both that she's in love with Junior.

That's when Spats shows up and registers at the hotel. The boys are about to leave when Spats spots them dressed as women. The chase is on, and Jerry and Joe hide under a hotel table, only to find they're at a gangster convention, where Spats is killed by his rival, Little Napoleon. With Spats dead, Joe and Jerry are ready to leave when Joe realizes he loves Sugar too much to leave her.

But now it's Little Napoleon who's after them, and the boys jump into Osgood's boat with Sugar in tow. Joe declares his love for Sugar, and as they kiss in the back, Osgood again proposes to "Daphne." Jerry frantically admits to Osgood that he's a man; undeterred, Osgood tells him, "Nobody's perfect." As they cruise off into the sunset, we get the feeling that everybody's going to live wackily ever after.

It's a frantic script, full of switches and surprises and some of the funniest dialogue ever written for the screen. It also contains far fewer scenes than the average movie. Wilder's love of dialogue forced him to write scenes that ran longer than average; he knew that his involved verbal riffs wouldn't work with shorter scenes and that he had to write a movie that was almost a play in disguise. This theatrical approach to writing had fallen out of favor by the late fifties, when terse dialogue had come into vogue. A new sort of audience was going to the movies in those years, the first generation that had grown up on TV, and they demanded quicker, telegraphic writing, which got to the point faster and moved like a shot to the next scene. Wilder and Diamond fought that trend, demanding that the audience stay seated for their much longer than average scenes, knowing they could enforce this demand only if their dialogue was so hilarious and fast paced that each scene was in effect ten scenes, telescoped together, employing a faster cadence than anything on TV. Their bet paid off: *Some Like It Hot* became a classic and, more to the point for the bean counters in Hollywood, a financial success. And it succeeded not only because of the brilliance of the writing, but because it employs a classic script structure. This Aristotelian structure was their foundation, one crafted so solidly that it permitted the erection of scenes that ran longer than was then popular. Let's examine this structure, beginning with the first act:

- Cops chase a hearse whose coffins are filled with bootleg booze.
- Mulligan the cop prepares to raid Spats's speakeasy.
- Joe and Jerry play in Spats's band; they're broke.

- Mulligan raids Spats's speakeasy; Joe and Jerry run for it.
- Joe and Jerry learn of the job for two women; they borrow a car and head out to a small gig.
- They witness the St. Valentine's Day Massacre; Spats is after them.
- Joe and Jerry dress up as women, join an all-woman's band, and jump on the train to escape Spats.

All very simple. The general problem of time and place is introduced when we first see the crazy world of Prohibition Chicago. This problem is made more specific when we see preparations for the raid. Only then, with the atmosphere established and the general contours of the external problem introduced, do we meet Joe and Jerry, our broke heroes. Normally it might be a little risky to start a movie with an examination of the times, but Wilder realized—just as the Epsteins and Howard Koch realized when they were creating *Casablanca*—the setting was so pertinent to the story, while at the same time something with which much of the audience might not be acquainted, that it was necessary to establish place and time before introducing the story; otherwise the audience would have had to spend much of the first act playing catch-up with characters moving through a mysterious setting. (The movie *Copland* tries to solve the same problem with a clumsy opening voice-over.) Wilder knew he was taking a risk by beginning his story with a general situation, but he solved it by making the opening scene so quick and clever that it doesn't slow up the narrative. Besides, the audience will give the filmmakers a few free minutes early on in a film, minutes they'd resent if imposed upon them later on. Joe and Jerry's money problem, which is their initial internal problem, is made worse when Mulligan the cop raids the speakeasy, effectively forcing Joe and Jerry into temporary retirement. We see more of Joe's internal problem when he reveals what an uncaring womanizer he is.

Joe and Jerry's decision to disguise themselves as women, something only our protagonists would do, provides the perfect avenue into a second act and the purest way of getting to know our characters. If Joe and Jerry had been a little less clever, they might have been discovered by Spats, who would have killed them on the spot, thereby ending the movie. On the other hand, if they'd been a little more clever, they'd have simply slipped away from Spats forever, again solving their problem, and the movie could have closed up shop right then and there. It's only the specific solution Joe and Jerry pick—to dress up as women and join a woman's band—that assures us that not only will the problem with Spats continue, but that we're complicating our initial crisis and thus powering into the second act:

- On the train "Josephine" and "Daphne" meet Sugar, on whom they both get a crush.
- Sugar tells "Josephine" that she has bad luck with male sax players, that she wants a rich husband.
- The band arrives in Florida; "Daphne" meets Osgood.
- Moving into their rooms, "Josephine" tells Sugar he has a feeling she'll soon meet a millionaire.
- Joe and Jerry learn they can't leave the band, that Spats is looking for them everywhere.
- Sugar meets Joe dressed as "Junior," the Shell Oil millionaire.
- Osgood invites "Daphne" to dinner.
- Joe and Jerry make a deal: "Daphne" will date Osgood, thus letting "Junior" use Osgood's yacht for his date with Sugar.
- "Junior's" date with Sugar; "Daphne's" date with Osgood.
- Back in the hotel Jerry tells Joe that Osgood proposed; Sugar tells them both she's in love with Junior.
- Spats shows up at the hotel.

This outrageously funny second act, so deceptively short, has three main actions. First, there's the evolution of the "Junior"/Sugar relationship, with Joe doing his best to get Sugar into bed. Second, there's the "Daphne"/Osgood relationship, with Jerry letting himself be wooed by the totally oblivious Osgood. Thematically both are romances based on use: Joe wants to use Sugar, while Jerry lets himself be used by Osgood. The third element is Spats, who, like the shark in *Jaws* or Howard Beale in *Network,* acts as a catalyst, kicking the plot forward whenever it's about to reach a moment of emotional closure. Spats first appears as a rumor just as the boys check into the hotel; Wilder knew he needed a motivation to keep his characters trapped in Florida, and the threat of Spats was his perfect motivation. Once he's locked his characters into the hotel, Wilder waits to bring back Spats until Joe's need for Sugar, Sugar's need for "Junior," and Osgood's love of "Daphne" have all been established. This second Spats appearance acts as the juncture into the third act. Everyone is at a low point, with each character loving the wrong person for the wrong reasons and with Spats ready to rub out everybody. It's the perfect time to kick into a third act:

- "Josephine" and "Daphne" ride up the elevator with Spats, who doesn't recognize them—yet.
- Joe and Jerry plan to leave; Joe gives Sugar the diamond bracelet Osgood gave "Daphne."
- Spats discovers Joe and Jerry as women.
- A chase through the hotel.
- Joe and Jerry hide under the banquet table as Little Napoleon kills Spats.
- Joe and Jerry again start to leave; Joe lovingly kisses Sugar good-bye, and she starts to fall for "Josephine."
- A new chase that leads to Osgood's launch.
- Joe and Sugar reconcile.
- Osgood remains determined to marry Jerry.

Spats's appearance this time forces Joe and Jerry to leave. But first, Joe gives Sugar the diamond bracelet that Osgood gave to "Daphne." Not only is this high burlesque, but it shows growth in Joe as he abandons his womanizing ways to commit to Sugar. But the boys still would be out the door, until Spats, always the catalyst stirring things up just when they seem to be settling down, discovers Joe and Jerry. But too much of Spats would become repetitive, so Wilder does what any self-respecting filmmaker-genius does to his monster when he's outlived his welcome: he kills him.

Unfortunately at this point, Wilder and Diamond, for the first time in the movie, run out of creative steam and kill their first monster with a new monster, this one named Little Napoleon. But when

Godzilla killed Mothra they'd at least had some screen time to get acquainted; here Spats and Little Napoleon barely have time to trade insults before Spats is pushing up daisies. Ideally Little Napoleon should have been brought in during the first act to lock in his relationship with Spats and, if possible, with Joe and Jerry. This problem of Little Napoleon's sudden appearance as a new character in the third act is made worse during the final chase: Little Napoleon has no stake in Joe and Jerry except the already used motivation that they are—once again—witnesses to a murder, in this case Spats's. It's the same tune, second verse, and Wilder and Diamond should have come up with a new motivation for Little Napoleon to be after them, ideally originating with something that passed between them in the first act. The only excuse for these two mistakes is that Wilder and Diamond may have been geniuses but they were also, after all, human. Besides, by now, with the movie charging toward the finish line, no one's going to question that Little Napoleon has taken over Spats's monster patrol.

As for the ending, our boys at last finally resolve not only their relationships, but who they really are: Joe admits his love for the beautiful Sugar (who stops fighting her attraction for sax players), while Jerry, it seems, will be doing just fine with Osgood.

But no discussion of *Some Like It Hot* is complete without mention of the brilliant Wilder and Diamond dialogue. Take, for example, the scene where Osgood dates "Daphne":

JERRY

You invest in shows?

OSGOOD

Showgirls. I've been married seven or eight times.

JERRY

You're not sure?

OSGOOD

Mama is keeping score. . . . Right now she thinks I'm on my yacht deep-sea fishing.

> JERRY
>
> Well, pull in your reel. You're barking up the
> wrong fish.

> OSGOOD
>
> Which instrument do you play?

> JERRY
>
> Bull fiddle.

> OSGOOD
>
> Do you use a bow or do you just pluck it?

> JERRY
>
> Most of the time I slap it.

> OSGOOD
>
> You must be quite a girl.

> JERRY
>
> Wanna bet?

It's setup to punch line to new setup to new punch line—all classic comedy writing that wonderfully emerges from specific character and circumstance. Not only that, but it sets up Osgood's yacht, tells us Osgood is definitely the marrying type, shows us "Daphne" is playing hard to get, turns a bass fiddle into a sexual reference, and prepares us for an upcoming date between Osgood and "Daphne." Jokes exist not simply to reveal character, but to advance plot, in a perfect marriage of wit and craft. It's not just brilliant, it's Billy Wilder.

PART TWO
CHARACTER

18. PRIZZI'S HONOR
The Passive Second Act Protagonist

▬ ▬ ▬ ▬

> *But dreadful is the mysterious power of fate; there is no deliverance from it by wealth or war, by fenced city; by dark, sea-beaten ships.*
>
> —Chorus, *Antigone*
> (title page of the script for *Prizzi's Honor*)

In 1963, Stanley Kubrick set out to make a serious examination of the dangers of thermonuclear war. But as soon as he sat down with his screenwriter he found that the issues were so titanic, the characters so over the edge, that it was impossible to write with a straight face. Whenever he started talking about someone giving the order to drop the Bomb, or considered a scene where the Russians were about to counterattack, the absolute insanity of the situation made him crack up and start laughing. Not only that, but *Fail-Safe*, another deadly serious detailing of the terrors of the Bomb, was already in preproduction and, with apologies to Dr. Johnson, nothing clarifies a man's mind faster than knowing the competition is already green-lit. Finding it impossible to deal in a levelheaded manner with the threat of total annihilation, Kubrick did the next best thing: he made his movie into a comedy and called it *Dr. Strangelove.*

Cut to 1984, when John Huston found himself faced with a similar situation. He wanted to make a movie about the Mafia, but *The Godfather,* parts one and two, had already defined that sordid world. What more could be said? What greater gravity could be lent to the subject? Huston was too smart to try to answer those questions. Instead, he took Richard Condon's delightful satire of the mob and made it into the wonderfully funny *Prizzi's Honor*. Besides the brilliant script by Condon and Janet Roach, *Prizzi* also boasts lustrous performances by Jack Nicholson, Angelica Huston, and Kathleen Turner. It is Huston at his best: wise, witty, sardonic, cynical, and in love with life. It is also one of the more complex and ambitiously structured scripts of the eighties, employing brilliant thematic and character parallels, and a passive second act protagonist who would have tommy-gunned almost any other movie.

The story revolves around Charley Partanna, who was adopted at the age of ten into the New York Prizzi crime family by the Don, a close associate of Charley's father, Angelo (Pop). As Charley reached young adulthood he swore eternal loyalty, on pain of instant death, should he ever place anything before his fealty to the Prizzis. By early middle age Charley has become the main hit man for the Prizzis.

Charley was once engaged to Maerose Prizzi, daughter to Dominic—who, along with Eduardo, is one of the Don's two sons—but Charley backed out just before the marriage. Maerose, enraged at Charley's desertion, made a public spectacle of herself, and has become the black sheep of the family. Now, ostracized and alone, she is allowed to show her face only at special family gatherings, such as the wedding of her sister. Charley is also at the extravagant affair, and soon spies a lovely blond Polish stranger who stands out in this sea of Italian faces. Charley is instantly smitten, but the beautiful woman runs off before he can get her name or address. Later the mystery lady calls, apologizing that she had to leave so quickly. Charley learns that her name is Irene, and that she lives in Los Angeles. Charley makes a date to see her for lunch the next day. There he declares his love for Irene, who agrees to marry him.

Charley soon gets an assignment from Dominic to kill Marxie Heller, who owes the Don money. Charley kills Marxie, only then to find that he was Irene's husband. Irene says that she was about to divorce Marxie, that she loves Charley, and that she knew nothing of Marxie's cheating the Don. Irene finds half of the money which Marxie owed the Don, but is unable to locate the other $360,000. Back home Charley explains what happened and is told that Irene isn't as innocent as she sounds; she is in fact a professional killer, like Charley, and probably stole the missing $360,000. Charley goes to Maerose to confess his confusion, only to find himself seduced by her; Maerose then urges Charley to marry Irene regardless of her career choice. Irene admits she's a hit man, but denies she's a thief, and marries Charley.

Charley gets his next assignment: to kidnap a rich man named Filargi and hold him for ransom. Charley, Pop, and Irene plan the kidnapping together, with Irene unfortunately killing a police chief's wife during the grab. Maerose meanwhile tells the Don of Irene's theft of the $720,000, of which only half has been returned. As Irene and Charley continue on happily in love, Charley begins to suspect that he is being set up by Dominic to be killed; in fact, Irene admits that Dominic hired her to do the killing. Irene begs Charley to escape with her, but Charley refuses. The police are putting pressure on the Prizzis to give up the police chief's wife; all mob activity has been stopped until the killer is found. Charley steals Filargi to use as a bargaining chip with the Don, hoping to win back his life. Charley begins to feel safe until Irene asks that the money that she stole be returned to her. Charley is told by the Don that Irene is a bad woman and that Charley must kill her. Only that way can he reenter the family and regain his position as heir to the Prizzi family command. Torn between his love for Irene and his loyalty to the Prizzis, Charley finally kills Irene. As the film ends he calls Maerose for a date; Maerose, out of the family doghouse, is about to reclaim not only Charley but also her honor.

It's a tangled tale (perhaps too tangled), with a complexity of plot that more appropriately attaches to a novel than a movie script. The dealing and double-dealing are at times hard to follow. Nevertheless, it begins in a simple enough manner:

- Before opening titles the young Charley swears eternal allegiance to the Prizzi family.
- Years later, Charley spies Irene at a wedding and falls instantly in love; Maerose is the black sheep at the family wedding.

- Charley tries to find Irene but can't; Maerose doesn't know where to locate her.
- Irene calls Charley; he makes a date with her in Los Angeles.
- Irene and Charley declare their love, make love, and agree to marry.

It's an elegant first act. The initial problem, introduced before titles, is internal: Charley has sworn a blood oath to the Prizzis and must honor this oath above all others, on pain of death. This oath hangs over the movie, defining and coloring all other actions, and it is Charley's escalating crisis of whether to honor or reject that oath that propels our story. But that internal problem is immediately complicated when the external crisis is introduced in the very next scene: Charley meets Irene and falls instantly in love. Like Michael Corleone when he meets the beautiful Apollonia in Sicily (and which this scene satirizes), Charley has been hit by the "thunderbolt." But since Charley has earlier rejected Maerose Prizzi, and since Irene is nothing if not an outsider, her very presence complicates and heightens the tension. Charley and Irene's declaration of love is a critical dramatic juncture because Charley's decision to marry outside of the family is the defining moment that powers us into the second act. Had Charley not fallen in love with an outsider (or had Irene not been the killer we'll soon find she is), then Charley's internal crisis of his absolute loyalty to the Prizzis would never have been tested, and he would have continued on forever, devoted killer and mob loyalist. Notice also how every scene in this first act has Charley not only as a protagonist but also as a catalyst; Charley powers forward every beat, creating and driving the plot. Now let's take a look at the second act. I've marked an A after each scene for which Charley is the prime activist, a B for every scene in which someone else propels the plot:

- Charley is ordered by Pop to kill Marty Gilroy. (B)
- Charley gets two checks from Marty. (B)
- Charley gets the assignment to kill Marxie Heller. (B)
- Charley kills Marxie. (A)
- Charley discovers Irene was married to Marxie; Irene gives Charley back half the money Marxie owed. (B)

- Charley reports the missing $360,000 to Dominic. (A)
- Charley learns Dominic thinks Charley took the $360,000. (B)
- Pop tells Charley that Irene is a hit man. (B)
- Maerose seduces Charley; she tells him to marry Irene. (B)
- Charley and Irene marry. (A)
- The Don tells Charley to kidnap Filargi. (B)
- Planning the kidnapping; Irene lays the plans. (B)
- Maerose tells Dominic she was "raped" by Charley. (B)
- The Filargi kidnapping; a cop's wife is killed by Irene. (B)
- Maerose finds Irene was involved in the Heller heist. (B)
- Dominic hires Irene to kill Charley. (B)
- Irene tells Charley she has a surprise for him. (B)
- Maerose tells the Don that Irene stole the Heller money. (B)
- The Don tells Irene to repay the $720,000 with interest. (B)
- Charley has phone-sex with Irene. (A)
- Pop is told the cops want the wife's killer; they're clamping down. (B)
- The Don tells Charley he's the heir to the Prizzi family. (B)
- Charley tells Irene he thinks he's being set up; Irene admits she was hired by Dominic to kill Charley; Irene begs Charley to escape with her; Charley refuses. (B & A)

It's a complicated second act. Notice how few of these scenes are generated by some action or decision made by Charley. Having made his decision to marry Irene, Charley's fate has literally been taken out of his hands; he's become the pawn of other forces. Turning an active first act protagonist into a passive second act protagonist can be terribly risky. Not only does it take the juice out of the movie's center but it also risks our losing sympathy for our hero and turns what was an active man into one unable to decide his own fate. In addition to his passivity, Charley also goes through a seeming change of character—his decisiveness turns into indecision—that is disorienting and alienating. But this all works because the fast-paced complexities of the second act, accompanied by its vigorous characterizations, power us along despite Charley's abdication as decision maker.

Notice also that two entirely new plot problems have been

introduced—the Marxie Heller killing, followed by the Filargi kidnapping. It probably would have been safest, and certainly more intelligible, if the script had stayed with one problem, rather than essentially resolving one problem only to introduce a second halfway through our second act. Although the two plot lines can be structurally justified, there certainly must have been some way to fold them together into one and still fulfill the story's narrative needs. On the other hand, this very complication is a virtue as the very convolutions of the plot give a stronger flavor to Charley's labyrinthine world.

A third plot line is also introduced here as well, something which begins small but, like Topsy, just grows; it is Maerose, who gradually insinuates herself back into Charley's life. But her movements are so subtle that her visible motivations are unreproachable; nevertheless, her growing power in the second act is a masterwork of accumulating narrative rhythm. Irene's machinations parallel Maerose's; by the end of the second act Charley has been surrounded by these two manipulative, plotting women—one trying to kill him, the other to marry him. Charley, the main plot catalyst for the first act, has become a passive observer upon whom everyone else acts.

It's only at the act break, as Charley prepares to power into the third act, that he at last makes a crucial plot decision: he refuses to go off with Irene and thereby seals both of their fates. The decision he made to marry Irene at the first act juncture has come full circle—committed to her and unable to relinquish his love for her, he powers into his third act decision to stay with her until death (Again, the A indicates Charley is motivating the scene, the B that someone else is in charge.)

- The cops clamp down on the Prizzis; they want the wife's killer. (B)
- Charley kidnaps Filargi and heads to the country. (A)
- Charley uses Filargi as a bargaining chip to save himself. (A)
- Dominic is killed. (B)
- The Don says they need Charley. (B)
- Pop makes moves to settle things with Charley. (B)

- Charley tells Irene they're at last safe; Irene says she still wants her money. (A & B)
- The Don tells Charley that Irene must die; Charley agrees. (B & A)
- Irene and Charley try to kill each other; Charley succeeds. (A)
- Charley calls Maerose. (A)

It's clear from these scenes how Charley has once again taken charge not only of the plot but also of his own life. First Charley acts against the family by kidnapping Filargi, thereby casting himself adrift from his roots. Then, while he's in a moral free fall, torn between his love for Irene, his desire to save himself, and his vow of loyalty to the Prizzis, Irene ups the ante by announcing she wants the money owed her. Charley is conflicted between maintaining his marriage to Irene and fulfilling his obligation to repay the family. With events rising to a crisis, Charley faces his internal climax when, in a brutally powerful scene, he agrees to prove his loyalty to the Prizzis by killing Irene. In doing so the internal problem of the movie, first seen before titles, of Charley's unbreakable bond of loyalty to the Prizzis, has been reconfirmed. From there it's only a matter of moments before the external problem of the film—his love for Irene—is resolved when he murders her. The icing on the cake is his phone call to Maerose, a call that will not only cement his loyalty to the Prizzis with his inevitable marriage to Maerose but will also allow Maerose back into the all-encompassing embrace of her family. Charley, around whom tidal forces have flowed during the film, is back where he began, utterly devoted to the Prizzis, forever in their thrall, doomed in love, enslaved to forces he can't understand, and yet eternally safe.

There are numerous other surprises in *Prizzi's Honor*. For example, let's look at the symmetries that run throughout the story. The movie begins with Charley falling in love with Irene and ignoring Maerose; it ends with Charley killing Irene and about to marry Maerose. It begins with Maerose as a black sheep, ostracized by her family, hated by her father, and yearning for Charley; it ends with Maerose accepted by her family, with her father dead, and about to marry Charley. These symmetries unite the script and give it a narrative coherence that transcends and yet strengthens the structure.

Similarly, almost without exception, the script is scrupulous in how it deals with the two major elements of the story: business and personal matters; business matters are discussed in abstractions and vicariously, whereas personal matters are always face-to-face. This dichotomy is subtle, not consciously perceived by the audience but, nevertheless, it once again unites the script, lending a thematic coherence that helps power the narrative.

Also, the word *honor* is used with meticulous care: the Don, Maerose, Dominic, the police lieutenant, even Charley himself use the word—it is a motif running throughout the story. "Where is your honor?" Dominic asks Maerose. "I have no honor," she replies. The police lieutenant, in explaining why the cops have shut down the Prizzi Family, says, "This one's a point of honor with us." When Charley is told he'll become the next head of the Prizzi Family, he says, "This is an honor beyond all my dreams." And when the Don discusses Irene's lying, he tells Charley, "She is a great sin against your honor." Only Irene never uses the word, and this very omission speaks volumes not only about Irene's character but also about the world into which she has married, one in which she will always remain an interloper. The repetition of the word *honor* echoed and reechoed by everyone in the script except Irene, becomes a litany from which Irene is excluded and damned. The only point of honor Irene allows herself is her insistence upon reclaiming the $900,000 she feels she's owed, a bundle of money that would be chump change when Charley accedes as head of the Prizzi Family; but for Irene her only honor lies in her bankroll and in this she assures her own doom.

As for Irene, she is trying to be reborn into a new identity, whereas Charley lives in a world in which you can never change your true self. But like the tiger who can't change his stripes, Irene can't change her soul. It is only Charley who changes in the movie; Irene, Maerose, the Don—all of these characters—are eternally set as the film begins. Only Charley, torn between his love for Irene and his duty to the Prizzis, sways like a confused limb caught in a hurricane until, at last, he settles back where he belongs.

Lastly, there is the character of Maerose, a diabolically clever woman who, like the gods in *A Midsummer Night's Dream*, or Shaw in *Pygmalion*, acts as puppeteer to the puppets, manipulating with invisible strings, shaping the plot and everyone's lives to her own purposes. Charley is her greatest creation: her love, her mainstay, her husband, and her pawn. In the end she is the true catalyst for the film, the hidden hand controlling all others, including even the Don, the genius unseen and unacknowledged—except by us.

19. THE DAY OF THE JACKAL

The Antagonist As Protagonist

▬ ▬ ▬ ▬

Fred Zinnemann is one of the great icons of the American cinema. His wonderfully crafted movies became famous not simply for their meticulous craftsmanship, but also because you could always tell a Zinnemann hero—someone faced with a deep moral crisis that defined and enlarged his or her life. It almost became a joke: Zinnemann . . . oh, yeah, he's the guy with his heroes always in some damn ethical turbulence. In *High Noon* the marshal, Will Kane, must choose between his sense of duty and his love for his bride. *From Here to Eternity* grappled with men in the United States Army who must keep or lose their honor in the days leading up to World War II. *The Nun's Story,* surely one of the most closely observed films ever made, meticulously shows how a nun must choose between her calling to Christ and her own personal needs. *A Man for All Seasons* is the tale of Sir Thomas More, who chooses to sacrifice his life rather than his beliefs. Yes, you could always tell a Fred Zinnemann film—until he made *The Day of the Jackal,* a film in which the moral crisis rested not with the hero, but with the audience, who find themselves rooting for a killer to murder an innocent man.

It is 1962. The OAS, a superconservative group of militarists, is outraged that President Charles de Gaulle of France has given freedom to the French colony of Algeria. They attempt to assassinate him but fail, done in by their own incompetence and the spies in their ranks. Their leader realizes he must go outside his organization and hire a professional killer, someone with no connection to the OAS and unknown to the French police; only such an anonymous killer has a chance to do away with de Gaulle. The OAS finds their man in the mysterious, supercompetent Jackal, who agrees to kill de Gaulle for $500,000. Banks are robbed to pay his price, and the Jackal meticulously proceeds to plan his killing. The OAS contacts the beautiful Denise, one of their operatives, to begin an affair with St. Clair, a member of the French State Department. She will act as a spy, ferreting out from St. Clair what the French are able to learn about the Jackal.

Eventually the French kidnap an assistant to the OAS leaders and, through torture, learn of the plot against de Gaulle. They order Claude Lebel, the best detective in the French police force, to find and stop the Jackal before he can get to de Gaulle. The Jackal learns of Lebel's pursuit but continues on, confident that his anonymity, coupled with his extraordinary talents, will permit him to succeed despite the efforts of the entire French police force. After many adventures the Jackal arrives in Paris and prepares for his hit. Only at the last moment does Lebel guess the Jackal's secret location and burst in upon him in time to stop de Gaulle's assassination. Lebel kills the Jackal and later watches as he is lowered into an anonymous grave, an enigma to the very end.

It's an utterly fascinating tale, one of the best pure thrillers ever made. Zinnemann has turned the tables on his usual moral universe, with the antagonist gaining our sympathy even as we're horrified at his growing list of murders; he has also played fast and loose with the most common rules for standard film structure by introducing both the Jackal and Lebel—the traditional antagonist and protagonist—far too late into the story and then conflicting our attachment to both of them. To top it off, he has us on the edge of our seats even though we know that Charles de Gaulle died in his sleep and that the entire plot is doomed to fail. Let's take a look at the first act:

- The OAS assassination attempt on de Gaulle fails.
- The leader of the plot is executed.
- Rodin, leader of the OAS, announces he will find a contract killer to assassinate de Gaulle.

- The Jackal is interviewed by the OAS; he agrees to kill de Gaulle.

Not bad. The failed assassination attempt that begins the film may run a bit long, but Zinnemann and his screenwriter, Kenneth Ross, knew that it would only make sense to hire a professional killer after it was shown how the OAS's own best efforts had failed. Only then can we understand why they'd seek out a total stranger to murder their nemesis. The act break comes naturally enough when the Jackal agrees to accept the challenge placed before him.

On the other hand, the argument can be made that the entire first act is an incredible mistake. After all, the Jackal, whom we know is going to be one of our main characters, shows up only a few minutes before the break. Thus we have a basically unknown tour guide leading us into the second act and through the next steps of the story. It's only upon reflection that we realize it is normally the protagonist, and not a ruthless professional killer, who accepts the challenge to move into the second act. In fact, we're entering the second act without a protagonist in sight. Not only that, but all the characters we've met in the first fifteen minutes are never seen again. To top it off, the movie doesn't give us an easy choice as to whom to root for. Is it de Gaulle, who's seen throughout the entire film as a shadowy presence, always photographed in long shot, and who hasn't a single line of dialogue? Is it the leader of the assassination attempt, who's executed just moments after we get to know him? Is it the OAS leaders, who seem a rather grim bunch, hunted and hiding in a distant hotel and whose job it is to kill a man for reasons that, unless you're a student of French history, seem obscure and irrelevant? The only saving grace is that the story takes off like a rocket once the Jackal does appear. And if a movie has to begin slowly and introduce characters who don't pay off in the main body of the narrative, then it's best to do so early on, when an audience will still give you a few minutes that they'd refuse you farther into the story. Not only that, but the events that do occur—an assassination attempt and an execution—are fascinating and mysterious enough in themselves to hold our attention apart from their dicey connection to the main story.

Let's take a look at the first beats of the second act:

- The OAS robs banks to get money to pay the Jackal's fee.
- The French police know the bank robberies are the work of the OAS; they set surveillance on the leaders of the OAS.

The last scene of the first act introduced us to the Jackal. The first scenes of the second act show us the OAS in action, followed by the French police. These three consecutive scenes establish the three main threads of the story. I'll mark each scene from now on with a 1 for the Jackal, a 2 for the OAS, or a 3 for the French police. On with the second act:

- The Jackal researches de Gaulle's habits. (1)
- The Jackal obtains phony identity papers as Paul Duggan. (1)
- The Jackal steals Per Lundquist's passport. (1)
- The Jackal buys hair dye. (1)
- The French police watch secret movies of the OAS; they see Wolenski, the courier for the OAS. (2 and 3)
- Denise gets her assignment to spy for the OAS. (2)
- The Jackal meets Gozzi, the gun maker, and orders his gun. (1)
- The Jackal meets the forger. (1)
- The Jackal scouts out the kill site. (1)
- Denise sees St. Clair, her assigned affair. (2)
- The French kidnap Wolenski. (2 and 3)
- Wolenski is kidnapped and tortured into talking. (2 and 3)
- Denise begins her affair with St. Clair. (2)
- The French police study Wolenski's "confession." (3)
- The French police realize that the OAS has hired a professional killer to assassinate de Gaulle. (3)
- The French minister informs de Gaulle. (3)
- The Jackal gets fake identity papers and kills the forger. (1)
- The Jackal gets his gun from Gozzi. (1)
- The French minister asks for the best detective in France; Lebel is summoned and agrees to find and stop the Jackal. (3)

So far we've been moving along nicely, with clever crosscutting among the Jackal, the French police, and the OAS. The Jackal has more scenes and more screen time than the others, but that's to be expected since he's (for want of a better word) our protagonist. Since he's operating in secret, and since his preparations are so complex and meticulous, it's only natural that we'd spend more time with him. Besides, since he came late into the movie, just at the first act break, we need to play catch-up with him all the more and get to know him as quickly as possible. But as this has been going on, some interesting countercurrents have also been created: Denise commences her spy affair, and the French police slowly find out about the Jackal—all beautifully done and interwoven with our main narrative thread. But then, out of nowhere, we're told halfway through the film that a new and major character is being thrown at us, someone named Claude Lebel, whose sole function for the rest of the movie is to catch the Jackal. Who the hell is this guy?

Just as the first act is a risky proposition, beginning with characters we'll never meet again and ending with the introduction of a character for whom, inevitably, we're going to root even while we know he's a professional killer, the introduction of Claude Lebel this late in the story is nothing short of astounding. How are we supposed to handle a completely new presence so late in the narrative? How much time can we spend getting to know him? And for whom do we root: the Jackal, with whom we've had plenty of time to grow comfortable and even admire, or this upstart Lebel (and a new character is always initially resented when he's brought into a story)? Sure, Lebel's on the side of God, mother, and apple pie, but he also wants to kill the fascinating Jackal. Are we supposed to root for the Jackal to murder de Gaulle? Or for Lebel to stop our favorite assassin? Obviously Fred Zinnemann wanted to play with us by stretching our moral boundaries and making us question everything we traditionally value in a movie. Alfred Hitchcock tried a similar switch in *Frenzy*, where the man we think is the villain and whom we want to kill turns out to be the hero. But what the filmmakers here are trying to pull off is a lot more troubling than anything Hitchcock tried in *Frenzy*.

Okay, back to the story. I'll denote Lebel's investigation with a number 4; the number 5 will represent the British investigation:

- Lebel makes inquiring phone calls to foreign police. (4)
- St. Clair innocently tells Denise the police know about the Jackal. (2)
- The Jackal tests his gun. (1)
- British policeman Thomas looks for the Jackal in England and learns his real name may be Charles Calthrop. (5)
- Thomas has the prime minister's support. (5)
- The Jackal hides his gun under a car. (1)
- Calthrop's apartment is searched; he's not there. (5)
- Lebel tells the French ministers about Calthrop. (4)
- Thomas finds Duggan is a false identity. (5)
- The Jackal crosses into France; he calls the OAS spy network and learns the French police know about him; he decides to continue on. (1 and 2)
- Lebel tells the ministers about Duggan. (4)
- The Jackal stops in a hotel, flirts with and then sleeps with Colette. (1)
- Police in the morning collect hotel cards. (3)
- Lebel heads for the Jackal's hotel. (4)
- Lebel finds the Jackal is gone from the hotel. (4)
- The Jackal learns the latest from the OAS spies. (1 and 2)
- The Jackal steals a car's license plates, keeps on driving. (1)
- Lebel questions Colette, who doesn't want to talk. (4)
- The Jackal paints his car; crashes; steals a new car. (1)
- The Jackal stays with Colette; he kills her; he becomes Per Lundquist and leaves. (1)
- The Jackal boards a train for Paris. (1)
- Lebel learns of Colette's murder; a manhunt begins. (4)

This is a very busy and ambitious second half of a second act. But take a look at the first half of this list, scattered with 5's, which then disappear for the rest of the movie. Why is there such a long British sequence, which, as in the first act, introduces characters we won't see again? True, this was the way Frederick Forsyth wrote his brilliant book, and true, the British sequence involves a number of steps necessary for the progress of the plot. But the price we pay is considerable: we lose Lebel, whom we've been getting to know, and replace him with Inspector Thomas, another late movie intrusion who'll drop out as soon as he's performed his plot tasks. In the purest of screenwriting worlds it should have been Lebel who finds out what Thomas discovers, and Lebel who alone powers us through the second act. Still, the screenwriter, besides whatever pressure he may have experienced to remain true to Forsyth's structure, most likely simply couldn't find a way to replace Thomas with Lebel and so decided to live with it. Should some other solution have been found? Most likely, yes.

Yet as soon as Thomas drops out, Lebel returns with a vengeance and occupies almost as much screen time as the Jackal. By the end of the second act, with the Jackal now a wanted murderer pursued by the entire French police force, Lebel has become the Jackal's equal not only in power and presence, but in that even rarer commodity, screen time.

There's just one other problem: While Lebel and the Jackal have evolved into the hunter and the hunted, there's not been one scene, nor will there be until at the very end, where these two opponents ever meet. And if the basis of drama is repeated collision, how can we sustain the narrative without their meeting even once? Even in *Chinatown,* where the antagonist, Noah Cross, appears only three times, each of his appearances involves a collision with the protagonist, Jake Gittes. As with so much in *The Day of the Jackal,* the answer to the separation of the protagonist with the antagonist lies in the necessities of the plot, which dictated such an unorthodox and risky approach. Short of inventing plot gymnastics that would have been unbelievable—and the movie hangs upon its utter believability—there simply was no way that Lebel and the Jackal could meet during the second act; not only are they separated physically, but were they ever to meet and recognize each other, one of them would have to die. We encounter the same situation in *High Noon,* where the protagonist, Will Kane, and the antagonist, Frank Miller, never meet until their fatal encounter at the climax; until then they're strangers waiting for the first and final meeting, which will resolve not only their conflict, but their very reason for being. Now on to the third act:

- Lebel just misses the Jackal as he enters Paris. (1 and 4)
- The Jackal, pretending to be homosexual, meets Jules at a Turkish bath. (1)

- Lebel tracks down Per Lundquist. (4)
- Lebel plays a secret tape recording of Denise telling St. Clair's secrets to the OAS. (2 and 4)
- Lebel realizes they have only two days until the Jackal tries to kill de Gaulle. (4)
- Lebel discovers St. Clair has committed suicide and captures Denise. (2 and 4)
- Lebel is dismissed from his job. (4)
- The Jackal kills Jules. (1)
- Lebel is rehired: they can't find the Jackal. (4)
- Liberation Day; a montage of the ceremony; the Jackal as a one-legged old man enters his hotel, kills the concierge, and prepares to kill de Gaulle; the Jackal misses his shot and is killed by Lebel. (1 and 4)
- The Jackal is buried, with Lebel as the only mourner. (1 and 4)

After such unconventional first and second acts, this third act is a textbook example of rising tension resolved at the climax. In a way, the entire structure looks like this:

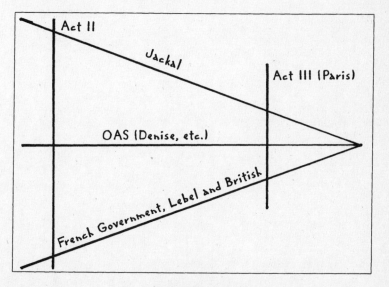

Jackal Chart #1

So, at long last, Lebel and the Jackal meet in the ending we've been waiting for. Only it's with an unexpected sadness that we find ourselves mourning for a vicious, near psychotic murderer and shaking our heads that the bland, uninteresting, and bureaucratic policeman has stopped a man of genius. If the Jackal has failed, then Fred Zinnemann has succeeded. Our world has been turned upside down. We mourn for Satan, that most beautiful of angels, cast out of heaven. We secretly hope that good didn't always have to triumph. We wish, though we'd hate to admit it, that the Jackal's exploding bullet had crashed into de Gaulle's innocent head. How wonderful the sight. How gratifying.

20. NETWORK

The Catalytic Monster

━━ ━━ ━━ ━━

Network is that rarest of movies (or, in fact, of any work of art)—it is a reverse time capsule. When it first appeared in 1976, it was viewed as a brilliant but over-the-top satire that, while making trenchant observations of television's effect on society, was in no way to be taken too seriously. Now, more than twenty years later, it seems less satire and more docudrama. The menagerie of grotesque characters who inhabit the story now seems all too real, while the plot, which appeared to be a silly series of ridiculous events, now reads like tomorrow's headlines.

But the script of *Network* doesn't simply reveal a grim view into the not so distant, absurd future. Paddy Chayefsky's dialogue may be the single greatest example of pure verbal fireworks ever written. His plotting, which at first seems so capricious and haphazard, is in fact a textbook example of catalytic structure, where all the characters react to one unchanging, central presence. And, perhaps as remarkable as anything else about this remarkable script, Chayefsky created it during what is generally considered the second phase of his extraordinary career, writing in a form and manner almost antithetical to his earlier scripts.

Born in 1923 as Sidney Stuckevsky, he began calling himself Paddy in World War II, pretending to be Irish Catholic and going to mass in order to avoid fatigue duty. He began writing for the theater but soon moved over to television in its fabled golden age, where his teleplays for *Marty* (which he later rewrote as a film and which won the Academy Award for best screenplay in 1955), *The Bachelor Party, The Mother, Holiday Song,* and many others remain classics of television writing. His use of "ordinary" everyday dialogue was a revelation in the early and middle fifties, as was his celebration of ordinary people in ordinary situations. He became, to put it too simply and too crudely, the Chekhov of early television.

However, after the early dramatic realism of television dried up, Chayefsky moved to Hollywood, where he labored successfully throughout the sixties. Then, in 1971 he authored *Hospital,* a scathing examination of the madness lurking just beneath the surface of a seemingly well-run hospital. Its riffs of ruminative, volcanic dialogue were as original as his celebrations of working-class lingo had been two decades earlier. The plot was more surreal, the characters more highly educated and superarticulate, and the themes more socially critical than anything he had attempted before. It was as if two writers, both named Paddy Chayefsky, were writing in completely different styles.

Network is the high point of this second phase of Chayefsky's career. Dazzling in its invention, breathtaking in its verbal gymnastics, astounding in its structure, it is one of the landmarks of American screenwriting. It is the tale of Howard Beale, newscaster for the fictional UBS network, who is fired by his friend, news manager Max Schumacher, because of low ratings. Beale threatens to kill himself on the air, but when Max lets him appear on TV for his valedictory address, he instead rants in apocalyptic tones. Ratings zoom, and Diana Christenson, head of programming, along with Frank Hackett, network head, use Beale to lift UBS out of the ratings cellar. She begins an affair with Max even as she turns Beale into a TV prophet. But as Beale's ratings again decline, and as Arthur Jensen, CEO of CCA Corporation, which owns the UBS network, refuses to fire him, Diana realizes the only way to reclaim high ratings is to have Beale assassinated on the air.

Crazy? Not in the hands of Paddy Chayefsky, who gives all the characters, even the most insane or obsessively driven, an air of almost documentary reality. Knowing he was writing a satire of immense proportions, Chayefsky rooted all of his situations and people in the real world. Bureaucratic infighting, boardroom palaver, and institutional hierarchies are all presented with absolute realism. Even the script's stage directions aim toward ultimate fidelity to the dynamics of office life.

But it is the extraordinary structure that holds the script together, by adhering to one of the most important guidelines of dramatic writing: Each scene should present a new problem or expand on an old one, creating a narrative imperative that powers the story past any hesitancies or questions. To this foundation Chayefsky added the cardinal guideline of, believe it or not, horror film writing: Bring out the monster at carefully chosen, and not too frequent, intervals. Like the shark in *Jaws*, or the monsters in *Alien(s)*, Howard Beale is not seen too often, and when he is, everything revolves around his next appearance and what he will do. To illustrate these two points, let's lay out the entire script, scene for scene, noting how each scene creates a new problem or expands an old one:

ACT ONE

- Max tells Beale he's fired for low ratings; Beale threatens suicide—first problem.
- Beale announces on TV that he will kill himself—the first problem is made more complex.

ACT TWO

- Hackett fires Beale and warns Max of the upcoming stockholder's meeting—two new problems.
- Max meets Diana; Beale asks for a last farewell on the air—two new problems.
- Diana tells her staff that she wants angry shows—new problem.
- In a stockholder's meeting, Max loses power in the news department—problem expanded (which also motivates Max to help Beale later).

- Beale's broadcast; Max lets Beale stay on the air; Max and Beale are in trouble—two new problems.
- Ruddy, head of UBS, fires Max—Max's problem expanded.
- Diana sees Beale on TV and sees boring TV ideas—problem expanded.
- Diana wants Beale kept on, Hackett is unsure—new problem.
- Hackett pushes to keep Beale on the air—problem expanded.
- Beale is told he can go back on TV—problem expanded.
- Ruddy rehires Max to fight Hackett—new problem.
- Beale does so-so as a TV prophet—new problem.
- Diana makes a play for Max and he accepts; they date; Max says Beale returns to doing straight news—two new problems.
- Beale hears a "voice" and must "make his witness"—new problem.
- Beale questions the "voice" why he's been chosen: Because you're on television, dummy—problem expanded.
- Beale tells Max he is imbued with mystical insights and faints—problem made more complex.
- Beale disappears in the night—new problem.
- Hackett fires Max; Max breaks up with Diana—one old problem revised, one new problem.
- Beale goes on TV, shouting, "I'm mad as hell, and I'm not going to take this anymore!"; Narrator says Beale is a hit—new problem.
- Diana in Los Angeles sets up radical programming with Laureen Hobbs—new problem ("B" plot developed).
- Laureen meets with the Great Ahmed Khan—problem expanded.
- Beale on TV announces that Ruddy is dead; Beale tells his audience to stop the UBS merger—new problem.
- CCA meeting, Hackett praised by Jensen—problem expanded.
- Max and Diana meet and become involved again—problem reintroduced.
- Max's wife learns of Max's affair; she "hurts badly!"—new problem.

- Max with Diana, Laureen with Khan, Diana with affiliates—three scenes that all equate the acquisition of money and power to the loss of humanity—problem developed.
- Beale on TV stops the CCA merger—new problem.
- Hackett is worried for his job, Jensen wants to meet Beale—two new problems.

ACT THREE

- Jensen tells Beale he will atone—new problem.
- Beale on TV repeats Jensen's message, but the ratings are bad—new problem.
- Diana and Max argue—old problem revisited.
- Diana can't find a Beale replacement, and Jensen won't fire him—new problem.
- Diana and Max break up—a scene that resolves their relationship, plus resolving the character arcs of both Max and Diana.
- Hackett can't get Beale fired—problem repeated.
- Beale is killed on the air—first problem of film resolved, all other problems resolved.

Notice how virtually every scene either introduces a new problem or develops and expands upon one already established. It is this continuing air of new crisis that lends the script its narrative urgency. You never know what's going to happen next, but whatever it is, you know it's going to be bad yet, in a strange way, horribly funny. The breakneck speed of the plot also allows us little time to reflect on the absurd events flashing before us. It's as if Chayefsky knew he was employing a plot that might not bear up under close scrutiny and, relying on the old saying that the best defense is a good offense, powered through plot point after plot point as fast as he could.

Now look back at that list of scenes and notice how Beale appears at regular intervals as a catalyst, regularly stirring events into unexpected and accelerating directions. It's similar to the structure of *The Godfather,* where all events hang upon the actions and decisions of Don Corleone, the unmoved central character.

And just as Don Corleone has far fewer scenes than the characters orbiting around him, so does Howard Beale appear far less often than Max, Diana, or Hackett, all of whom, like attendants at some court ceremony, live and die upon the slightest word or glance from the king. It's as if Howard Beale, filled with the ability to control and shape all events, is dramatically radioactive: a little of him illuminates the story, while too much would burn us to a crisp. The shark in *Jaws* and the monsters in *Alien(s)* are similar in their explosive power, as is the Glenn Close character in *Fatal Attraction*, who is seen less and less frequently as the film turns from a character drama into a monster movie.

The act breaks in *Network* are also uniquely arranged: typically a central protagonist's decision to jump into a situation marks the beginning of the second act. But since *Network* is really a monster movie, in which an unchanging catalyst generates the entire plot, the act break has been moved up to page eleven in the script, much earlier than usual. Since neither Max nor Diana decides to commit to a course of action, but rather have events thrust upon them, Chayefsky wisely kicked Beale into gear as soon as possible.

In a similar sense *Network* breaks the accepted guidelines for how a third act should function. Normally a third act involves the decision of the protagonist, reduced to his lowest point, to overcome the story's problems and thus end the story. But since Max largely drops out of the third act (he is used only to allow Beale to stay on the air and then becomes a "B"-line love story), Chayefsky has the third act revolve around Jensen, the multibillionaire conglomerate owner, whose intransigence, as catalytic and monsterlike as Beale's, forces events to come to a final head. Dropping out a major character like Max, and then introducing an entirely new character two-thirds of the way through the story as a foil for the monsterlike Beale, is a risky decision. In effect, as if fighting fire with fire (or Godzilla fighting Mothra), he created a new monster (Jensen) to fight the old monster (Beale). Chayefsky was thus able to skate by conventional structure with his headlong plot and narrative rush.

Finally, no discussion of *Network* would be complete without examining Chayefsky's astounding use of dialogue. Arguably, no one in American screenwriting, with the possible exception of Joseph L. Mankiewicz, whose *All About Eve, Cleopatra,* and *A Letter to Three Wives* are as verbally adroit as they come, has ever dared to write such long, complex, and intellectually daunting dialogue. Movies are by their very nature more visual than aural (they were called movies long before they were called talkies). Relying on the spoken word to convey ideas and plot is a little like throwing a football while wearing mittens: you can do it, but there are so many better ways to go about it. But Chayefsky wrote dialogue of such brilliance that he overcame film's natural tendency to keep talk short and poetic in its density.

Let's take a look at one such speech, which takes place just after Max has told his wife, Louise, that he is in love with Diana:

LOUISE

Then get out, go to a hotel, go anywhere you want, go live with her, but don't come back! Because after twenty-five years of building a home and raising a family and all the senseless pain we've inflicted on each other, I'll be damned if I'll just stand here and let you tell me you love somebody else!

(now it's she striding around, weeping, a caged lioness)

Because this isn't just some convention weekend with your secretary, is it? Or some broad you picked up after three belts of booze. This is your great winter romance, isn't it? Your last roar of passion before you sink into your emeritus years. Is that what's left for me? Is that my share? She gets the great winter passion, and I get the dotage? Am I supposed to sit at home knitting and purling till you slink back like a penitent drunk? I'm your wife, damn it! If you can't work up a winter passion for me, then the least I require is respect and allegiance! I'm hurt. Don't you understand that? I'm hurt badly.

She stares, her cheeks streaked with tears, at MAX *standing at the terrace glass door, staring blindly out, his own eyes wet and welling. After a moment, he turns and regards his anguished wife.*

> LOUISE
>
> Say something, for God's sake.

> MAX
>
> I've got nothing to say.

He enfolds her; she sobs on his chest.

> LOUISE
> *(after a moment)*
> Are you that deeply involved with her?

> MAX
>
> Yes.

> LOUISE
>
> I won't give you up easily, Max.

Notice how her wonderful, rolling, roaring tirade is then followed by a few brief lines with completely different rhythms. Not only does that change the pace of the scene, it subtly tells us that a different emotional beat is being introduced. And it's fabulous how Chayefsky, after first letting Louise rant and bellow her rage, then ends the scene simply by stating the opposite of what you'd expect: she proclaims her love for the man she has just castigated. Very daring scene. Very great screenwriting. Very great screenwriter.

21. CHINATOWN

The Elusive Antagonist

▬▬ ▬▬ ▬▬ ▬▬

You see, Mr. Gittes, most people never have to face the fact that at the right time and right place, they're capable of anything.

—Noah Cross in *Chinatown*

But Noah Cross has faced that fact, and it is his dark presence that looms over *Chinatown* like a shroud of evil. Nor is he some mindless, remorseless psychotic, randomly bringing his horror onto the world; rather, he is a nuanced, intelligent man who performs his terrible deeds not for personal gain, but for what he thinks will better the lot of mankind and return to him the daughter he loved and lost. It's the very nobility of his motives that makes his actions all the more horrifying and that paints Noah Cross as a villain equal in menace to the terrible Keyser Sose. But while Keyser Sose is the surprise narrator of *The Usual Suspects,* and therefore omnipresent, Noah Cross appears in only three scenes in all of *Chinatown,* and his very absence from the story makes his shadow all the darker, his deeds farther reaching.

A detective mystery is one of the guilty little pleasures of life. A murder is committed, and only our hero, the detective, can snake his way through the labyrinth of conflicting testimony, lies, coverups, and half-truths to find the villain. In the old days these detective stories seemed the exclusive province of British writers; Agatha Christie's Miss Marple and Hercule Poirot, and Sir Arthur Conan

Doyle's Sherlock Holmes, dictated the terrain for almost a century. It was only in the 1920s, when Dashiell Hammett created his Continental Op, Sam Spade, and Nick and Nora Charles, and Raymond Chandler invented his Philip Marlowe, that the classic American detective was born. Unlike the older, more refined British detectives who, while brilliant at solving the most complicated of mysteries, were never themselves emotionally touched by the evil deeds around them, these new detectives were grim paladins, existential heroes, modern-day knights who involved themselves personally in the lives of those they investigated, and went through their own catharsis. Sam Spade, to give just one example, fell in love with the beautiful, homicidal, dissembling Brigid O'Shaughnessy, only to give her up to the police rather than sacrifice his morals. These new detectives made their own code and swam through immoral waters while holding true to their frontier ethics. They stood apart from society and carried their personal morality with them, like a shield, to protect themselves from the dark forces that only they had the brains and street smarts to overcome. For them truth was not some simple exercise in logic, such as the wonderfully complex puzzles Miss Marple untangled, but rather an endless journey into treachery, where truth always lies unreachably deeper. These new detectives dealt with elemental forces and the darkest passions of the human soul, and their ability to stay aloof from the moral grime was both their triumph and their cross.

It was with these more modern, hard-bitten detectives in mind that Robert Towne, in 1973, wrote his extraordinary *Chinatown*. Not only is it recognized as one of the great films of the seventies, it is also acclaimed as one of the decade's great screenplays. Directed by Roman Polanski at the height of his powers, it features Faye Dunaway and John Huston in the brilliant supporting cast. Its elegantly precise yet bawdy dialogue, pristine structure, and amazing characters combine in a film that is close to perfection.

But it's the character of Jake Gittes that holds it all together. As portrayed by Jack Nicholson in his Academy Award–winning performance, Gittes is a man pummeled by life, cynical and yet vulnerable underneath, a man who has retreated from the moral ambiguities of his beat as a cop in Chinatown to work as a detective, living off the agonies of others. Gittes is a man who has touched bottom and is now just struggling to keep his head above water when he takes on a case that seems simple (all cases in hard-bitten detective stories begin simply) but spirals into a soul-wrenching journey into the depraved depths of human temptation. Yet the person most tempted is Gittes himself. Will he be bought off by the corrupt forces around him? Will he believe, just one last time, that love and hope can survive in an immoral world? In the end it isn't the forces of evil that are on trial, but Gittes's very soul.

Los Angeles in the 1930s. Jake Gittes is a successful detective, specializing "in matrimonial work" (such as proving adultery to irate, jilted spouses), when he's asked by a Mrs. Mulwray, wife of Hollis Mulwray, the head of the Department of Water, to spy on her husband and catch him in an affair. Gittes follows Hollis Mulwray and sees him with an attractive blonde, but he also sees him investigating water ducts and arguing with an old man. When the scandal breaks that Mr. Mulwray is having an affair, Gittes is sued by a very beautiful woman who says that she, and not the woman we first saw, is the real Mrs. Evelyn Mulwray. Angry at being used, Gittes tries to find out who was exploiting him. His investigation leads to Hollis Mulwray's death, which the cops report as accidental but which Gittes suspects was murder. He becomes intrigued by the real Mrs. Mulwray, who hires him to find out who killed her husband. She seems to be hiding some terrible secret and grows especially nervous whenever talk leads in the direction of her father, Noah Cross, the fabulously wealthy man who gave Los Angeles the land upon which the city relies for its water supply. Gittes meets Cross, who hires him to search for the young girl with whom Mulwray was having the affair.

The investigations grow more and more complex. Gittes finally discovers that Cross has been secretly buying up land in the nearby San Fernando Valley, destroying small farmers in the process. As for the girl he was hired to find, Gittes learns from Evelyn Mulwray, with whom he has begun an affair, that the girl is the result of an incestuous union between Cross and Evelyn. Gittes talks to Cross, who admits that he fathered his own daughter's child; he further admits that he is illegally bringing water into the San Fernando Valley, a vast section of farmland that Cross now largely owns, and which, when he has it incorporated into greater Los Angeles, will not only transform Los Angeles into a major city, but will also make Cross millions. Gittes tries to stop Cross both from buying up the Valley and from getting his clutches on the innocent girl whom Cross fathered; but his efforts only end up getting Evelyn murdered in Chinatown. As the tale ends Gittes walks off into the night, shattered by all he has witnessed. Evil has triumphed.

The very elegance of the theme is matched by the elegance of its structure. Let's look at the first act:

- Gittes shows Curly proof of his wife's infidelity.
- "Mrs. Mulwray" hires Gittes to follow her husband.
- Gittes sees Mulwray speak against building a new city dam.
- Gittes follows Mulwray to the Los Angeles River, where he talks with a boy on a swaybacked horse.
- Gittes watches Mulwray sit by an empty water duct all night.
- Gittes sees pictures of Mulwray arguing with an old man.
- Gittes sees Mulwray with a pretty, blond young woman.
- Gittes follows Mulwray and the young woman to an apartment.
- Gittes is derided for exposing Mulwray's affair.
- The real Evelyn Mulwray sues Gittes.

It's a straightforward first act, whose only structural surprise is the beginning, where Gittes proves to the working-class Curly that his wife has been unfaithful to him. Although Curly will return later, he isn't introduced here as a part of the main story, nor does he introduce any external problem to be solved. Rather, by first showing us what Gittes does for a living, Towne is telling us that the greatest problem to be solved in the movie isn't "who done it," but rather Gittes himself, a man profiting from human agony. It's Gittes's soul with which we're dealing first and finally, the soul of a man who is so slick in his trade that his very success tastes like ashes in his mouth.

Having set up Gittes's soul as the internal problem, Robert Towne immediately brings in the external problem—or at least what we think is the external problem—of proving Mulwray is having an affair. Like any self-respecting detective story, nothing is what it seems. Not only is "Mrs. Mulwray" not the real Mrs. Mulwray, but Gittes begins an investigation that constantly eludes his comprehension. The first act also introduces the two plot skeins of the movie. First, Gittes witnesses Mulwray's obsession with water ("The guy's got water on the brain," as Gittes's associate, Walsh, says) as he wrangles against a proposed dam, argues with an as yet unidentified old man, and investigates the barren Los Angeles River. In the second skein Gittes tails Mulwray on what seems to be a lovers' date first to a boat ride on a lake and then to a hotel, where we assume Mulwray and the girl are conducting their affair. After establishing these two plotlines, Towne surprises us with the act-ending revelation that "Mrs. Mulwray" is an impostor, that Gittes has been set up for some reason, and that the real Mrs. Evelyn Mulwray is suing Gittes. Surprise upon surprise, twist after twist, as Gittes sinks deeper into the confusion.

Towne now gives us a traditional first act break in which the protagonist is faced with a plot-determining choice: either give up or forge ahead. Gittes could simply refer Mrs. Mulwray's lawsuit to his lawyer, where it would most likely be dropped in time. He could also legitimately forget about his investigation of Hollis Mulwray and return to his "matrimonial work." Instead Gittes decides to keep on snooping, not for profit this time, but because his own moral code won't allow him to be used and makes him determined to seek out the truth, no matter where it leads. It's this decision by Gittes to satisfy his own curiosity that defines his character, establishes him as a protagonist, sets the tone for the rest of the movie, and rockets us into the second act. I'll mark a 1 after each second act scene that deals with the water theme and a 2 after each scene that deals with Evelyn and the mystery of the young woman.

- Gittes meets Assistant Water Commissioner Yelburton. (1)
- Gittes at Mulwray's; the gardener says something is "bad for glass"; Evelyn drops the lawsuit and says her husband is at a dam. (1 and 2)
- Gittes finds Hollis Mulwray drowned at the dam. (1)
- Gittes helps Evelyn get away from reporters. (2)
- At the morgue Gittes learns an indigent drunk was drowned in a dry riverbed. (1)

- Gittes sees the unlikely spot where the drunk "drowned," sees the boy on the swaybacked horse who says Mulwray asked when the water flowed. (1)
- Gittes gets his nose slit at the city reservoir by Mulvihill and a bad guy. (1)
- Ida Sessions calls, tells Gittes to look in the obituaries. (1)
- Gittes learns Evelyn is Noah Cross's daughter; Gittes tells Evelyn she is hiding something. (2)
- Gittes tells Yelburton he doesn't want to nail him and learns that Noah Cross donated the land that became the city water system. (1)
- Evelyn tells Gittes that Cross and Mulwray had a falling-out. (1)
- Noah Cross hires Gittes to find the girl with whom Mulwray had the affair. (2)
- Gittes checks the Hall of Records and sees that much land in the Valley has recently changed hands. (1)
- Gittes gets beat up by irate Valley farmers. (1)
- Evelyn helps Gittes; he tells her no water is going to the Valley, despite Yelburton's claims that it is. (1)
- Gittes and Evelyn at a convalescent home; he learns many of the old people "own" large tracts of the Valley and are supported by the Albacore Club charity; Mulvihill nearly beats up Gittes; Evelyn helps him escape. (1)
- Gittes and Evelyn make love; he learns Cross owns the Albacore Club. (1 and 2)
- Gittes follows Evelyn to a house where she's keeping the young woman; Evelyn says "it's not what you think it is." (2)
- Gittes gets a call to see Ida Sessions. (1 and 2)
- Gittes sees Ida has been murdered and that she was the woman posing as Mrs. Mulwray. (1 and 2)
- Policeman Escobar says they can't find any dumped water; Gittes is in trouble. (1)

Complicated, isn't it? But it's all right if you don't understand the plot, because at this point neither does Gittes. He's been beat up, had his nose slit, been hired and fired and threatened repeatedly.

He knows that someone is buying up land in the Valley and that it seems to be connected with Noah Cross. He also knows that there's a mysterious young woman who's being secretly hidden by Evelyn. But beyond that it's all largely conjecture. We're at an act break because events have taken Gittes about as low as he can go: he's about to lose his job, and he feels estranged from Evelyn, with whom he's fallen in love. It's at this point, much as at the first act break, that Gittes must decide whether to forge on to the end or give up. Gittes's decision to go ahead regardless of the consequences is the catalyst of a second act break and powers us into the third act. Notice how neatly Towne has balanced the two themes in the second act—1's and 2's are pretty equally divided, with Gittes, like a tennis ball, bouncing back and forth between the two plotlines. Notice also that the scenes in which 1's and 2's combine are almost all placed at the last section of the second act. The two themes converge beautifully at the midpoint of the movie, when Gittes first meets Noah Cross. From then on the two themes increasingly weave together, braided by Gittes's obsessive investigation. It all looks like this:

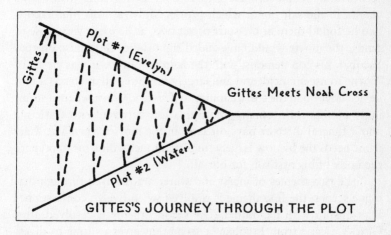

Chinatown Chart #1

As you can see, Noah Cross is the catalyst for the plot, propelling Gittes forward. Like the shark in *Jaws* or the Howard Beale character in *Network,* Noah Cross appears minimally in the movie, with his very absence lending greater menace to his power: like an unseen puppeteer, he manipulates the visible characters. With events colliding and Gittes near his end, we move into the third act:

- Gittes at Mulwray's finds Mulwray's glasses in the saltwater pond, proving Mulwray was murdered. (1)
- Evelyn confesses to Gittes that the young woman is her daughter through an incestuous relationship with her father. (2)
- Gittes escapes from Escobar with Curly's help. (1)
- Cross admits everything to Gittes: that he killed Mulwray, is stealing water, and had incest with his daughter. (1 and 2)
- Gittes finds Evelyn in Chinatown; she is killed; Cross literally gets away with murder; the water scam will go on; Gittes walks off into the night. (1 and 2)

After such a complicated second act, Towne wisely gives us a brief and simple third act to wrap things up. Notice how earlier scenes and people are cleverly reused. Gittes finds Mulwray's glasses in the salt pond, which proves Mulwray was murdered—had he found them at the start of act two, as he came very close to doing, the movie would have ended right there. Gittes also escapes Escobar, his cop nemesis, with the help of Curly—it was clever of Towne to use an incidental and largely forgotten character as a plot device later on in the story (similar to *The Godfather,* where a seemingly unimportant opening conversation between Vito Carleone and a funeral director pays off later in the movie, when Vito Carleone needs the by now largely forgotten funeral director to prepare the body of his first son for burial).

The two themes of incest and water are resolved through dialogue scenes: the first theme is resolved when Evelyn confesses her relationship with her father. The second theme is resolved after Gittes's escape from Escobar (a scene that gives us time to digest the revelation of incest that Evelyn has just dumped on us), when Cross admits in a devastating scene to being behind everything. Two dialogue scenes, like a one-two punch, which round off and explain all of the action that has preceded them. Normally a screenwriter would go for physical action to serve as the climax of the movie, but Towne, having packed his second act with tails, chases, and beatings, gives us the opposite—words here are far more terrible than any explosion.

Notice also how Towne uses exposition. Take, for example, the scene where Gittes finds out that Mulwray was asking where and when the water flowed in the Los Angeles River. This is important plot information, which could have easily been told to the audience through, say, a phone call, a check into Mulwray's daily planner, or any of a hundred other devices. Instead Towne has Gittes ask a mysterious boy on, of all things, a swaybacked horse, who tells what is needed to advance the plot. This striking and creepy visual is the sweetener that helps the medicine of plot exposition slip down without our noticing. Or take a look at the scene where Gittes visits the Hall of Records and finds out the necessary plot information that much of the land in the San Fernando Valley has been bought up recently. Again, a phone call or a simple clerical search would have sufficed; Gittes could have even had one of his assistants squirrel out the information. Instead Towne has Gittes speak with a weaselly clerk who, like any good bureaucrat, tells as little as possible. Gittes has to goad the loathsome toad into talking and then literally rips out the needed information (which he could have just as easily copied down) and steals it, out of spite against the horrible little toad. Again, the clerk is the sweetener, letting us swallow without choking the needed plot information.

Chinatown is filled with many such clever plot devices that, while always unexpected, are always right and always let us learn what we need to know without feeling force-fed.

There are a few problems with the script. Evelyn never shows any reaction to Hollis Mulwray's death; she never even comments upon it. While this makes her more intriguing, it seems unlikely that Evelyn would show so little reaction to the death of the one man who has protected her from her horrendous father. There's also a scene where Gittes speaks of his old cop days in Chinatown and how he had tried to help someone, only to find out too late that he had made things worse. This is a heavy-handed foreshadowing of what's to come, and it wasn't necessary. In fact, Towne should have realized that the less said about Chinatown, the better.

Like Rosebud in *Citizen Kane,* Chinatown is a metaphor for the always elusive truth, forever unknowable.

As for the actual ending, which takes place in Chinatown, the story goes that Towne hated it. He felt that Gittes, having gone through so much, must at least partially "win" in the end. Perhaps, while the water scam might go through, Cross could have gone to jail; perhaps Evelyn could have survived to go off with Gittes; perhaps the young woman, Cross's daughter/granddaughter, could have escaped his clutches. But whatever ending Towne may have wanted, Polanski was determined to demonstrate (as he would be equally determined to demonstrate in his equally brilliant *Rosemary's Baby*) that evil must triumph. Towne raged at Polanski, begging, cursing, and threatening, demanding that good must, at least in some small way, triumph. But Polanski wouldn't hear of it; he insisted that Towne write the last scene as an utter defeat of the forces of good. Towne, while swearing for years afterward that the ending he wrote was "dogshit," nevertheless did as he was told. It was only twenty years later that Towne finally admitted that Polanski had been right, and that Gittes must lose to the evil that is Noah Cross.

22. CASABLANCA

The Antihero As Protagonist

■■■■

By 1977 *Casablanca* had become the movie most frequently screened on American television. In 1983 the British Film Institute declared it to be the best film ever made. In 1988 Sam's piano—not even the one used in Rick's Café in Casablanca, but the one he played in Paris—fetched $154,000 in an auction at Sotheby's. A poll of the readers of *TV Guide* called it the most popular film of all time. A Mafia subchief christened his home "Casablanca." Woody Allen named his hit play and movie *Play It Again, Sam*. Billy Crystal recently starred in a movie with Debra Winger entitled *Forget Paris*. And in 1996 the brilliant Christopher McQuarrie won an Academy Award for his script titled *The Usual Suspects*.

So what exactly is the mysterious allure of *Casablanca*? Why does it grab hold of our collective consciousness like almost no other film? Is it the deep psychological resonance of the characters, in which, as film critic Richard Corliss claimed, Rick represents in Jungian terms the animus while the "radiantly corrupt" Renault is the anima? Or is it, according to William Doneley's *Love and Death in Casablanca*, "a standard case of the repressed homosexuality that underlies most American adventure stories"? Psychoanalyst Harvey Greenberg feels that the situation is Oedipal: ". . . the sacrosanct stolen treasure [is] the wife of a preeminent older man; her husband is the one murdered—and by the love thief. Thus, the essence of this 'combination' of offenses is the child's original desire to kill his father and possess his mother." Literature professor Krin Gabbard and psychiatrist Glen O. Gabbard suggest that "Rick kills the principal enemy of his father surrogate, thereby becoming a man himself." Jacques Lacan suggests that Rick's famous toast, "Here's looking at you, kid," is in fact reflective of a castration complex.

Certainly the screenwriters, Howard Koch, Julius J. Epstein, and Philip G. Epstein, had nothing of the sort in mind. To them it was simply an ordinary assignment to adapt a third-rate play into a "B" movie for "B" actors, a quickie production, nothing more, nothing less. "Slick shit" is what Julius Epstein called it when he and his twin brother began work on it. When the Epsteins got the job they were on their way to becoming legends in Hollywood, famous as much for their pranks as for their witty dialogue. They had saved *Yankee Doodle Dandy* for Jimmy Cagney and were considered right for turning the play *Everybody Comes to Rick's* by Joan Alison and Murray Burnett into a love story that would promote the war effort.

The Epsteins labored with producer Hal Wallis and director Michael Curtiz over several drafts, all of which dealt with an expatriate American named Rick refalling in love with an American named Lois. But Wallis had become intrigued by the rising young Swedish beauty Ingrid Bergman, whose career had stalled with mediocre projects, and decided to go with her. However, Bergman was under contract to David O. Selznick, who agreed to loan her out to Wallis in return for eight weeks' work from Olivia de Havilland, under contract to Wallis. The trade was made, Lois became Ilsa, and the rewrites continued.

Wallis was also dissatisfied with the characterization of Rick and the story line in general, and brought in Howard Koch, who had recently distinguished himself with *The Sea Hawk* and *The Letter*. Koch was a serious, historically minded writer, who took the Epsteins' witty, bantering script and began adding the needed character, weight, and back story, or character history. The Epsteins, aware of Koch, kept on writing, with Koch rewriting the Epsteins' rewrites. Wallis also brought in screenwriters Casey Robinson and Lenore Coffee for editorial advice. It was Robinson who suggested that Ilsa and Rick meet late at night in the cafe, and outlined much of the still-deficient Rick/Ilsa relationship. If it sounds like chaos, then chaos was probably what it was.

Even with all this preparation *Casablanca* began shooting without a finished script. Koch and the Epsteins, still working separately, still trading script pages back and forth, kept writing even as the cameras rolled. When they left, three weeks into shooting, Casey Robinson took over, writing scenes just days and sometimes even hours ahead of their going before the cameras. Still, the ending remained a problem. Everyone knew that Rick must give up Ilsa, but no one could figure out what would happen next. Would Rick go to jail? Would he kill Strasser? Would he escape? The story goes that the Epsteins were driving together in a car, mulling over the seemingly unsolvable problem, when, simultaneously, they shouted out, "Round up the usual suspects!" They called Wallis and explained that Louis Renault would cover for Rick's killing of Strasser. From there on it was clear sailing, with Wallis the one who came up with the wonderful exit line: "Louis, I think this is the beginning of a beautiful friendship."

But this is no way to write a movie. In fact, perhaps the greatest miracle of *Casablanca* is that it works at all, let alone so marvelously. It went on to win five Academy Awards, including Best Screenplay, which would have gone to Casey Robinson as well as to the Epsteins and Howard Koch, except that Robinson refused to share credit on a film. As Arnold Schwarzenegger would say, "Big mistake."

Let's take a look at *Casablanca*'s structure, which is remarkable for its integration of external with internal problems and which employs flashbacks with the precision of a marksman. Here's our first act:

- The narrator talks about Casablanca, one of the few ways out of Nazi-occupied Europe.
- A courier is killed in Casablanca.
- Major Strasser arrives, tells Louis he wants the killer of the courier captured; Louis says they should begin the search that night at Rick's Café.
- At Rick's Café—we explore the cafe and finally see Rick.
- Ugarte gives the letters of transit to Rick to hold.

- Ferrari wants Sam to work for him; Sam wants to continue playing piano for Rick.
- Yvonne yearns for Rick; he rejects her.
- Louis with Rick: "I came to Casablanca for the waters"; Louis tells Rick that Victor Lazslo is in town and will be captured.
- Ugarte is arrested.
- Rick and Strasser discuss Lazslo.
- Lazslo enters with Ilsa.

This is a wonderful first act. The writing is witty and evocative, and there has rarely been such a perfect marriage of script with actors. The external problem of desperate refugees trying to get away from the Nazis is first told to us through a narrator, then shown by the murder of the courier; thus, a bit like the opening beats of *Some Like It Hot,* an external historical event is first generalized, then made into a particular problem. It is made yet more particular when Strasser arrives and tells us of the valuable letters of transit (which never existed in real life and were invented by the screenwriters). With fine economy, we move from the problem of Casablanca in general, through the murder of a courier, to Strasser, who tells us of the mysterious letters of transit that might be found at Rick's Café. Like the Wizard waiting at the end of the Yellow Brick Road, spoken of but not seen until well into *The Wizard of Oz,* Rick begins to take on larger-than-life dimensions before we even meet him, while the external problem of the letters of transit segues beautifully into the internal problem of the mysterious Rick.

To build this sense of mysterious anticipation, the writers don't have us meet Rick until we've first had time to explore his cafe and meet some of the customers and workers. It's only when a hand reaches into the frame to sign a gambling chit, and the camera pans up to see the wonderful face of Humphrey Bogart, that we know the long wait to meet Rick has been worthwhile. Just as the first half of the first act is taken up with explaining the external problem of Casablanca and the missing letters of transit, the second half of the first act is devoted to exploring the internal problem of Rick's character. We see him revealed through his talks with Ugarte, Ferrari, Yvonne, Louis, and Strasser, five distinct conversations, each of which unveils a differing facet of Rick's elusive personality. And while we learn a good deal about Rick from these conversations, he still seems to retain a secret we've yet to discover, a secret revealed only at the fantastic act break when the beautiful Ilsa arrives.

There's only one problem in the entire first act, and it's dealt with so swiftly that we realize only later that it makes absolutely no sense for Rick to hold Ugarte's stolen letters of transit, even for the brief hour that Ugarte asks: doing favors for anyone, let alone for sniveling murderers like Ugarte, isn't Rick's style, yet Rick takes the letters without explanation or motivation. But he does it so quickly, it's over before you have time to question why it's done. Still, unless Rick takes Ugarte's letters of transit we have no movie, so the screenwriters slipped the single most crucial plot point of the film past us without giving us time to think. It helps that it all takes place in such a swirl of brilliant dialogue and fascinating characters that the audience is swept up in the story without being given any pause to reflect or question.

Rather, it's Rick we concentrate on, Rick who dominates the story, who seems utterly in command of his world, absolutely unflappable and unafraid, the catalyst for everyone else's dreams; yet he is a man who seems to have no dreams of his own, whose disillusionment is complete, someone without values or ideals, the ultimate antihero. Rarely has cinema showcased such a cynical, disillusioned, negative character in a central role. If Fred C. Dobbs in *The Treasure of the Sierra Madre* begins as an ordinary man who ends personifying all the base instincts of the human soul, then Rick is the opposite, someone who begins as a man who has lost his ideals, whose bitterness consumes him, yet who ends with those ideals rediscovered, his faith in humanity restored.

It is this transition from antihero to hero that is the central bridging device of the script, and a central problem for the screenwriters, since it asks the audience to care for a character who is portrayed negatively in the first part of the film; it's only when Rick meets Ilsa that some vestige of his submerged humanity surfaces to excite our compassion. Until then he is a distant, largely unlikable man, whose only saving grace seems to be the affection with which his staff treats him. But this is respect from a distance, similar to the respect Paul Newman is given in *Hud,* one of the few other films that treats an antihero as its central character. Like the professional killer in *The Day of the Jackal,* Rick displays supreme competence, and this is perhaps why he demands our respect and even affection (that, plus Bogart's extraordinary ability to portray the deeper aspects of the human heart compassionately). In fact, it was the fear of placing such an antihero in a central role that doomed *The Bonfire of the Vanities.*

In the end, it is our innate love for the underdog, the alienated, the beautiful misfit, that is behind our affection for antiheroes. But it's a tightrope for writers who create these curious creatures, as well as for the actors who have to portray them: too little alienation and the antihero seems merely whiny, too much and he appears psychotic; a balance must be struck that, when it's (so rarely) found, holds a fascination greater than that for any other personality.

But *Casablanca* shows no such fears of finding that balance—Rick is portrayed without blush or apology, and his bitter disillusionment is the keystone of the script, which never blinks from depicting Rick as a man whose self-imposed damnation is stopped by only one fantastic event: the arrival of Ilsa. With her appearance our cast of characters is complete, our environment explored, our external and internal problems introduced. She is the complicating factor that powers us into the second act, the one person who can move Rick, the one ingredient that can integrate the external and the internal problems and bring both to a crisis.

Now to the second act, which picks up as part of the same long mise-en-scène at Rick's Café:

- Lazslo talks with Strasser.
- Louis flirts with Ilsa.
- Ilsa with Sam: "Play it, Sam."
- Rick, Ilsa, Lazslo, and Louis talk; Ilsa, Lazslo, and Louis leave.
- Rick with Sam: "Play it [again, Sam.]"
- Rick's flashback: his love affair with Ilsa in Paris; as the Nazis approach they promise to meet and escape together, but she never shows up.

- Rick comes out of his flashback as Ilsa returns; he tells her of his anguish and she leaves; Rick gets drunk.

Here we learn that Rick's internal problem is his unresolved love for Ilsa and his bitterness at her leaving him. Howard Koch fought against the flashback and fortunately lost the battle; the flashback not only perfectly explains Rick's problem and his relationship with Ilsa, it does so without having to fall back upon the awful "tell me about it" that would have been the only other way to handle the problem. Showing is almost always better than telling, because showing is always more direct, less vicarious, and more visual. Not only that, but the flashback flows naturally into the next scene, where Ilsa ironically returns to Rick. We can directly contrast the love affair they blissfully experienced in Paris with the bitter recriminations and hesitancies that characterize their relationship in Casablanca. As for the famous "Play it again" scene, it uses music as an emotional keynote to conjure up all the magic happiness of Paris; the music reinforces the flashback and acts as an emotional bridge running throughout the film, much as the song "Do Not Forsake Me" runs through *High Noon*.

Having established the nature of Rick's internal crisis, let's return to the external problem that is powering so much of our plot:

- Louis and Strasser want the letters of transit, while Strasser is desperate to arrest Lazslo.
- Strasser tells Lazslo that if he gives names, he can go free; we learn Ugarte is dead.
- Annanina and Jan with Ferrari, who can't help them escape.
- Ferrari asks Rick about the letters of transit.
- Ilsa tells Rick that Lazslo has always been her husband.
- Lazslo with Ferrari, who can get a letter of transit for Ilsa but not for Lazslo.
- Ilsa tells Lazslo that since he didn't leave her before, she won't leave him now.
- Ferrari tells Lazslo that Rick might have the letters of transit.

Most of these complicated plot developments are designed to place the characters in a straitjacket, limiting their range of choices.

Ilsa won't leave without Lazslo, but Lazslo can't leave without going to Rick, who has little reason to give the letters to him. The only wrinkle is the Annanina scene, where a desperate couple can't find a way out of Casablanca. This is that old standby, a "B" story, used to crosscut against the main plotline and to dramatically extend the wait for the main story's resolution. Like all self-respecting "B" stories, this echoes back on the main story, reinforcing and enhancing it. The drama might have been stronger if we had seen Ugarte killed—preferably by Strasser, thereby reinforcing his evil—rather than only hearing about it, but the screenwriters probably felt they hadn't the time to devote an entire scene to a secondary character's death. With the plot tightening, and the range of choice diminishing for the characters, let's see where we go next:

- At Rick's Café, Rick stops a near fight between some French and Germans.
- Strasser threatens to kill Lazslo.
- Annanina pleads with Rick for help; Ilsa and Lazslo enter; Rick lets Annanina win at roulette.
- Rick refuses to give Lazslo the letters of transit.
- The singing scene; Strasser demands Louis close Rick's Café; Louis closes Rick down.
- Lazslo suspects Ilsa is having an affair with Rick.
- Ilsa demands the letters of transit and pulls a gun, they kiss and make love; Ilsa explains her past life with Lazslo; Ilsa tells Rick, "You'll have to think for both of us."

This last scene, where Ilsa tells Rick to decide their fates, marks the act break. The noose is tightening around Lazslo, Rick's Café has been shut down, tension is mounting between the French and Germans, and Lazslo is suspicious of Ilsa. Things can't get much worse than this, and the decision of who is to live and who is to die has been thrown to Rick. We can now see why it was so important for Rick to get those letters of transit, no matter how suspect his motivations to take them off Ugarte's hands—with them he holds the MacGuffin, the "thing" that everyone else wants, and thus holds power over the characters and the plot. Not only that, but when Ilsa redeclares her love for Rick, it resolves his initial dilemma only to give him a new and greater one. Does he go off to live happily ever after with Ilsa and thereby almost certainly condemn Lazslo to death? Or does he help the cause he has so often disavowed and thereby give up the woman he loves? Although we won't know Rick's decision until the final scene, it is in fact here, at this second act break, that Rick makes up his mind; anything that happens after this is simply the unveiling of Rick's plan.

Ironically, until now we've been invited into the deeper workings of Rick's mind. But it's just at the point that he's making his greatest decision that we're locked out and left to observe him from the outside. On the other hand, Rick's decision to help Annanina foreshadows his later decision regarding himself and Ilsa, and thus plays fair with us, letting us read at least a little of his mind. From now on Rick writes the script, and all the other characters are merely pawns in the game he's playing. The antihero has come full circle and become a hero:

- Rick tells Lazslo to go off with Ilsa.
- Rick tells Louis he's leaving with Ilsa and makes a deal to get Lazslo arrested.
- Rick tells Lazslo he'll get him the letters for a lot of money.
- Rick sells out his cafe to Ferrari.
- The ending, where Rick kills Strasser and forces Ilsa and Lazslo to fly away; Louis covers for Rick.

All of this maneuvering, designed to make Rick look duplicitous, is a charade to trick Strasser and Louis into placing Lazslo and Ilsa on the airport runway. The character of Rick is no longer the antihero. The script, which at first uneasily asked us to care for the wrong man in the wrong place, now asks us to cheer for the right man in the right place; our waiting has been worthwhile, our hopes are realized, our fears buried. It is only now that we realize it was the very tension of waiting and hoping for Rick to recapture his ideals that has all along been the narrative fuel propelling the story forward; only an antihero can command such tension and sustain the plot—had Rick begun the movie as a hero, then his climactic decision to sacrifice his love for his ideals would have been preordained. Only his own inner journey sustains the tension of waiting for his external decision to save Lazslo. This tension is further sustained by the fact that there are only six times when Rick and Ilsa talk; it's their separation, and the sparsity of their meetings, which heightens the suspense; rarely has the saying "Less is more" been more dramatically appropriate. Had Rick spent more time with Ilsa, then his true humanity would have inevitably risen to the surface and the tension been reduced or even destroyed.

But Rick's character is not the only avenue into the complexities of the script. We can also view it in terms of the major problems, both internal and external, that propel the story forward:

1. Where are the letters of transit? (the external)
2. Who is Rick and what's his problem? (the internal)
3. Rick keeps the letters of transit.
4. Ilsa arrives in Casablanca.
5. Rick's Café is shut down.
6. Ilsa admits her love for Rick.

On a graph, with the internal converging with the external, we have this:

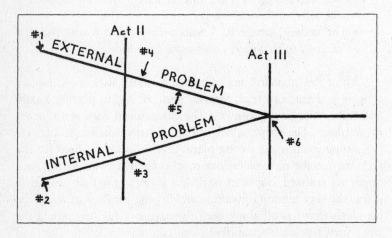

Casablanca Chart #1

It's the joining of the internal problem with the external problem at the moment when Ilsa admits her love for Rick that powers us into the third act and accelerates the narrative drive. Each problem creates a new problem, worse than before, so that the escalating line of problems forces the plot forward.

Finally, let's take a look at the various characters in the story, noting what they do to advance the plot:

- Ugarte—gets the letters of transit and gives them to Rick; he then has the good sense to die.
- Ferrari—tells Lazslo that Rick has the letters of transit.
- Strasser—is after Lazslo and closes down Rick's Café; by having the good manners to be shot by Rick, he lets Rick get away and Louis reclaim his self-respect.
- Louis—changes sides at just the right time to save Rick.
- Lazslo—is the obstacle that prevents Rick from going off with Ilsa; he is the plot's primary catalyst that causes the collision of all the other characters.
- Sam—plays it again, bringing Ilsa and Rick closer together.
- Ilsa—by demonstrating her love for Rick helps him reclaim his idealism; she is a catalyst that enables Rick to reclaim his ideals.
- Annanina—foreshadows and motivates Rick's growing idealism.

With the exception of a few atmospheric characters, everyone in the cast, while being fully realized and motivated in themselves, also serves a number of specific plot purposes that could have been performed by no one else. No one is there simply to create thematic effects; everyone also advances the plot. Here's looking at you, kid.

23. HAVANA

Casablanca Lite

▬ ▬ ▬ ▬

You can hear the pitch now: We remake *Casablanca,* see, only instead of Bogie running a bar, we have a dissolute, cynical gambler. Instead of Ilsa Lund, we have a beautiful freedom fighter. For her freedom fighter husband, we substitute a freedom-fighting plantation owner. And for Casablanca, we substitute Havana, just weeks before the 1959 revolution. Love, war, intrigue, angst—sign on the dotted line, we start shooting in a month.

Nor is this an entirely bad idea for a movie. *Casablanca* is one of the seminal American films. Its antihero, Rick, not only made Humphrey Bogart a star, but defined the antihero for all time. His love affair with the fabulously attractive Ingrid Bergman is one of the great romances in all cinema. And the setting of exotic Casablanca during World War II, peopled with goose-stepping Nazis, corrupt French officials, frightened expatriates, and unscrupulous human traders, was ideal for creating a complex world of intrigue. Who could resist trying it again? The only problem was that a strict remake was out of the question because Bogart's and Bergman's unforgettable performances meant no one could ever play Rick or Ilsa again. When Rick forever gave up Ilsa to the cause of freedom, a sequel became impossible. Instead studio executives needed not only new characters, but a new location and time in which to reset the love story. Perhaps the only surprise is that it took twenty years until someone realized that while Castro may have tried and failed to give his people freedom, he at least succeeded in giving Hollywood a great setting for a remake.

Havana was one of the most expensive films of the eighties. Directed by Sydney Pollack, starring Robert Redford, and based on a script by the brilliant Judith Rascoe, it was the "can't miss" project of the year. And even when it failed, its star was so luminous, its director so "A" list, that no one really took the fall for a movie for which everyone should have taken the plunge.

So where did it go wrong? It wasn't with Sydney Pollack's direction, which was largely clean and intelligent. Nor was it with Robert Redford's fine characterization of Jack Weil, the gambler. It certainly wasn't the expert set design, the camerawork, the editing, or the secondary actors. The movie went wrong with one of the most ill-considered big-budget scripts in history. While it suffers from obscure secondary characters, a diffuse plot, and poorly articulated motivations, its largest problem is its astoundingly passive voice, where characters endlessly "talk about" their problems, deadening the narrative, stalling the plot, and destroying the movie. More than many of the bad scripts this book considers, the script for *Havana* was a train wreck waiting to happen, and one that the filmmakers should have seen coming a mile away. Let's take a look at the first act:

- Batista's Cuba: police search an incoming boat for contraband. The beautiful Bobby (Roberta) asks Jack to help her smuggle in some radios. He helps her get past customs.
- Jack meets Volpi, the gambling boss, and asks him for a game. They talk about politics.
- Jack meets Bobby, tries to pick her up, they talk about getting involved.

So far, so good. We've got our first act break. We've met Jack and seen he's adept both at smuggling in contraband and at making a pass at the beautiful Bobby. We've seen the corruption of Batista's Cuba and that Jack desperately wants a high-stakes poker game. In other words, both an external danger (Batista's Cuba) and an internal danger (Jack's unrequited fascination with Bobby and his need for a game) have been created. So far there's only one danger sign: the second and third scenes both involve Jack "talking about" something; twice in a row we hear about something rather than having it shown to us. Still, it's just two scenes, with the setting interesting enough and the characters unusual enough that we'll forgive it. But let's see where our second act goes:

- Jack meets Bobby's husband, Arturo—they talk about the political situation.
- Jack has sex with two tourists.
- Jack talks about Arturo's death.
- Bobby is tortured while Jack plays cards.
- Jack makes a deal to get Bobby out of jail.
- Bobby and Jack talk about her life.
- Jack is threatened by the Cuban police.
- Jack and Ramos talk about politics.
- Volpi and Jack talk about cities.
- Jack and the professor talk about women and leaving Cuba.
- Jack searches for Bobby and finds her.
- Jack and Bobby talk about leaving Cuba—they make love.
- Jack drives Bobby to Havana—they make love.
- Jack and Bobby talk about whether to leave or stay.

The upshot of these scenes is that Jack does what any self-respecting movie hero is supposed to do: he puts himself at risk to save the woman he loves. This is the kind of action that creates tension, illustrates the politics of Batista's Cuba, and increases the love between Jack and Bobby (although their back-to-back lovemaking scenes diminish rather than build up their love affair; in sex, as in so much else, less is more).

But what distinguishes the second act is that eight of its fourteen scenes are wholly "speculative" in nature, in which people discuss their situations and how they plan to act. Furthermore, people routinely show up for a scene and then disappear; the professor,

Volpi, Arturo, Ramos, the women Jack makes love to—all appear for a scene and then vanish. It is hard to imagine a combination more guaranteed to ruin a script: nonrecurring characters who talk about situations rather than live them. As for Arturo, Bobby's husband, we meet him only once in the entire second act, yet he's Bobby's husband and thus, along with Bobby's devotion to the revolution, the major obstacle to Jack's love for her. The less we see of Arturo, the less of an obstacle he presents to their love.

But the intimations of structural disaster in the second act are fulfilled in the third:

- Jack confronts Chigwell.
- Jack helps Arturo.
- Jack and Bobby are about to leave when he tells her Arturo is alive—she leaves Jack to go to Arturo.
- Jack talks about what to do now.
- Jack and Bobby say good-bye.
- Jack, alone in Key West, talks about his hopes of seeing Bobby again.

The central idea for this act isn't bad: Jack saves Arturo and, in so doing, guarantees that he will never see Bobby again. In other words, the ignoble antihero performs a heroic act that leaves him alone but ennobled; Bogie would eat it up with a spoon. But take another look—Bobby and Jack say good-bye twice (!), and we again have two of those awful "talk about" scenes, one inserted between the two good-byes and the other at the end of the movie. We are provided with the summation of a film whose main structural feature is that it's already summed up everything that's happened.

But even if this script wasn't a memorial to passive narrative and emotional avoidance, it fails on a deeper level, as the following list explores. Time after time the filmmakers, even with the blueprint of *Casablanca* before their eyes, made choices for *Havana* that diminish the drama, reduce the tension, abbreviate the emotional range of its characters, and sublimate the action.

CASABLANCA	HAVANA
Hero has power	Hero has little power
Hero won't take sides	Hero won't take sides
Heroine in a good cause	Heroine in an ambiguous cause
Hero saves the husband	Hero saves the husband
Hero fights evil	Hero is out for himself
Evil is personified	Evil is complex, ambiguous
Hero is active	Hero is largely passive
Hero talks about little	Hero talks about much

The list could undoubtedly be made longer. But while there are a few similarities in these two films, the dissimilarities greatly outweigh them, and, more to the point, all of these dissimilarities diminish the hero, the heroine, the evil, or the narrative line itself. *Havana* commits movie suicide—a state of affairs that could have been avoided by some clear thinking. Rick's power in operating his cafe, and in holding the letters of transit, causes everyone to orbit around him—surely a stronger position for a protagonist than to strip him of power and thus limit his influence. Ilsa, by fighting the evil of Nazism, confronts Rick with a difficult moral choice, whereas Bobby supports a revolution for which Jack could care less and thus creates in him no moral conflict. While Rick is constantly active, powering the plot from point to point, Jack is much more passive, causing the plot of *Havana* to sag and tilt. Rick's emotional reticence makes him a greater figure of fascination and later of compassion than Jack's loquacious and less mysterious character. Even the setting of pre-Castro Cuba, while intriguing, has none of the resonance of World War II Casablanca, where good guys fought bad guys and moral lines were clearly drawn. *Havana* carries around its neck the albatross of the audience's knowledge that Castro's Cuba became an ambiguous revolution, to say the least. While Batista was a monstrous villain, the dictatorship Castro created to supplant it was not that much of an improvement. Thus Bobby and Arturo's devotion to Castro mutes their moral stance; certainly it calls their political intelligence into question. (Incidentally, Arturo is one of the liberal landed gentry. One can't help wondering how glad he was for having supported Castro after the revolution when the Bearded One took away his land and turned it into a state-owned farm; he probably had plenty of time to ponder the irony as he languished in some Cuban worker's paradise prison.)

Some of *Havana*'s failings can be written off as a product of the times in which it was made. The eighties were years of moral sloppiness, where the notion of fighting for noble causes was looked at askance. The moral certainties of the forties had given way to the anguished aftermath of Vietnam and Watergate: heroes, even of the antiheroic variety, seemed stale and ironic, while the desire to "talk about" situations, anathema to drama, had become the calling card of eighties intellectuals lost in a world they could neither control nor escape. If art is a mirror of life, then too often the reverse is just as true, with the times dictating the art we create. A passive political time gave birth to a passive political film. Still, while this may serve as an explanation, it doesn't excuse *Havana*. Nothing excuses *Havana*. Like Castro, it broods over a barren landscape, giving endless speeches to an audience that is looking for the exit.

24. THE TREASURE OF THE SIERRA MADRE

The Greatest Adventure

■■ ■■ ■■ ■■

. . . going with a partner or two is dangerous. All the time murder's lurking about. Hardly a day passes without quarrels—the partners accusing each other of all sorts of crimes, and suspecting whatever you do or say. As long as there's no find the noble brotherhood will last, but when the piles begin to grow, that's when the trouble starts.

Directed by John Huston working from his own screenplay of the B. Traven novel, *The Treasure of the Sierra Madre* is the greatest adventure movie ever made. Now, you're probably thinking, What about *The Guns of Navarone*, the Indiana Jones movies, *The Terminator*, or any of a dozen other wonderful movies; how does a film from the late 1940s come off leaving them so far in the dust? The answer is easy: *Treasure* may not have the greatest physical adventures ever filmed (though they're nothing to sneeze at), but it does have the greatest adventure that really counts—an adventure into the heights and depths of the human soul. That may sound pretentious and intellectual, but it's quite the opposite; the greatest study of man is man, and the greatest adventure is the one that takes place inside ourselves.

Tampico, Mexico, in the 1920s. Fred C. Dobbs, down on his luck, begs for pennies and takes a chance on a lottery ticket. He meets Curtin, another American bum, and together they sack out at a flophouse and hear an old-timer named Howard speak of the eternal lure of gold and of the evil things it does to men's souls.

Later, Dobbs and Curtin take a tough job for several weeks, only to learn they've been stiffed by their boss, Pat. They find Pat, beat him up, and take the money that was owed them. Knowing it's only a matter of time before they're flat broke again, they look up Howard and ask him to accompany them on a treasure hunt. Howard readily accepts, and after Dobbs wins the lottery and adds his prize to their stash, they find they have just enough to buy provisions and burros for a trek deep into the unexplored wilderness of the Sierra Madres.

After a torturous journey, including an attack by bandits led by Gold Hat, whom Dobbs nearly kills, they find a mountain containing a vein of gold. They speak of their dreams for the future: Howard just wants to relax, and Curtin hopes to own a fruit orchard, while Dobbs plans to spend his money on fancy food and women. After weeks of backbreaking work they accumulate $5,000 worth of gold dust, and just as Howard prophesied back in the flophouse, the three begin to distrust each other. Each hides his private stash of gold from the others, and they soon find themselves at each other's throats, with Dobbs growing nearly mad in his paranoid distrust of Curtin and Howard.

It's just then, with the men almost ready to kill each other, that Cody, an American whom Curtin had met while buying provisions in town, arrives and asks to throw in with them. Although the three are tempted to take in Cody as a partner, they finally vote to protect their gold by killing him instead. Just as they're about to shoot Cody they spot bandits headed their way. When Gold Hat and his crew arrive in camp, the four shoot it out with them and are about to be overwhelmed when Federales drive off the bandits. The three discover that Cody has been killed in the fight, and in reading a letter from his wife, they learn that Cody owned a fruit orchard in California.

With the vein of gold playing out, the three decide to return to civilization. On the way back they encounter Indians who ask for Howard's help tending a sick boy. Curtin and Dobbs take Howard's gold to protect it from the Indians and continue on, planning to give Howard his gold when they meet in Durango. But Dobbs again grows insane, disarms Curtin, and shoots him, leaving him for dead. Dobbs, troubled by his conscience, journeys on with all the gold. But Curtin is saved by the Indians, who reunite him with Howard. The two ride out after Dobbs, swearing revenge.

Dobbs, meanwhile, has run into Gold Hat and the last remnants of his band, who kill Dobbs for his shoes and burros. Finding what they think are sacks of sand on the burros, they split open the sacks and let the gold dust dribble onto the ground. When Gold Hat and his two compadres enter town, their burros are recognized as belonging to Dobbs, Curtin, and Howard, and the bandits are promptly executed. A "norther" windstorm begins, and by the time Curtin and Howard arrive, all the gold has literally blown back from whence it came—all their work for nothing. Howard and Curtin laugh at the immensity of their misfortune, and the two part. Howard will become the medicine man of the Indians, who will treat him royally for as long as he lives, and Curtin will seek out Cody's widow and, we assume and hope, finally get the peach orchard he always dreamed of owning.

It's a fascinating plot, filled with twists and turns. Now let's look a little deeper, analyzing how it plays out scene by scene, beginning with the first act:

- Dobbs begs a small coin called a *tosten* from an American named White Suit.
- Dobbs buys himself a meal and a portion of a lottery ticket.
- Dobbs meets Curtin; they talk of hard times in Tampico.
- Dobbs begs a second *tosten* from White Suit.
- Dobbs gets a haircut.
- Dobbs begs a third *tosten* from White Suit, who says from now on Dobbs must make his way in the world without his help.

Hold on here—what's going on? We follow Dobbs moving from *tosten* to *tosten,* hand to mouth, without getting anywhere, until he's finally warned he must make his way in the world without White Suit's help. (White Suit, by the way, was played by John Huston, in one of his first acting jobs.) Just what's this movie about? Is it about Dobbs's poverty? About how he's not getting anywhere? The movie's after bigger game; it's really saying that

Dobbs, in relying upon others, has cursed himself to a dead-end life and that beyond the simple initial problem of Dobbs's poverty is the underlying theme of whether or not—and to what extent—we can take control of our own destiny. It asks how much luck and even fate control our lives. We're not ten minutes into the movie and some pretty potent thematic material is already being broached. Now let's see where the rest of the first act takes us:

- Dobbs takes a camp-rigging job from Pat; he meets Curtin on the way to the job.
- Dobbs and Curtin work hard for three weeks without pay; Pat promises them their money when they return to Tampico.
- Getting off the ferry, Pat is "surprised" not to find the money waiting for him; he tells Dobbs and Curtin to wait for him at a bar, where he'll give them the money soon.
- At the bar Dobbs and Curtin learn that Pat has stiffed them.
- Dobbs and Curtin stay at a flophouse, where they hear Howard speak of the lure of gold and how it twists men's souls; Dobbs swears it wouldn't happen to him.
- Dobbs and Curtin find Pat; they beat him up and take the money due them.
- Their lives at a dead end, Dobbs and Curtin decide to seek out Howard and learn how to look for gold.
- Dobbs, Curtin, and Howard pool their money; they're $100 short until Dobbs wins the lottery and throws in his winnings; they're going to look for gold.

The second part of the first act, in addition to reintroducing the motif of coincidence, expands upon the idea that Dobbs can't rely upon the kindness of strangers and that he must take charge of his own life. Pat's thievery impresses both Dobbs and Curtin that they can't rely upon others and that no one is to be trusted. Huston now throws the problem of greed into the mix, with the warning that gold destroys men's souls. In other words, while Huston is giving Dobbs and Curtin a way out of the vicious treadmill they're on, he's also warning them that the way out may come at a terrible price. And on a deeper level, Huston is telling us that the theme of this movie will be the way greed destroys men, drives them mad, and sets them at each other's throats. The movie, in other words, is playing fair with us, not only alerting us what's to come, but foreshadowing themes and ideas that will animate the rest of the story. White Suit may be right that from now on Dobbs will have to make his own way in the world, but Howard is also right that the dark side of self-reliance is the distrust of others.

But notice something else: when Dobbs and Curtin beat up Pat for cheating them, they take only what's due them and not a penny more (in fact, Dobbs pays the bar bill out of his own pocket, rather than robbing Pat of even that small amount). Dobbs and Curtin are, even in their desperate poverty, still creatures of civilization, obeying and living by standards of accepted morality. Huston takes this social contract a step further by having Dobbs, flushed as he is with the "noble brotherhood," as Howard calls it, throw his lottery winnings into the common pot without regret or charge, thereby giving them all the money they need to mount their treasure hunt. Notice how coincidence has played its hand again: Dobbs's money comes through a lottery drawing—luck is still a silent partner on the gold hunt, throwing its own caprice into the mix.

Nor is luck at work only in the script for *The Treasure of the Sierra Madre*. It is a common presence in some of the finest screenplays ever written. When Charles Foster Kane, on his way to visit Rosebud, gets waylaid when he runs into the woman who will soon become his second wife, it's luck that scripted the coincidence. When Lawrence of Arabia is forced to execute the same man whose life he saved, it's luck at work. Luck's latest credit might be *Pulp Fiction*, where again the theme is interwoven with human greed and compassion.

So a first act that initially seems a series of unrelated events is in fact tied together through its steadily mounting theme of the collision of character with destiny, which Huston is using as his narrative glue. Huston here is working on two levels: he writes movingly of his characters while simultaneously orchestrating the events that will determine their fate.

So we've met our characters, seen the problem of their poverty, how they come up with the idea to search for gold, and how they get the money necessary to finance the expedition. We're at a second act break because our characters have made a decision to accept the challenge of the first act (poverty and the need to take charge of their lives) by seeking gold. Other characters in this situation might have given up and sunk into deeper poverty or simply cleared out and headed back to America. But Dobbs and Curtin opt to look for gold and thereby not only define their characters, but propel themselves into the second act. Howard, who is always "at your service" to seek for gold, plays a toothless Cassandra, knowing the future, unable to stop it, and yet willingly going once more into the madness he knows is to come. He's our silent guide, a grizzled Greek chorus commenting occasionally upon the unfolding events. But on a deeper level, we've seen thematic resonance coming into play: luck and coincidence already play a dominant force in the lives of the three men, perhaps every bit as dominant as their own decisions to take charge of their fate. It'll be the collision between these two forces that will energize the rest of the movie, beginning with the first sequence of the second act:

- The three take a train into the mountains; they're attacked by bandits led by Gold Hat; Dobbs nearly kills Gold Hat but a spur of the mountain gets in the way; driven off by Federales on the train, Gold Hat lives to rob another day.
- They buy burros and supplies.
- They head into the mountains—the going is hard.
- Dobbs and Curtin think they've struck it rich; Howard tells them it's fool's gold.
- They weather a "norther" windstorm, hack through a jungle, and sleep, exhausted.
- Howard finds gold and does a dance.
- Howard shows them how to find gold; he tells them that "soon you'll know it all."

Let's call this sequence "the Trek into the Wilderness." Like the journey that Michael Caine and Sean Connery make into the depths of "Kafiristan" in Huston's *The Man Who Would Be King*, Dobbs, Curtin, and Howard are cutting themselves loose from the constraints and comforts of civilization; they are becoming men of nature, without any law or morality except that which they invent for themselves. That's why Huston lets this sequence linger as long as it does. Leaving civilization, both as a physical and as an ethical consideration, is not just a hell of a journey, it's a journey into hell, one not undertaken lightly or easily. And when Howard shows them how to find gold and tells them, "Soon you'll know it all," he's not speaking simply of mining techniques, but rather is alerting us of bigger stakes to come.

Notice how even on this all but impossible journey luck and coincidence still lend a hand: they meet Gold Hat, are nearly killed by him and his band, and escape only because Federales happen to be on the train; and Dobbs is about to kill Gold Hat when the train's progress causes a bit of mountain to come in his way—one can only wonder how the movie would have played out had Gold Hat died here. But that's a question for later. For now, let's see how our next sequence shapes up:

- Having found $5,000 worth of gold, they decide to divide it three ways and hide their stash from the others.
- Dobbs gets caught in a cave-in; Curtin nearly lets him die but saves him instead.
- They discuss what they'll do when they return to civilization: Howard will just relax; Curtin will own a fruit orchard; Dobbs will buy fancy meals and make love to women. Dobbs argues he could demand more profit from his lottery ticket but agrees to split things three ways; they agree to dig for six months or $40,000 each, whichever comes first.
- At night each checks that the others haven't robbed his stash.
- Dobbs, growing mad and paranoid, starts talking to himself.
- Dobbs accuses the others of wanting him dead.
- Dobbs sees Curtin about to open Dobbs's stash; he nearly shoots Curtin until they see Curtin was really looking for a Gila monster.

Let's call this sequence "Dobbs's Descent #1." In a few short scenes we've come a long way from the "noble brotherhood" with which we began the gold hunt. Curtin has nearly turned murderer, as has Dobbs, who's growing mad. The descent into hell has begun, the very same descent Howard prophesied back in the Tampico flophouse. We're barely halfway through our movie and murder is in the air—is Huston introducing these elements too soon? Where can he go from here without being redundant? Why make the descent into savagery occur so quickly? Not only does Huston risk losing credibility by having the men at each other's throats so soon, he also risks the movie itself, which may become anticlimactic from now on. Has Huston dug himself into a hole? Let's see what happens next:

- In town to get supplies, Curtin meets Cody, who asks to come along and look for gold; Curtin says he's a hunter and refuses Cody's company.
- Cody appears in camp; the three deny they're looking for gold.
- The three keep watch all night, wary of Cody.
- In the morning Dobbs hits Cody; Cody says that the three have three choices: kill him, run him off, or make him a partner.
- The three decide to kill Cody and are about to carry out their sentence on him when Cody spots bandits headed their way.
- The four band together and prepare their defenses.
- The bandits appear, led by Gold Hat; a brief shoot-out.
- The four wait for the next attack.
- Second shoot-out—the bandits are temporarily driven off.
- The bandits are about to overpower the four when Federales run them off.
- The three find that Cody has been killed; they read his letters; Cody's wife waits for him back at their fruit orchard.

This sequence, which I call "Cody and the Bandits," is filled with surprises. Cody's appearance throws a wild card into the proceedings. The three, who a moment before were at each other's throats, find themselves united against Cody. And while this sudden comradeship might be unexpected, the movie takes an equally unexpected turn when Cody poses a problem to the three: run him off, make him a partner, or kill him. The three, ready to kill each other, barely able to decide their own fates, now have to unite to decide another's. The decision to kill Cody, while barbaric and horrifying, is probably inevitable.

It's here that the device of coincidence-as-catalyst, which has been lurking subtly throughout the first half of the movie, becomes more apparent. Just as the three are about to murder Cody they spot bandits coming up the mountain toward them. The "noble brotherhood" is re-formed once more, with Cody added to the mix. If the bandits had appeared five minutes earlier, the three would never have had to go through the grim business of voting whether or not to become murderers but would have simply let Cody join them to fight the new intruders. If the bandits had appeared five minutes later, the three would have been shoveling Cody into his grave (and, without a fourth gun to protect them, would most likely have guaranteed their own slaughter as well). But the coincidences don't end there; in the shootout with the bandits it's Cody, the wild card, who's killed—it's as if Cody left his wife and traveled all the way to this desolate mountain just to sacrifice himself so that the three partners could live. But this coincidence is followed by the equally fortuitous event that the three, about to be killed by the bandits, are rescued by the serendipitous arrival of the Federales, who drive them off. This third coincidence is followed by a fourth and equally unlikely coincidence that Cody owned a fruit orchard—remember that Curtin planned to buy one with his share of the loot—which he had left to hunt for gold: a search that is ultimately "fruitless."

Normally four coincidences like these would be a death sentence for a movie. But Huston has planned them well. Not only are they individually believable, containing none of the unlikely interventions that characterize a deus ex machina, but Huston has prepared us for them with his carefully laid out first act, which lets us know just how much of a role luck plays in our lives—a greater role than we'd like to admit or, in the case of this sequence, normally even believe. Huston, by telling us that luck is an invisible character along for the ride, has prepared us for Cody's ironically brief life and death and for the three men to survive into a second act that still bears them many terrors and uncertainties:

- The vein of gold almost played out, the three decide to quit digging and head back to civilization.
- They leave the mountain, thanking it for its generosity.
- Howard and Curtin decide to give a fourth of their gold to Cody's widow in thanks for his saving their lives; Indians appear and ask Howard to help tend a sick boy.
- Howard tends the sick boy.
- On the trail, the Indians insist that Howard return and receive their thanks; Dobbs and Curtin take Howard's gold and promise to return it to him in town.
- Dobbs and Curtin begin to argue on the trail.
- Night camp; Dobbs wants to steal Howard's gold; Curtin refuses; Dobbs, going mad, says Curtin wants to kill him; they fight and find themselves in a standoff.
- Dobbs grabs Curtin's gun and shoots Curtin, leaving him for dead.
- Dobbs runs off with all the gold.
- Curtin is rescued by the Indians.
- Dobbs hurries on; his burro dies; he's growing increasingly desperate.
- Howard learns of Curtin's near murder; Curtin starts to heal.
- Dobbs is lost on the trail.

This sequence, which I call "Dobbs's Descent #2," reprises and expands the themes that animated Dobbs's Descent #1 at the beginning of the second act and were interrupted only by the Cody and the Bandits sequence. The ethic of the "noble brotherhood" temporarily returns when the three stop mining and head off the mountain and even prompts them to parcel out some of their gold as a present to Cody's widow; on the verge of returning to civilization, the men once again feel the pull of social and moral obligations.

But once they're on the trail, the "noble brotherhood" turns to sand. With Howard removed from the equation, Dobbs's smoldering paranoia reignites. Once again the role of fate is underscored: had the Indians not happened upon the three, then the Indian boy would most likely have died, but the three would have returned to civilization, divided up their gold, and gone their separate ways.

The moral good of trying to cure the sick boy causes Howard to leave, which in turn creates a moral vacuum for Dobbs; it's just him against Curtin, and the madness is born again.

But the coincidences don't end there. It's conceivable that Curtin could have overpowered Dobbs and led him back to civilization. Instead it's Dobbs who gets the upper hand, and in a grotesque reenactment of White Suit's advice from the first act that he must make his own way in the world, he tries to kill Curtin and steal all the gold. The screenplay is adroit in revealing Dobbs's self-justification for his theft and attempted murder—even Dobbs's evil is three-dimensional and compassionately drawn.

But what if Dobbs had succeeded in killing Curtin? Then Dobbs would have ridden on and met the same fate awaiting him in the third act. But Dobbs misses his chance to kill Curtin, and at close range. How? Dobbs himself says it's his conscience playing on him, but destiny is again at work. By allowing Curtin to live, the moral drama can play itself out in all its irony and cosmic justice. Curtin lives because fate and Huston want him to live (as does Dobbs, subconsciously not a murderer—an explanation that, on a simpler level, might justify why his bullet went astray).

Now we see why Huston tipped his hand so soon in Dobbs's Descent #1; he risked an anticlimax by introducing the distrust among the men with the film not even at its midpoint, but he knew it was necessary in order to expand upon his already established themes of luck and fate. Not only that, but the Cody and the Bandits sequence gives us time to digest the growing madness and murderous distrust, so that when it returns it's like a boxer hitting us first with a left (Dobbs's Descent #1), then an unexpected right (Cody and the Bandits), and finally finishing us off with another, even more terrible left (Dobbs's Descent #2). Two lefts in a row, or one single tremendous left, wouldn't have packed the emotional punch of this deadly series of hits.

With things at their lowest, we move into our third act:

- Curtin recovers; he and Howard go off after Dobbs, seeking revenge.
- Dobbs is killed by Gold Hat and his two remaining bandits, who steal Dobbs's gold-laden burros.

- Gold Hat and his men find "sacks of sand" and slash them, emptying the gold onto the earth.
- Gold Hat and his men are caught and executed.
- Curtin and Howard ride through a "norther"; they find their gold has blown back to the mountain; Howard and Curtin part, Howard to become a medicine man and relax, Curtin to seek out Cody's widow on her fruit orchard.

So we see why Huston let Curtin live: it wasn't to get revenge on Dobbs, which would have simply turned him into a murderer on Dobbs's level. Nor was Curtin allowed to live in order to claim his gold, which returns from whence it came. Rather, Curtin has been allowed to live in order to find his heart's desire in the person of a grieving widow trying to run a fruit orchard. Just as Cody died in order to save the three and create a widow, Curtin lives in order to meet that widow, fall in love with her, and manage her fruit orchard. Similarly, Howard will get his heart's desire of relaxing for the rest of his life; but it won't be gold that will buy his rest, but his act of humanity toward a sick Indian boy. And Dobbs, by trying to murder Curtin, earns his reward at the hands of bandits. Each man has gotten what he deserves; each has found justice.

In a way *Treasure* is the opposite of *High Noon,* which explores the limitations of civilization and concludes that all moral choices are finally made by the individual, without the sanction or help of society. *Treasure,* on the other hand, strips us of civilization and comes to the same conclusion—that while civilization acts as a carrot and stick to hold our baser selves in check, in the end it's the individual who maps his own conscience and charts his own morality. Both films conclude that human nature isn't set by society but is, rather, ours to choose and shape. We don't all have to become Fred C. Dobbs, destroyed by greed, or even Will Kane, who takes command of his fate at the price of losing his faith in mankind; we can choose to be Curtin, tempted and nearly destroyed but finally emerging as someone who retains his hope for humanity while choosing to be that rarest of creatures, a man.

If destiny has written the lives of Dobbs, Curtin, and Howard, then its agents on earth include Gold Hat and his bandits. In the beginning of the second act, destiny saves Gold Hat from Dobbs's bullet by placing a mountain in the way. We now see that had Dobbs killed Gold Hat at the train robbery, Dobbs might have successfully gotten away with the gold—and justice wouldn't have been done. But Gold Hat isn't simply an agent for doling out justice to Dobbs. By killing Dobbs, Gold Hat stops Curtin and Howard from ever catching up with Dobbs and becoming morally damned as murderers—rather, Gold Hat takes on that burden and pays the price. Gold Hat also kills Cody, thereby giving Curtin the opportunity to get his fruit orchard. And it's Gold Hat who slashes the gold sacks, thereby letting the wind return the gold back to the mountain. The bandits' ignorance of the wealth they have always sought, and which they literally let slip through their fingers, turns them into cosmic agents for a sublime justice. The bandits' actions affect the ethical choices of all they meet, and they die when their role is finished, the moral drama played out.

Nor does destiny limit itself to using Cody and the bandits as its agents. The Indians, with their sick boy, permit Howard to do a good deed for another, thereby justifying and earning his life's dream of rest. It's also the intervention of the Indians, in taking away Howard, that forces Dobbs and Curtin to be alone together, a situation that foments Dobbs's madness and final reckoning with fate. Even Pat, by cheating Dobbs and Curtin out of their pay, and then giving it over to them only after they beat him up, makes the two men desperate and thereby all the more aware of their need to take control of their lives. Only they never really had control of their lives, did they? It was destiny, using coincidence as its grammar and luck as its language, that has truly written the script, employing B. Traven and John Huston as its brilliant secretaries to tell a tale filled with madness, redemption, greed, charity, fellowship, treason, horror, and hope.

25. FALLING IN LOVE

The Good Guys Ought to Be the Bad Guys

Can a vacuum love another vacuum?

—Pauline Kael

The year was 1983. Meryl Streep was the biggest female movie star in the world, an actress who had displayed her amazing talents by portraying extraordinary women living extraordinary lives. But now Streep wanted more than anything to be ordinary. Not only that, she wanted to be ordinary with Robert De Niro, that extraordinary actor who had reached near the top of the slippery pole of movie stardom through his astonishing portrayals of unusual personalities. The two had acted together in *The Deer Hunter* and enjoyed the experience. Now, Bobby D not only also wanted to be ordinary, he wanted to be ordinary with Meryl Streep. They wanted to be ordinary together.

Problems, problems, problems. But a solution was found in the script *Falling in Love* by the Pulitzer Prize–winning playwright Michael Cristofer. It was the tale of Molly, a graphic designer, and Frank, a construction supervisor, who meet in a bookstore and slowly fall in love. Both Molly and Frank are married, and their anguish over leaving their bland marriages is the dynamic that animates the drama. The dialogue was hyperreal, filled with pregnant pauses, half sentences, unfinished thoughts, and inarticulate emotions. It was a script owned by Paramount Pictures, which had commissioned Cristofer to write a love story about two nice people who fall in love at the wrong time but who—filled with the moral angst understood only by movie stars who don't want to alienate their fans by being unfaithful—never go to bed together. But the characters, while unimaginative, undeveloped, and celibate, were also, if nothing else, ordinary.

Sam Cohn, the powerful agent, showed the script to Meryl and Bobby and got their approval. In fact, they were so enamored with the tremendous potential of a love story about ordinary people who never make love that they agreed to cut their price, making up for it with greater participation in the much anticipated profits to come. Cohn then brought on board Ulu Grosbard, the theatrically trained director who had worked with De Niro on *True Confessions*. Cohn presented the package of Grosbard and a bargain-basement De Niro and Streep to the head of Paramount Studios, who read the Cristofer script and called in Streep and De Niro for a conference.

"Why," he is said to have asked, "should I make this movie? These characters are ordinary; they have no special traits or individual characteristics; all they do is mouth inanities and leave their spouses. Who the hell likes people who do that? Besides, not once in the entire script do they shtup. Now how the hell can you make a movie about people falling in love with no shtupping? In other words, why the hell should anyone want to see this picture?"

"But," Meryl Streep said, including Robert De Niro with her, "that's why you employ us."

The head of Paramount sat back and considered. True, Streep and De Niro were arguably the two greatest film actors in the world. They weren't exactly sex symbols, but perhaps that made the no-shtupping part easier to swallow. Besides, they'd worked miracles with difficult material before, while this script was so . . . well, ordinary, how could they screw it up? Maybe she was right; maybe that was why he hired people like Streep and De Niro— because they could take ordinary material and make it special. Besides, if he passed on *Falling in Love*, then Sam Cohn would within hours take it over to Warners or Twentieth or Columbia or some other damn studio, which would jump at the chance to have two living legends acting in one of *their* upcoming pictures—and then gleefully let the rumor fly that they'd grabbed the project right out from under his nose. Not only that, but if the picture made money, he'd look like the greatest fool who ever drove his Mercedes into slot one of a movie studio's executive parking lot. He leaned forward and shrugged; okay, they could make the picture.

So *Falling in Love,* a movie born of a banal script, fueled by the egos of two movie stars and the fears of a studio executive, came to be. The Paramount ad people were leery of it from the beginning. They saw there wasn't much sexual juice between Streep and De Niro, and concerning the no-shtupping part, well, how do you sell a supposedly hot love story where no one winds up in the sack, starring two actors not exactly renowned for their talents below the belt? As for the ordinariness of the characters, well, how do you persuade people to get a baby-sitter and drive to God knows what theater so they can watch people who are even less interesting than themselves?

After *Falling in Love* inevitably wound up one of the big losers of 1984, industry wags began searching for a scapegoat. It couldn't be the head of production, who was about to jump ship for another studio at a greatly increased salary. Nor could either the incredibly talented Meryl Streep or the terrifically talented Robert De Niro be held accountable for the fiasco. As for Michael Cristofer; hey, the guy won a Pulitzer, didn't he? Who, then, should take the fall for *Falling in Love*? Apparently the last man standing was the director, Ulu Grosbard, whose meticulous direction had done so much to distinguish the otherwise undistinguished project. Years were to pass before Grosbard ever again directed a picture.

But justice was served, the guilty (or at least the defenseless) were punished, and the ones really responsible for *Falling in Love* went on to years of righteous employment. Who said life was fair?

Rather than discuss the structure of *Falling in Love,* which is a straightforward, predictable affair, let's instead take a look at a few of the scenes and examine Cristofer's approach to dialogue. Take, for example, this exchange between Molly and Frank as they meet secretly during one of their initial flirtations:

FRANK

Hi.

MOLLY

Hi. Oh. Hello.

FRANK

What's the matter?

MOLLY

You look different.

FRANK

Well . . .

MOLLY

No. You look nice. You just look different.

MOLLY

What?

FRANK

Nothing.

MOLLY

What did you do? Did you get a haircut?

FRANK

No.

MOLLY

You sure?

FRANK

Yes, I'm sure.

MOLLY

Did you have a mustache before?

FRANK

What?

MOLLY

What did you do?

FRANK

I didn't do anything.

MOLLY

You're lying.

FRANK

I didn't.

MOLLY

Come on.

FRANK

I didn't. . . .

They talk like this through the whole script. The rhythms are interesting, the inarticulateness almost refreshing after watching so many other movies where people speak in perfectly crafted phrases. But even though there are people for whom this sort of dither passes for conversation, the only justification for having to sit through it is if there's some deeper profundity, some unexpressed resonance to keep us hanging around. The equally inarticulate musings in *Tender Mercies* reveal deeply sensitive and feeling characters. The banalities of *Fargo* perfectly capture people whose longings run ocean-deep. The characters in *2001: A Space Odyssey,* mouthing their commonplace utterances, are Stanley Kubrick's vehicles for describing a civilization in desperate need of an extraterrestrial injection of soul. But this scene is all text without subtext, surface without depth, affect without meaning. What you see is what you get. Nor is this shallow dialogue specific only to Frank and Molly's interaction. Here's a glimpse of Molly at dinner with her doctor husband, Brian, just a few scenes later:

BRIAN
The Shaffer woman died today.

MOLLY
Oh, no.

BRIAN
Yes.

MOLLY
Was it bad?

BRIAN
The husband was there. I made my little
speech. He kept looking at me. They always
look at you, like you should have something
more to say.

(pause)

Do you want to go to a movie?

MOLLY
No.

BRIAN
Are you going into town tomorrow?

Again, the rhythms are interesting, and the dialogue feels very
"real." And it's not as if people don't relate to each other like this;
they do. A doctor, distraught and a little drunk, starts to reveal to
his wife his anguish at telling a husband that his wife has died. It
happens all the time. And so are there wives like Molly, who have
no words of consolation, no sympathy or compassion. And it
wouldn't be so bad except, first of all, we're supposed to care for
Molly, who comes off as the unsympathetic bitch of the world, and
second because just a few scenes earlier we've seen her mumbling
similar inanities to her beloved Frank, whom she doesn't even recognize is wearing a tie for the first time. It is for people like these
that mercy killings were invented. But we're not supposed to put

her out of her misery, we're supposed to root for her, cheering that in Frank she's at last found a kindred spirit, light-years in sensitivity above her oh-so-very-boring husband. Only it isn't the men in her life who are Molly's problem, it's Molly herself, brooding in her self-absorption, unable to feel or care for others. Our heroine, the egomaniacal moron.

But Molly isn't the only one who should be placed on the euthanasia list. Here's Frank telling Ann, his wife, who already suspects he is having an affair, that he is in love with Molly:

> FRANK
> I met a woman on the train. I . . . uh . . . I
> don't know. Nothing happened. I mean, we
> didn't . . . we never . . . well. It's over now.
> Nothing happened. I'm not seeing her. I'm
> not having an affair. It's nothing like that.

> ANN
> No. It's worse. Isn't it?

Another pause. Then Ann hits Frank in the face. Then she leaves the room.

Once again, the emotional antagonist is rejected by the unemotional protagonist, only this time it took us a lot longer to get there. It's not that this scene, of which this is only an excerpt, is poorly written—it has a rising line of tension, an interesting emotional reveal when Frank admits he's in love with Molly, and the final beats where Ann reacts to this bombshell are sharply drawn. Nor is the problem that scenes like this don't happen in real life. Of course there are people who are afraid and hesitant to reveal embarrassing or hurtful truths.

But Frank and Molly are just not the people with whom we want to live for two hours in a dark theater. No audience will hope they'll live happily ever after, continuing to hide their deeper feelings and shrug off relationships. Rather, the audience is conflicted whether to root for them or throw tomatoes at them. These characters are a vast miscalculation, who can only alienate an audience and lose box office. The paint-by-the-numbers calculations in so many other movies that too often make for predictably likable characters at least can be justified by the bottom line. The choice to create characters like those in *Falling in Love* was a choice to make the movie about the wrong people: Frank and Molly should be the antagonists, while Ann and Brian, with their deeper emotions, willingness to risk, and greater compassion, should be the protagonists. Mel Brooks, in his brilliant *The Producers,* made a Broadway musical whose hero is Adolf Hitler—only that was made for laughs. *Falling in Love* is deadly serious, and that's one of the reasons it died.

Not only that, but in all of these scenes there are no specifics of character that make Frank and Molly different from a million other people in these circumstances. Their words and their silences never reveal a reaction that they and only they would make. Their individuality is never revealed through these scenes—they are merely generic fill-in-the-blanks, subtext personified, people without affect, without personality, characters as interchangeable as identical grains of sand.

In case you're curious, Frank does leave his wife, and Molly does leave her husband, and they do come together at the end, to live happily ever after. The two happiest nonentities in the history of drama.

Resources

▬ ▬ ▬ ▬

Finding Scripts

Many screenplays are published and can be obtained through any bookstore. The following outfits sell reprints of actual scripts:

> Script City
> 8033 Sunset Boulevard
> Box 1500
> Los Angeles, California 90046
> 213-871-0707

> Hollywood Book and Poster
> 6562 Hollywood Boulevard
> Hollywood, California 90028
> 213-465-8764

Information on the History of the Films in This Book

Information on the making of some of the more recent films in this book was obtained through interviews with people involved in their production; I will honor their wish to remain anonymous. However, the following books can be consulted for further information on the making of some of the films in this book:

Singin' in the Rain. Lorrimer Publishing, 1986.

Pulp Fiction. Miramax Books, 1994.

Round Up the Usual Suspects—The Making of Casablanca, by Aljean Harmetz. Hyperion Books, 1992.

America's Favorite Movies: Behind the Scenes, by Rudy Behlmer. Frederick Ungar Publishing, 1982. Contains information on *High Noon* and *Singin' in the Rain.*

Three Screenplays, by Horton Foote. Grove Press, 1989.

Adventures in the Screen Trade, by William Goldman. Warner Books, 1983.

The Citizen Kane Book—Raising Kane, by Pauline Kael. Limelight Editions, 1984.

Television Plays, by Paddy Chayefsky. Simon & Schuster, 1955.

Hit & Run—How Jon Peters and Peter Guber Took Sony for a Ride in Hollywood, by Nancy Griffin and Kim Masters. Simon & Schuster, 1996.

The Devil's Candy—The Bonfire of the Vanities Goes to Hollywood, by Julie Salamon. Houghton Mifflin Company, 1991.

Scenario magazine, vol. 1, no. 3—script of *The Usual Suspects,* with an interview with Christopher McQuarrie.

Scenario magazine, spring 1995—an early script of *Groundhog Day* with an interview with Danny Rubin.

About the Author

——— ——— ——— ———

THOMAS POPE has worked as a professional screenwriter for twenty-five years. He did his undergraduate and graduate work in cinema with an emphasis in screenwriting at the University of Southern California. His credits include *Fraternity Row, A Great Ride, The Manitou, Hammett, The Lords of Discipline,* and *Cold Dog Soup.* He also worked on *F/X, Someone to Watch over Me,* and *Bad Boys.* He has sold or optioned scripts to Columbia, Disney, and Miramax. He has worked for Penny Marshall, Frank Oz, Francis Coppola, Barry Levinson, and many others. He is married to the poet and novelist Freya Manfred; they live with their twin sons in Shorewood, Minnesota.